Ready®
Common Core

3 Mathematics
INSTRUCTION

Vice President of Product Development: Adam Berkin
Editorial Director: Cindy Tripp
Project Manager: Grace Izzi
Executive Editor: Kathy Kellman
Supervising Editors: Pam Halloran, Lauren Van Wart
Cover Design: Matt Pollock
Cover Illustrator: O'Lamar Gibson
Book Design: Jeremy Spiegel

ISBN 978-1-4957-0550-2
©2016–Curriculum Associates, LLC
North Billerica, MA 01862
No part of this book may be reproduced
by any means without written permission
from the publisher.
All Rights Reserved. Printed in USA.
30 29 28 27 26 25 24 23

Table of Contents

Mathematical Practices Handbook . . . . SMPi

Standards in boldface are the focus standards that address major lesson content.

©Curriculum Associates, LLC   Copying is not permitted.

Table of Contents continued

Standards in boldface are the focus standards that address major lesson content.

Standards in boldface are the focus standards that address major lesson content.

MATHEMATICAL PRACTICES HANDBOOK

We use our math thinking to figure out all kinds of problems, even hard problems from real life.

There are eight math habits that will help make your math thinking grow stronger.

Keep practicing! You'll be learning to think like a math pro. Then you'll be ready to take on any problem.

THE 8 MATH HABITS

1 Solve problems.
Keep looking for clues until you solve the problem.

2 Think and reason.
Make sense of the words and the numbers in a problem.

3 Show and explain.
Share your math ideas to help others understand you.

4 Use math in the real world.
Solve problems in real life.

5 Choose a tool.
Decide when to use tools like a ruler, a pencil, or mental math.

6 Be clear and precise.
Try to be exactly right in what you say and do.

7 Zoom in and zoom out.
Look for what's the same and what's different.

8 Use patterns.
Look for patterns in math to find shortcuts.

Read more about each math habit on the pages that follow.

MATH HABIT ①

Solve problems.

Keep looking for clues until you solve the problem.

For some math problems, you may not know where to start. Try different ways to find a solution. Look for clues about which way works best. Always check that your answer make sense.

To solve problems

Ask Yourself

- Can I say what the problem is asking for?
- Can I ask questions to understand it better?
- Can I think about what does or doesn't make sense?
- Can I try a different way if I need to?

Then, Discuss with a Partner

- I made sure I understood the problem when I …
- I know my answer makes sense because …

MATH HABIT ②

Think and reason.

Make sense of the words and the numbers in a problem.

Reasoning is thinking in a way that puts ideas together. If you know one thing, then you know another thing. Reasoning is using math rules and common sense together.

To use reasoning to solve a problem

Ask Yourself

- Can I use addition to solve a subtraction problem?

- When I see an equation, can I think of a story that could go with it?

- Can I write an equation to find the answer to a problem?

- Can I try out my answer to see if it makes sense in the story?

Then, Discuss with a Partner

- I turned the problem into numbers when I …

- I checked my answer by …

MATH HABIT ❸

Show and explain.

Share your math ideas to help others understand you.

When you explain your math ideas to others, it helps you understand them even better. And that helps you solve other problems later. It also helps to listen to other people. You can get new ideas too!

To show and explain your ideas

Ask Yourself

- Can I use words to show how to solve the problem?
- Can I use pictures or act out the problem with objects?
- Can I ask questions to understand another person's ideas better?

Then, Discuss with a Partner

- I showed my ideas when I wrote …
- I explained my ideas when I said …

MATH HABIT ④

SMP 4 Model with mathematics.

Use math in the real world.

Solve problems in real life.

One of the best ways to use your math thinking is to solve real problems. Words tell the story for the problem. Math can turn the words into a model, like a picture or equation.

You can use models to solve problems about shopping, sports, or . . . almost anything!

To solve a real-life problem

Ask Yourself

• Can I draw a picture or write an equation to show the math?
• Can I use my math model to solve the problem?
• Can I check that my answer makes sense?

Then, Discuss with a Partner

• I used a math model when I . . .
• I know my answer makes sense because . . .

MATH HABIT ⑤

SMP 5 Use appropriate tools strategically.

Choose a tool.

Decide when to use tools like a ruler, a pencil, or mental math.

There are many tools to use in math. You can use a pencil to do a lot of math. Sometimes you can use base ten blocks. Often you can just do the math in your head.

To choose the best tools

Ask Yourself

- Can I do any part of the problem in my head?
- Can I write the problem on paper?
- Can I make a table or diagram?
- Can I use a ruler to solve the problem?

Then, Discuss with a Partner

- The tools I chose for this problem are …
- I chose these tools because …

MATH HABIT ❻

SMP 6 Attend to precision.

Be clear and precise.

Try to be exactly right in what you say and do.

Everybody likes to be right when they do math. But sometimes people make mistakes. So it's good to check your work. And it's good to say exactly what you mean when you talk about your math ideas.

To be exactly right

Ask Yourself

- Can I use words that will help everyone understand my math ideas?
- Can I find different ways to check my work when I add or subtract?
- Can I always think about whether my answer makes sense?

Then, Discuss with a Partner

- I was careful to use the right words when I …
- I checked my answer by …

MATH HABIT ⑦

Zoom in and zoom out.

Look for what's the same and what's different.

Math has rules. Look at these problems.

$2 + 0 = 2$
$3 + 0 = 3$

You see rules by *zooming out* to look at what's the *same* about problems. They show that any number plus 0 is that number.

You can also *zoom in,* to see what's *different* about problems. The number added to 0 is different in each problem.

To zoom in and zoom out

Ask Yourself

- Can I see how different whole numbers are all made from hundreds, tens, and ones?
- Can I see what happens when I add numbers in any order?

Then, Discuss with a Partner

- I zoomed out and used a math rule when I …
- I zoomed in and found a difference when I looked at …

MATH HABIT ⑧

SMP 8 Look for and express regularity in repeated reasoning.

Use patterns.

Look for patterns in math to find shortcuts.

It's important in math to pay close attention. You might find a pattern or see a math idea.

Think about the pattern you see when you count by tens:

  10, 20, 30, 40, 50 …

You can use the pattern to make a good guess about what comes next.

To use patterns

Ask Yourself
- Can I find a pattern in a math problem?
- Can I use math words to describe your pattern?
- Can I make a good guess about what is next?

Then, Discuss with a Partner
- I saw a pattern in this problem when I looked at …
- I used the pattern to make a good guess when I …

Unit 1
Operations and Algebraic Thinking, Part 1

Let's learn about multiplying and dividing.

Real-World Connection How many 4-ounce bags of carrots will you need to make a salad that calls for 12 ounces of carrots? How many 3-inch blocks will you need to stack to make a 12-inch tall tower? How will you share a box of 12 erasers with 3 classmates?

Sure, you could just guess how many bags of carrots to buy and start handing out erasers until you run out. Or, you could use math facts to help you.

In This Unit You will learn how multiplication and division are related. The number sentences $4 \times \square = 12$ and $12 \div \square = 3$ may seem like mysteries at first. But, by learning to make math connections using multiplication and division, you can start to solve these mysteries. These new math connections can be really helpful whether you are sharing erasers, stacking blocks, or making a salad!

✓ Self Check

Before starting this unit, check off the skills you know below. As you complete each lesson, see how many more you can check off!

I can:	Before this unit	After this unit
explain multiplication using equal groups and arrays.	☐	☐
use order and grouping to make multiplying easier, for example: $6 \times 2 \times 5$ is equal to $6 \times (2 \times 5)$.	☐	☐
break apart numbers to make multiplying easier, for example: 3×8 is equal to $(3 \times 4) + (3 \times 4)$.	☐	☐
understand division as a multiplication problem, for example: $10 \div 2$ can be shown as $2 \times \square = 10$.	☐	☐
use multiplication and division facts up through the facts for 10.	☐	☐
find the rule for a pattern and explain it.	☐	☐

Think It Through

What is going on when you multiply numbers?

When you multiply, you work with equal groups.

These groups of shells are equal.

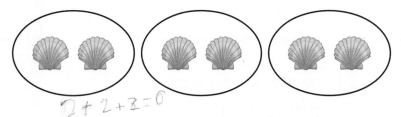

2 + 2 + 3 = 6

These groups of shells are NOT equal.

Think Multiplication is a way to find how many in all.

When you have equal groups of objects, you can **multiply** to find a total.

Groups are called equal groups when they all have the same number of objects.

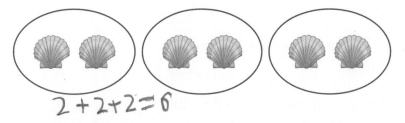

2 + 2 + 2 = 6

There are **3 groups**. There are **2 shells** in each group.

You can write this as **3 × 2**. Think of 3 × 2 as "3 groups of 2."

3 groups of 2 shells is 6 shells in all. 3 × 2 = 6

> ✏️ **Underline** the sentence that tells you what equal groups are.

Think You can use pictures and models to understand multiplication.

A picture can help you see what **multiplication** means.

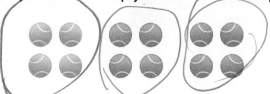

3 groups of 4 balls is 12 balls in all.

One factor tells
how many groups.

→ $\boxed{3 \times 4} = 12$ ←

The **product** is
the result. It tells
how many in all.

The $\times$ means
"groups of."

The other factor tells how
many are in each group.

$3 \times 4 = 12$ is a
multiplication equation.
The numbers you
multiply are called
factors.

When you see $3 \times 4 = 12$, you say, "Three times four equals 12."

You can arrange the equal groups into rows and stack them
on top of each other. This is called an **array**.

Array

3 rows with 4 balls in each row is 12 balls in all.

$3 \times 4 = 12$

▶ Reflect

1 Do the chairs in your classroom make an array? Explain why or why not.

_____

_____

_____

Think About > **Equal Groups in Multiplication**

🔍 **Let's Explore the Idea** Using a picture to show equal groups can help you think about multiplication.

Use the picture to answer problems 2—5.

2 How many fish tanks are there? _____ 3 _____

3 How many fish are in each tank? _____ 6 _____

4 How many fish are there altogether? _____ 18 _____

5 What multiplication equation could you write to tell about the fish? _____

Now try these two problems.

6 There are 4 apple trees in Nell's backyard. She picked 5 apples from each tree. Draw a picture to show the equal groups.

4 × 5 = 20

5 + 5 + 5 + 5 = 20

7 What multiplication equation could you write about the apples? _____

Let's Talk About It

Solve the problems below as a group.

8 Look at the picture you drew for problem 6. Explain how you decided what to draw to help you solve the problem.

_____

_____

9 Look at problem 6 again. Draw an array to show the equal groups.

10 Look at the array below.

What multiplication equation can you write for this array? Explain what each number in the multiplication equation tells you. $2 \times 1 = 18$ $2 \times 9 = 18$

_____

▶ **Try It Another Way** **Work with your group to use rectangles to understand multiplication.**

11 You can push the tiles in an array together to make a rectangle. Write the multiplication equation the rectangle below shows. $3 \times 7 = 21$

12 Draw a rectangle made up of square tiles that shows $5 \times 3 = 15$.

Connect > Ideas About Equal Groups in Multiplication

Talk through these problems as a class, then write your answers below.

13 Explain Travis used the picture below to write the multiplication equation $4 \times 6 = 24$.

What did he do wrong?

_____

_____

14 Create Write a problem that could be solved using the multiplication equation $9 \times 4 = 36$.

_____

_____

_____

15 Analyze Amelia used the array at the right to write the multiplication equation $3 \times 2 = 6$.

What multiplication equation would Amelia write if she added another row of 2 triangles to the bottom of the array?

_____

_____

Look at the array above. How would it change if Amelia added 1 more triangle to each row? What multiplication equation would she write?

_____

_____

Ideas About Equal Groups in Multiplication

16 Put It Together Use what you have learned to complete this task.

Tucker arranged his pennies in an array.

Part A Write the multiplication equation the array shows. Explain what each number means.

_____

_____

_____

_____

Part B Draw a model for the multiplication equation. Show equal groups.

🔵 Use What You Know

In Lesson 1, you learned about the meaning of multiplication. This lesson will help you solve multiplication problems using what you already know. Take a look at this problem.

> Ava's mom bought 2 packs of 3 T-shirts. Her dad bought 3 packs of 2 T-shirts. How many T-shirts did each of Ava's parents buy?
>
> **Mom**  **Dad**

a. How many packs of T-shirts did Ava's mom buy? _____

b. How many T-shirts were in each of her mom's packs? _____

c. What multiplication equation could you write to find out how many T-shirts Ava's mom bought? _____

d. How many packs of T-shirts did Ava's dad buy? _____

e. How many T-shirts were in each of her dad's packs? _____

f. What multiplication equation could you write to find out how many T-shirts Ava's dad bought? _____

g. Explain what is the same and what is different about the two multiplication equations you wrote. _____

_____

_____

On the previous page you saw that the order of the factors in a multiplication problem does not matter. If you know that 2×3 is 6, then you also know that 3×2 is 6.

Sometimes you need to multiply three numbers together. You can use parentheses ( ) to show which two numbers you want to multiply first. Look at the problem below.

> Jayden bought 4 boxes of hot dogs. Each box has 2 packs.
>
> Each pack has 5 hot dogs. How many hot dogs did she buy?

- **One way** to think about this is to first find how many packs there are. Then multiply by the number of hot dogs in each pack, 5.

4×2 packs is 8 packs.

8 packs with 5 hot dogs each is 40 hot dogs.

$(4 \times 2) \times 5 = 40$

- **Another way** to think about this is to first find how many hot dogs are in each box. Then multiply by the number of boxes, 4.

2×5 is 10 hot dogs in a box.

4 boxes with 10 hot dogs is 40 hot dogs.

$4 \times (2 \times 5) = 40$

▷ Reflect

1 What did you just learn that can help you with multiplication?

_____

_____

_____

Learn About ▶ **Using Order to Multiply**

Read the problem below. Then explore ways to show you can multiply factors in a multiplication equation in any order.

> Chad read books at the library each week for 6 weeks. He read 3 books each week. Mia read books at the library each week for 3 weeks. She read 6 books each week. Who read more books at the library, Chad or Mia?

▶ **Picture It** **You can use equal groups to help you understand the problem.**

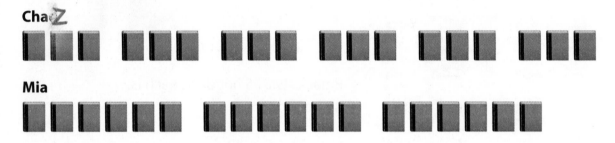

▶ **Model It** **You can also use arrays to help you understand the problem. Each row in the arrays shows the number of books Chad or Mia read each week.**

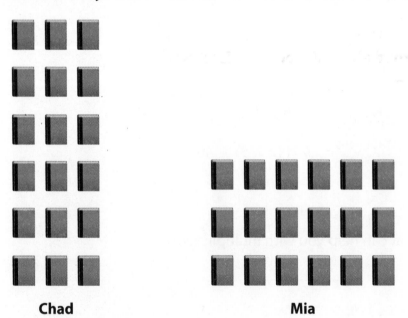

Connect It Now you will solve the problem from the previous page using equations.

2 What multiplication equation could you write to find the number of books Chad read? _____

3 What multiplication equation could you write to find the number of books Mia read? _____

4 Who read more books? _____

5 Explain how you could know that Chad and Mia read the same number of books without finding the product in each multiplication equation.

_____

_____

_____

6 Your teacher tells you that $8 \times 9 = 72$. Explain how you know what 9×8 equals.

_____

_____

Try It Use what you just learned about the order of factors to solve these problems. Show your work on a separate sheet of paper.

7 Josie has 5 cups with 4 tokens in each cup. Ian has 4 cups with 5 tokens in each cup. Draw a model to show that Josie and Ian have the same number of tokens.

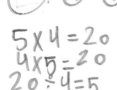

$5 \times 4 = 20$
$4 \times 5 = 20$
$20 \div 4 = 5$
$20 \div 5 = 4$

$5 \times 5 = 25$
$5 \times 5 = 25$
$25 \div 5 = 5$
$25 \div 5 = 5$

8 Ashish has 6 drawers in his dresser. He puts 8 shirts in each drawer. Gita has the same number of shirts in all as Ashish. She has 8 dresser drawers. She wants to put an equal number of shirts in each drawer. How many shirts should Gita put in each drawer? _____

Learn About ▶ **Using Grouping to Multiply**

Read the problem below. Then explore different ways to group factors to help you multiply three numbers.

Nykole decorates her gloves with plastic jewels. She glues 3 jewels onto each finger and thumb. How many jewels does she use?

▶ **Picture It** **You can multiply 5 fingers × 3 jewels on each finger to find that she has 15 jewels on each glove. Then multiply the 15 jewels × 2 to find how many jewels on both gloves altogether.**

You could also multiply 2 gloves × 5 fingers on each hand to show there are 10 fingers, including thumbs. Then multiply 10 fingers × 3 jewels to find how many jewels she uses.

▶ **Model It** **You can write the multiplication problem and use parentheses to show which two numbers you will multiply first.**

$(3 \times 5) \times 2 \longrightarrow 15 \times 2 = 30$

You could also choose to multiply different numbers first.

$3 \times (5 \times 2) \longrightarrow 3 \times 10 = 30$

▶ **Connect It** **Now you will solve the problem from the previous page using equations.**

9 Use parentheses to show one way to group $3 \times 5 \times 2$. _____

10 Use parentheses to show a different way to group $3 \times 5 \times 2$. _____

11 Which way would you choose to find the product? Explain why.

_____

_____

_____

12 Explain how you can use grouping to make multiplying three factors easier.

_____

_____

_____

▶ **Try It** **Use what you just learned about grouping factors to solve these problems. Show your work on a separate sheet of paper.**

13 Use parentheses to show two different ways to group $7 \times 2 \times 4$. Then choose one of the ways and show the steps to finding the product.

_____

_____

14 Use parentheses to show two different ways to group $2 \times 4 \times 3$. Then choose one of the ways and show the steps to finding the product.

_____

_____

Learn About > **Using Order and Grouping to Multiply**

Read the problem below. Then explore different ways to order and group factors to make multiplication easier.

> Joelle bought 2 bags of bananas. There are 9 bunches in each bag, and there are 5 bananas in each bunch. How many bananas did Joelle buy?

▶ **Model It** **Think of the multiplication problem you can write: $2 \times 9 \times 5$.**

You can use what you have learned about multiplying in any order and grouping to help make the problem easier.

Start with $2 \times 9 \times 5$.

First, change the order of the numbers. Switch the 2 and the 9.

Now you have $9 \times 2 \times 5$.

Then, group it like this: $9 \times (2 \times 5)$.

Multiply the numbers in parentheses: $2 \times 5 = \mathbf{10}$.

Then do the last multiplication: $9 \times \mathbf{10} = 90$.

▶ **Model It** **You can use diagrams to help you understand the problem.**

The first two diagrams show two ways you can solve the problem using just grouping. The third diagram shows how you can solve the problem by changing the order of the numbers before using grouping.

```
  2 × 9 × 5          2 × 9 × 5          9 × 2 × 5
   \ /  |             |  \ /             |  \ /
   18 × 5             2 × 45            9 × 10
     \  /              \  /              \  /
      90                90                90
```

Connect It Now you will choose which way to solve the problem from the previous page.

15 You can order and group the factors in the multiplication expression $2 \times 9 \times 5$ in different ways. Look at the ways shown below. Fill in the missing numbers.

$(9 \times 2) \times \underline{\hspace{1cm}} = 90$ $(5 \times 2) \times \underline{\hspace{1cm}} = 90$ $\underline{\hspace{1cm}} \times (9 \times 5) = 90$

16 Remember that you must multiply numbers inside parentheses first. Look back at the multiplication equations in problem 15. Multiply the numbers in the parentheses, then fill in the missing numbers below.

$(\underline{\hspace{1cm}}) \times \underline{\hspace{1cm}} = 90$ $(\underline{\hspace{1cm}}) \times \underline{\hspace{1cm}} = 90$ $\underline{\hspace{1cm}} \times (\underline{\hspace{1cm}}) = 90$

17 Which of the three multiplication equations in problem 15 do you think is the easiest to solve? Explain why you think so.

_____

_____

_____

18 Explain how you can use grouping and multiplying in any order to make multiplying three numbers easier.

_____

_____

_____

Try It Use what you just learned about ordering and grouping factors to solve these problems. Show your work on a separate sheet of paper.

19 Change the order of the factors and use parentheses to show one way to solve $3 \times 7 \times 3$. Then show the steps to finding the product.

_____

20 Change the order of the factors and use parentheses to show one way to solve $4 \times 9 \times 2$. Then show the steps to finding the product.

_____

Practice ▶ Using Order and Grouping to Multiply

Study the example below. Then solve problems 21–23.

Example

There are 8 rows of tables in the cafeteria. Each row has 5 tables. Maria knows that 5 × 8 is 40. How can she use this to figure out how many tables there are?

Look at how you could show your work using arrays.

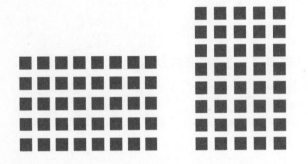

Solution ___You can multiply numbers in any order.___

5 × 8 = 40, so 8 × 5 = 40. There are 40 tables.

The first array shows 5 × 8. The second array looks the same, just turned on its side. It shows 8 × 5.

Pair/Share
If two arrays have the same total, how do they show two different multiplication facts?

---

21 There are 2 classes of third graders. In each class, there are 3 rows of desks, with 7 desks in each row. Write a multiplication expression to find the number of desks in both classes. Show how to group the factors to find the product. Then write the answer.

Show your work.

Which two numbers have a product that would be easy to multiply by in your head?

Pair/Share
How would solving the problem be different if you grouped the factors another way?

Solution _____

22 AJ needs to solve $3 \times 8 \times 2$. Show one way to find the answer. Use parentheses to show how you grouped the numbers.

Show your work.

I think it would be easiest if you changed the order of the factors before you grouped them.

Solution _____

Pair/Share
How did you decide which two numbers to multiply first?

---

23 Matt knows $4 \times 6 = 24$. What other math fact does this help Matt remember? Circle the letter of the correct answer.

A $6 + 4 = 10$

B $8 \times 3 = 24$

C $24 - 6 = 18$

D $6 \times 4 = 24$

Sadie chose **A** as the correct answer. How did she get that answer?

What have you learned about the order of factors in multiplication?

_____

_____

_____

_____

Pair/Share
Does Sadie's answer make sense?

Practice **Using Order and Grouping to Multiply**

Solve the problems.

1 Jackson knows $9 \times 7 = 63$. He needs to solve _____ $\times 9 = 63$. What number goes in the blank?

A 5

B 6

C 7

D 8

2 Which of the following is NOT true?

A $3 \times 6 \times 3 = 6 \times 3 \times 3$

B $3 \times 6 \times 3 = 9 \times 3$

C $3 \times 6 \times 3 = 9 \times 6$

D $3 \times 6 \times 3 = 3 \times 18$

3 Gisell's service group is making sandwiches for a community picnic. There are 7 children in the service group. Each child is making 5 sandwiches. It takes 2 slices of bread to make a sandwich. What is the total number of slices of bread the children need to make the sandwiches?

Answer _____ slices of bread

4 Lyn's mom has pictures arranged on her refrigerator in rows. There are 3 rows of pictures. There are 7 pictures in each row. Which of the following expressions or arrays could be used to find the total number of pictures? Circle the letter for all that apply.

A 3 × 7

B 7 × 3

C 7 × 7 × 7

D
□□□
□□□
□□□
□□□
□□□
□□□
□□□

E
□□□□□□□
□□□□□□□
□□□□□□□

5 Dan has 2 photo albums. Each photo album has 8 pages. Dan can fit 4 pictures on each page. How many pictures can Dan fit in the albums?

Show your work.

Answer _____ pictures

 **Self Check** Go back and see what you can check off on the Self Check on page 1.

Split Numbers to Multiply

⟳ Use What You Know

In Lesson 2, you learned some ways to make multiplying numbers easier. Take a look at this problem.

Ty has 6 bunches of carrots. There are 3 carrots in each bunch. How many carrots does Ty have altogether?

a. Circle 5 of the bunches.
What multiplication equation can you write to find how many carrots are in 5 bunches? _____

b. Circle the 1 bunch that is left.
What multiplication equation can you write to find how many carrots are in 1 bunch? _____

c. Look at the two sets of bunches you circled. You found the number of carrots in each set.
Explain how you could use those two numbers to find the total number of carrots.

_____

_____

_____

▷▷ Find Out More

You can break apart numbers to help you figure out multiplication problems you do not know.

Ty did not know what 6 groups of 3 were, but he did know what 5 groups of 3 were. That left 1 group of 3.

Ty broke apart **6** into **5 + 1**. Then he multiplied each part by 3 and added the products together.

You can write 5 bunches of 3 carrots plus 1 bunch of 3 carrots like this:
(5 × 3) + (1 × 3)

The parentheses show you that you multiply each set of numbers first, and then add the products together.

You can also show this using an array.

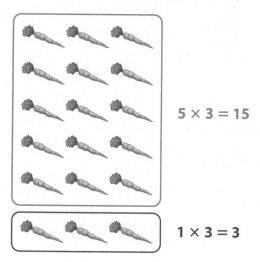

$5 \times 3 = 15$

$1 \times 3 = 3$

You can write what the array shows three ways:
6 × 3   or   (5 + 1) × 3   or   (5 × 3) + (1 × 3)

▶ Reflect

1 What if Ty had 4 carrots in each bunch instead of 3? Explain how he could break apart the numbers to find the product of 6 × 4.

_____

_____

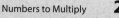

Read the problem below. Then explore different ways to break apart one of the numbers to solve the problem.

> Mario has 6 vases of flowers. There are 4 flowers in each vase. How many flowers does Mario have in all? Break apart one of the numbers to find the answer.

▶ **Picture It** **You can use equal groups to help understand the problem.**

Mario chose to break apart the number of groups to find the answer.

▶ **Model It** **You can also use an array to help understand the problem.**

Mario made an array and then broke apart the rows to show the new groups.

▶ **Solve It** **You can also use words to help understand the problem.**

6 vases of 4 flowers is the same as 4 vases of 4 flowers plus 2 vases of 4 flowers.

Connect It Now you will explore different ways to solve the problem from the previous page.

2 What numbers did Mario break 6 into to help him solve the problem?

_____

3 What two multiplication equations did Mario use then?

_____

4 What is another way you could break apart 6?

_____

_____

5 What numbers could Mario break 4 into to help him solve the problem?

_____

6 What two multiplication equations would Mario use if he broke apart the 4?

_____

7 Explain why Mario's way of solving the problem is not the only way.

_____

_____

_____

Try It Use what you just learned to solve this problem.

8 Show two different ways to break apart the numbers to solve 4×3. Draw models and show the math equations you used.

_____

_____

Learn About ▶ **Breaking Apart Numbers to Multiply**

Read the problem below. Then explore ways to break apart a number to make one hard multiplication equation into two easier multiplication equations.

> Matt shared some crackers with 8 friends. He gave each friend 7 crackers. How many crackers did Matt give away? Break apart one of the numbers to find the answer.

▶ **Model It** **You can use an array to help understand the problem.**

Instead of breaking apart the rows (the number of friends), Matt broke apart the columns (the number of crackers).

 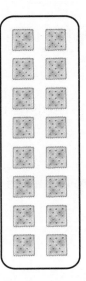

▶ **Solve It** **You can also use words and multiplication expressions to help understand the problem.**

Giving 8 friends 7 crackers is the same as giving 8 friends 5 crackers each, then giving each of them 2 more crackers. You can write the multiplication three ways:

8×7 or $8 \times (5 + 2)$ or $(8 \times 5) + (8 \times 2)$

Connect It   **Now you will think more about the problem from the previous page.**

9 What numbers did Matt break 7 into to help him solve the problem? _____ 5 + 2

10 What two multiplication expressions did Matt use then? _____ 8 × 5 + 2 × 8

11 Show how to use the two multiplication expressions to find the answer.

_____ 8 × 5 = 40   8 × 2 = 16 _____ 4 + 16 = 56 _____

12 Madison knows the answer to 4 × 7. How can this help her multiply 8 × 7?

_____

_____

13 Explain why someone might want to break apart one of the numbers in a multiplication equation.

_____

_____

Try It   **Use what you learned about breaking apart numbers to solve these problems.**

14 Alice knows the answer to 5 × 7. How can that help her find the answer to 6 × 7? Draw a model and show the math equations you used.

_____

15 Tim knows the answer to 6 × 7. How can that help him find the answer to 6 × 9? Draw a model and show the math equations you used.

_____

Practice ▶ **Breaking Apart Numbers to Multiply**

Study the example below. Then solve problems 16–18.

Example

Stacy is making 4 bracelets. Each bracelet uses 7 silver beads. How many silver beads does Stacy need? Show how to break apart one of the numbers to make the problem easier to solve.

Look at how you could show your work using an array.

$2 \times 7 = 14$

$14 + 14 = 28$

$2 \times 7 = 14$

Solution _28 silver beads_

The student broke apart the 4 into $2 + 2$ and then added the two products together.

💬 **Pair/Share**

How else could you have broken apart one of the numbers to solve this problem?

---

16 There are 6 bowls of apples. There are 6 apples in each bowl. Show how to break apart the number 6 to make the problem easier to solve.

What ways do you know to break apart the number 6? Which way do you think is easiest?

💬 **Pair/Share**

What is another model you could have used to show how to break the number apart?

---

17 Joe has 8 shelves with 9 books on each shelf. How many books does Joe have altogether? Show how to break apart one of the numbers to make the problem easier to solve.

You can break apart the number 9 many different ways.

Pair/Share
How did you and your partner decide how to break apart one of the numbers?

Solution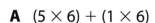

---

18 Jordan found 6×8 by breaking apart the 6 into $5 + 1$. Which of the following correctly shows the next step in finding the result? Circle the letter of the correct answer.

A $(5 \times 6) + (1 \times 6)$

B $(6 \times 8) + (1 \times 8)$

C $(5 + 8) \times (1 + 8)$

D $(5 \times 8) + (1 \times 8)$

Jordan broke apart the 6 in 6×8. What will he do with the 8?

Avery chose **A** as the correct answer. How did she get that answer?

Pair/Share
Does Avery's answer make sense?

Practice ▶ **Breaking Apart Numbers to Multiply**

Solve the problems.

1 Tucker solved 7 × 5 by breaking it apart as shown below.

$$(7 \times 3) + (7 \times \underline{\hspace{1cm}})$$

What number belongs in the blank?

A 1

B 2

C 4

D 8

2 Cole has 8 packs of pencils. There are 5 pencils in each pack. He wants to know how many pencils he has in all. The model below shows how he breaks apart one number in the problem.

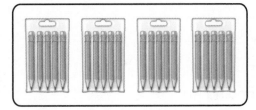 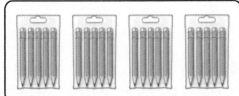

Which expression shows how Cole solves the problem?

A (4 × 5) + (4 × 5)

B (8 × 2) + (8 × 2)

C (4 × 2) + (4 × 2)

D (3 × 5) + (5 × 5)

3 Use the array below to solve 8 × 8. First draw circles to break the array into two groups. Then fill in the blanks to show how you broke the numbers apart.

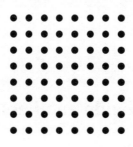

$$8 \times 8 = (8 \times \underline{\quad}) + (8 \times \underline{\quad})$$

4 Is each expression equivalent to the product of 6 and 9? Choose *Yes* or *No*.

a. (6 × 3) + (6 × 3) ☐ Yes ☐ No

b. (6 × 4) + (6 × 5) ☐ Yes ☐ No

c. 6 × (6 + 3) ☐ Yes ☐ No

d. 9 × (2 + 4) ☐ Yes ☐ No

e. (9 × 3) + (9 × 3) ☐ Yes ☐ No

5 There are 9 rows in Mrs. Mitchell's flower garden. Each row has 9 flowers planted in it. How many flowers are planted in the garden? Show how to break apart the numbers to find the answer.

Answer There are _____ flowers in the garden.

✔ **Self Check** **Go back and see what you can check off on the Self Check on page 1.**

Think It Through

What is going on when we divide numbers?

When you **divide**, you separate a number of items into equal-sized groups.

Suppose you have a total of 6 socks. One way you can divide the socks is to make 3 groups and put 2 socks in each group.

There are 6 socks in all. There are 3 groups. There are 2 socks in each group.

Think You can use division to find the number in each group.

When you know the total and the number of groups, you can divide to find how many to put in each group.

✏️ **Circle** the division equation.

Jake has 8 cookies and 2 plates.
There are 8 cookies in all.
There are 2 groups.

He puts the same number of cookies on each plate. 8 ÷ 2 tells you how many cookies Jake puts on each plate.

There are 4 cookies on each plate.

8 ÷ 2 = 4

Think You can use division to find the number of groups.

When you know the total and the number in each group, you can divide to find how many groups you can make.

Missy has 15 balloons. She ties them into groups of 3.

15 balloons   5 groups of 3 balloons

15 ÷ 3 tells you how many groups Missy can make.

There are 15 balloons in all. There are 3 balloons in each group.

There are 5 groups of balloons.

You can write the **division** equation 15 ÷ 3 = 5.

Did you notice that a division equation always starts with the total amount?

▶ Reflect

1 Use your own words to explain how drawing a picture can help you solve a division problem.

_____

_____

_____

_____

_____

Think About **Equal Groups in Division**

🔍 **Let's Explore the Idea** **Using a model to show equal groups can help you think about division.**

Use the pictures of shells and pails to answer problems 2–5.

2 How many shells are there? _____

3 How many pails are there? _____

4 Ben wants to put the same number of shells in each of the pails. How many shells should he put in each pail? _____

5 What division equation can you write to tell about the shells? _____

Now try these two problems.

6 Marc's dad picked 24 oranges. He wants to put all the oranges in bags. He decides to put 6 oranges in each bag. Draw a model to show how many bags he needs.

7 What division equation can you write about the oranges? _____

Let's Talk About It

Solve the problems below as a group.

8 Look at the picture you drew for problem 6. Explain how you decided what to draw to help you solve the problem.

_____

_____

9 Look at problem 6 again. Imagine Marc's dad changes his mind. Instead of putting 6 oranges in each bag, he decides to put all the oranges in 6 bags. He will put the same number of oranges in each bag. How does this change the division in problem 6?

_____

_____

10 Draw a model to show how many oranges will go in each of the 6 bags.

▶ **Try It Another Way** Work with your group to use the arrays to solve the division equations.

11 45 ÷ 5 = _____

■ ■ ■ ■ ■ ■ ■ ■ ■
■ ■ ■ ■ ■ ■ ■ ■ ■
■ ■ ■ ■ ■ ■ ■ ■ ■
■ ■ ■ ■ ■ ■ ■ ■ ■
■ ■ ■ ■ ■ ■ ■ ■ ■

12 42 ÷ 7 = _____

▲ ▲ ▲ ▲ ▲ ▲
▲ ▲ ▲ ▲ ▲ ▲
▲ ▲ ▲ ▲ ▲ ▲
▲ ▲ ▲ ▲ ▲ ▲
▲ ▲ ▲ ▲ ▲ ▲
▲ ▲ ▲ ▲ ▲ ▲
▲ ▲ ▲ ▲ ▲ ▲

Connect ▸ **Ideas About Equal Groups in Division**

Talk through these problems as a class, then write your answers below.

13 **Explain** Maddy used this array of stars to show the division problem $8 \div 4 = 2$.

What did she do wrong?

_____

_____

14 **Create** Write a problem that could be solved using the division equation $16 \div 2 = 8$.

_____

_____

15 **Compare** David and Mitch each bought a box of pears at the grocery store. Look at how each boy divided his pears into equal groups.

David   Mitch

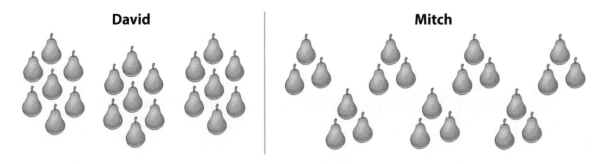

What is the same about the two boxes of pears?

_____

_____

What is different about the way the boys divided their pears into groups?

_____

_____

16 Put It Together Use what you have learned to complete this task.

> Cory has 20 crayons. He wants to give the same number of crayons to each of his friends.

Part A Write two different questions about Cory's crayons that can be answered using division.

1. _____

_____

_____

2. _____

_____

_____

Part B Choose one question to answer. Circle the number of the question you chose. Show how to find the answer using pictures or an array. Then write the division equation that shows the answer to your question.

_____

_____

_____

_____

_____

_____

Think It Through

How are multiplication and division related?

Multiplication joins equal groups to find a total, or product. Division starts with a total and breaks it up into equal groups. The result is called the **quotient**.

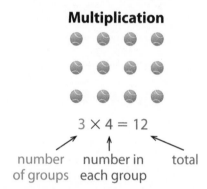

Multiplication

$3 \times 4 = 12$

number of groups · number in each group · total

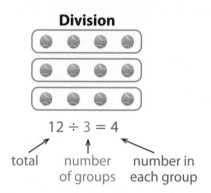

Division

$12 \div 3 = 4$

total · number of groups · number in each group

Think **You can use multiplication or division equations to describe a problem.**

Juan arranges pennies in an array.

✏️ **Circle** the total in each equation.

You can use multiplication to tell how many pennies there are in all.

$4 \times 8 = 32$ pennies   or $8 \times 4 = 32$ pennies

You can use division to tell how many pennies are in each row and how many rows there are.

$32 \div 4 = 8$ pennies in each row   or $32 \div 8 = 4$ rows of pennies

Notice that all of the equations use the same three numbers: 4, 8, and 32.

Think   Division equations have related multiplication equations.

To help you solve a division problem, you can write a multiplication equation that uses the same numbers. Look at the problem below.

> Nina buys 20 stickers. She puts the same number of stickers on each of 5 pages in her scrapbook. How many stickers does she put on each page?

5 times what number equals 20?

You know the total number of stickers is 20. You also know the number of groups, or pages, is 5. The unknown number you need to find is how many in each group, or the number of stickers on each scrapbook page.

One Way
You can write a division equation.

$$20 \div 5 = \square$$

$$20 \div 5 = 4$$

Nina puts 4 stickers on each page.

Another Way
You can write a multiplication equation.

$$5 \times \square = 20$$

$$5 \times 4 = 20$$

▶ Reflect

1 Use your own words to explain how you could use multiplication to find $35 \div 5$.

_____

_____

_____

_____

Think About ▶ **Multiplication and Division Connections**

🔍 **Let's Explore the Idea** **You can think about a problem as division or multiplication.**

Read the following problem. Then answer problems 2–5.

A pet store has 18 hamsters. The shop owner wants to put 3 hamsters in each cage. How many cages does the shop owner need for all the hamsters?

2 Draw a model using equal groups or an array to show the problem.

3 Write a division equation for the problem. Use a ☐ for the unknown number.

_____

4 Write a multiplication equation for the problem. Use a ☐ for the unknown number.

_____

5 How many cages does the shop owner need? _____

Now read this problem and answer problems 6–8.

Manuel has 42 quarters. He puts them into 7 piles. He puts the same number of quarters in each pile. How many quarters are in each pile?

6 Write a division equation for the problem. Use a ☐ for the unknown number.

_____

7 Write a multiplication equation for the problem. Use a ☐ for the unknown number. _____

8 How many quarters are in each pile? _____

Let's Talk About It

Solve the problems below as a group.

9 Look at your answer to problem 6. Explain how you knew what equation to write.

_____

_____

_____

Look at your answer to problem 7. How can you use your multiplication equation to solve the problem?

_____

_____

_____

10 Justin knows that $8 \times 7 = 56$. What related division equations can he write?

_____

_____

Try It Another Way Work with your group to find the number that goes in the ☐ for each problem.

11 $3 \times \square = 24$

$24 \div 3 = \square$ $\square = $ _____

12 $\square \times 9 = 54$

$54 \div \square = 9$ $\square = $ _____

Connect ▸ **Multiplication and Division**

Talk through these problems as a class, then write your answers below.

13 **Identify** Elisa planted the same number of flowers in each pot. Look at the picture below. Then write two multiplication equations and two division equations that the picture shows.

4

$3 \times 4 = 12$ $4 \times 3 = 12$ $12 \div 3 = 4$ $12 \div 4 = 3$

14 **Explain** Yasmin saw the problem $63 \div \square = 7$. She thought, "There are 63 things in all that are divided into groups. There are 7 in each group." Explain how Yasmin can use multiplication to help her find the number of groups.

You can use your fact family,
ask your self what is $7x — = 63$

15 **Analyze** Marissa has 4 boxes of markers with 6 markers in each box. She wrote the following equations:

$4 \times 6 = 24$

$6 \times 4 = 24$

$24 \div 4 = 6$

$24 \div 6 = 4$

Circle the number in each equation that shows the total number of markers.
Put a box around the number in each equation that shows the number of groups.
Underline the number in each equation that shows the number in each group.

Apply **Ideas About Multiplication and Division** **41**

16 Put It Together Use what you have learned to complete this task.

Part A Write a problem that can be solved using the equation $5 \times \square = 15$.
Make the problem about arranging desks in a classroom.

_____

_____

_____

_____

Part B Solve your problem. Draw a model that shows your problem and solution.

Use What You Know

You learned that multiplication and division are related. Look at this problem to see how multiplication can help you with division facts.

Kenny has 24 marbles. He puts the same number of marbles into each of 3 bags. How many marbles are in each bag?

a. Write a division equation you need to solve to answer this question. _____

b. Think about finding the number of marbles in each bag as a multiplication problem. How many equal groups are there? _____

c. You don't know how many marbles are in each group. Write a

multiplication equation that says 3 groups of ☐ marbles is 24. _____

d. Multiplication facts for 3 are shown below.

$3 \times 1 = 3$	$3 \times 2 = 6$	$3 \times 3 = 9$	$3 \times 4 = 12$	$3 \times 5 = 15$
$3 \times 6 = 18$	$3 \times 7 = 21$	$3 \times 8 = 24$	$3 \times 9 = 27$	$3 \times 10 = 30$

Write the fact for this problem. _____

e. What number is ☐? _____

f. How many marbles are in each bag? _____

g. How could you check your answer?

_____

_____

_____

Fact families are sets of related multiplication and division facts. Here is one example:

$$3 \times 8 = 24 \qquad 8 \times 3 = 24 \qquad 24 \div 8 = 3 \qquad 24 \div 3 = 8$$

This fact family has two multiplication facts and two division facts. All the facts use the same three numbers: 3, 8, and 24. If you know one fact in the family, you can find all the others, too.

The unknown number in a multiplication or division problem can be any one of the three numbers in a fact family. You can choose any fact in the family to help you find the answer.

For example, you might need to solve $\square \div 9 = 6$ to answer a question. You can write each fact in the family to find one that you might know. You can also use an array to help you complete this fact family.

$6 \times 9 = \square$

$9 \times 6 = \square$

$\square \div 6 = 9$

$\square \div 9 = 6$

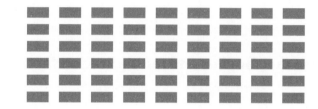

The array can help you to see that $6 \times 9 = $ **54** and $9 \times 6 = $ **54**. You can use these facts to write the related division facts: **54** $\div 6 = 9$ and **54** $\div 9 = 6$.

▶ Reflect

1 How are the multiplication facts in a fact family alike? How are they different? How are the division facts alike and different?

_____

_____

_____

Learn About ▶ Working with Division Facts

Read the problem below. Then explore different ways to find the unknown number in a division fact.

Jo knows nickels are worth 5 cents, and she needs 40 cents altogether. She wants to find how many nickels she needs. Jo writes $40 \div 5 = \square$.

▶ **Model It** **You can use a number line to help you understand the problem.**

Skip count by 5s to find the answer. Start at 0 and jump by 5s until you get to 40.

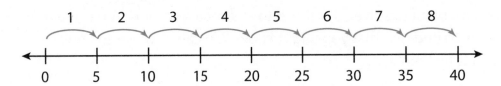

▶ **Model It** **You can use fact families and multiplication facts you know.**

Here are the facts in this family:

$5 \times \square = 40$ $\qquad$ $\square \times 5 = 40$ $\qquad$ $40 \div \square = 5$ $\qquad$ $40 \div 5 = \square$

Write the multiplication facts for 5:

$5 \times 1 = 5$	$5 \times 2 = 10$	$5 \times 3 = 15$	$5 \times 4 = 20$	$5 \times 5 = 25$
$5 \times 6 = 30$	$5 \times 7 = 35$	$5 \times 8 = 40$	$5 \times 9 = 45$	$5 \times 10 = 50$

Look for the fact that has the numbers you know from the fact family, 5 and 40. Use that fact to fill in the unknown numbers above.

Connect It Now you will use fact families to solve another problem like the one on the previous page.

2 Mo wants to know how many nickels he needs to make 45 cents. He writes $45 \div \square = 5$. What other division fact can he write to model this problem?

_____

3 Write the two multiplication facts that are in the same fact family. Use $\square$ for the unknown number.

_____

4 Look at the list of multiplication facts for 5 on the previous page. Which fact will help Mo answer his division problem?

_____

5 Explain how you know which multiplication fact you can use to help you find the unknown number in a division fact.

_____

_____

_____

_____

_____

Try It Use what you just learned about fact families and the relationship between multiplication and division to solve these problems.

6 Write the missing product. Then complete this fact family.

$2 \times 3 =$ _____   _____   _____   _____

7 Write two multiplication facts Brice can use to solve $\square \div 3 = 7$.

_____

_____

Learn About ▶ **Using a Multiplication Table**

Read the problems below. Then explore different ways to use a multiplication table to complete multiplication and division facts.

Find the missing numbers.

$2 \times \square = 10$ $24 \div 6 = \square$ $6 \times \square = 48$ $\square \div 9 = 8$

▶ **Picture It** **You can use a multiplication table to find the numbers in multiplication and division fact families.**

A multiplication table shows both multiplication and division fact families.

	0	1	2	3	4	5	6	7	8	9
0	0	0	0	0	0	0	0	0	0	0
1	0	1	2	3	4	5	6	7	8	9
2	0	2	4	6	8	10	12	14	16	18
3	0	3	6	9	12	15	18	21	24	27
4	0	4	8	12	16	20	24	28	32	36
5	0	5	10	15	20	25	30	35	40	45
6	0	6	12	18	24	30	36	42	48	54
7	0	7	14	21	28	35	42	49	56	63
8	0	8	16	24	32	40	48	56	64	72
9	0	9	18	27	36	45	54	63	72	81

▶ **Model It** **Use the table above to complete the fact family.**

The multiplication table shows the three numbers that belong in the fact family for $2 \times \square = 10$. Look at the row for 2. Go across to find 10. Then look up to the top of that column to find the third number in the fact family. Fill in the blanks below.

$2 \times \underline{\quad} = 10$ $10 \div 2 = \underline{\quad}$

$\underline{\quad} \times 2 = 10$ $10 \div \underline{\quad} = 2$

Connect It Now you will use the multiplication table to find the unknown numbers in the other three facts from the previous page.

8 Look at the multiplication table. What are the three numbers in the fact family for $24 \div 6 = \square$?

_____

Now fill in the blank: $24 \div 6 =$ _____

9 What are the three numbers in the fact family for $6 \times \square = 48$?

_____

Now fill in the blank: $6 \times$ _____ $= 48$

10 What are the three numbers in the fact family for $\square \div 9 = 8$?

_____

Fill in the blank: _____ $\div 9 = 8$

11 Explain how you can use a multiplication table to find the three numbers in any fact family.

_____

_____

_____

_____

_____

Try It Use what you just learned about using a multiplication table to find the answers.

12 Use the multiplication table to write the equations in the fact family that includes 42 and 6. Show your work on a separate sheet of paper.

_____

13 Fill in the blank: $56 \div$ _____ $= 8$

Practice ▶ **Solving Problems with Facts**

Study the example below. Then solve problems 14–16.

Example

Today some students will give an oral report. The teacher is planning to have all the reports done in 15 minutes. Each student will get 3 minutes. How many students will give reports? Solve $3 \times \square = 15$.

Look at how you could show your work using a number line.

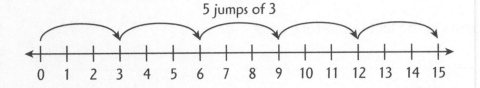

5 jumps of 3

Solution ___5 students___

Each jump on the number line shows the amount of time a student gets.

Pair/Share
What other equations can be used to solve this problem?

---

14 There are 35 students in the math club. They break into groups of 5 to work on a project. How many groups are there? Solve $35 \div \square = 5$.

Show your work.

How can you find the third number in this fact family?

Pair/Share
What are the other facts that belong to this fact family?

Solution _____

15 Each package contains 4 party favors. Sheila buys 9 packages. How many party favors does she buy? Solve $4 \times 9 = \square$.

Show your work.

> Are you looking for a factor or a product?

Solution _____

> **Pair/Share**
> Explain how you solved this problem.

---

16 Mrs. Tobin needs 30 juice boxes for her class. The juice boxes come in packages of 6. How many packages does she need? Solve $30 \div 6 = \square$. Circle the letter of the correct answer.

A 4

B 5

C 6

D 36

Pia chose **D** as the correct answer. How did she get that answer?

_____

_____

_____

_____

> Do you know a multiplication fact that can help you solve this problem?

> **Pair/Share**
> Does Pia's answer make sense?

Lesson 6 Multiplication and Division Facts   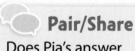 **49**

Practice ▸ **Solving Problems with Facts**

Solve the problems.

1 Which equation does NOT belong to the same fact family as $12 \div \square = 4$?

A $\square \times 4 = 12$

B $\square \times 2 = 12$

C $4 \times \square = 12$

D $12 \div \square = 4$

2 Which fact can you use to solve $5 = 20 \div \square$?

A $5 \times 5 = 25$

B $4 \times 5 = 20$

C $5 + 15 = 20$

D $6 \times 4 = 24$

3 Jan and Jon pick 18 apples. They share them equally. Which facts can be used to find the number of apples each person gets? Circle the letter for all that apply.

A $6 \times 3 = 18$

B $2 \times 9 = 18$

C $18 \div 2 = 9$

D $18 \div 3 = 6$

E $18 \div 9 = 2$

4 Does putting the number 8 in the box make the equation true? Choose *Yes* or *No* for each equation.

a. $9 \times \square = 64$ ☐ Yes   ☐ No

b. $6 \times \square = 48$ ☐ Yes   ☐ No

c. $56 \div \square = 8$ ☐ Yes   ☐ No

d. $32 \div \square = 4$ ☐ Yes   ☐ No

5 Ho says that some fact families have only one multiplication equation and one division equation. Fill in the blanks to show an example.

_____ × _____ = _____   _____ ÷ _____ = _____

6 Sasha has 32 stickers to use in her scrapbook. The scrapbook has 8 pages, and she wants to put the same number of stickers on each page. Write two multiplication facts Sasha can use to find how many stickers to put on each page.

Solution _____

_____

_____

_____

 **Self Check** **Go back and see what you can check off on the Self Check on page 1.**

3.OA.D.9

Understand Patterns

Think It Through

What is a pattern?

A **pattern** is something that repeats. Sometimes you see patterns in shapes or letters. Other times numbers make a pattern. You can create patterns when you add, subtract, multiply, or divide.

You can see patterns in things around you. Look at the line of trees and shrubs below.

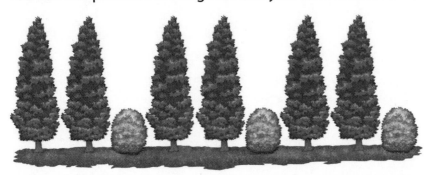

Think How can you describe a pattern?

The **rule** of a pattern tells how to go from one number or shape to the next. A rule for the pattern shown in the line of plants is *tree, tree, shrub*.

You can also use numbers to describe this pattern.

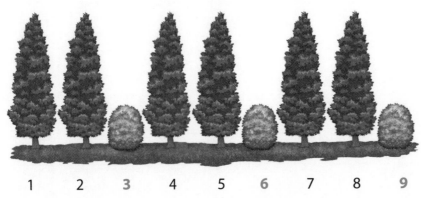

| 1 | 2 | 3 | 4 | 5 | 6 | 7 | 8 | 9 |

The numbers 3, 6, 9, . . . tell where the shrubs are in line. Look for a change that repeats over and over to get from one number to the next number.

> ✏️ What do you add to get to the next number in the pattern? _____

Think How do you know what numbers come next in a pattern?

To go from one number to the next number in the pattern 3, 6, 9, . . . ,
you add 3. You can use the rule "add 3" to find other numbers in the pattern.

The number pattern 3, 6, 9, . . . is shown in the chart below.

1	2	3	4	5	6	7	8	9	10
11	12	13	14	15	16	17	18	19	20
21	22	23	24	25	26				

> Putting the numbers on a number line or in a chart helps me notice things I might not see if I just made a list of numbers.

You may also notice other things about the pattern you can use
to find what numbers come next:

- The numbers form diagonals in the hundred chart. You can use them to tell the next number in the pattern is 27.

- The numbers in this pattern also alternate: odd, even, odd, even. Since 27 is odd, you know the number that comes after 27 in the pattern will be even.

▶ Reflect

1 Write your own number pattern that has at least six numbers in it. Then, describe the rule and one other thing you notice about the pattern.

_____

_____

_____

_____

_____

Think About ⟩ **Exploring Number Patterns**

🔍 **Let's Explore the Idea** Use the information below to help you think about patterns in addition.

> Rick has a pack of 100 baseball cards and likes to sort them into 2 piles. He notices that when he has a pile of 20 cards, the other pile has 80 cards. When he has a pile of 30 cards, the other pile has 70 cards. When he has a pile of 40 cards, the other pile has 60 cards. Finally, when he has a pile of 50 cards, the other pile has 50 cards too.

2 Rick shaded 20 squares and left 80 squares white in the first 100 grid. He did this to show how many baseball cards were in the first pair of piles he made. Shade the rest of the grids to show the other pairs of piles he made.

 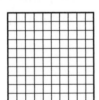

3 What do the shaded squares show in each grid?

_____

4 What do the white squares show in each grid?

_____

5 What happens to the number of shaded squares as you move from one grid to the next? _____

6 What happens to the number of white squares as you move from one grid to the next? _____

7 Describe the rule for the pattern of shaded squares. _____

Describe the rule for the pattern of white squares. _____

Let's Talk About It
Solve the problems below as a group.

8 The grid on the left shows Rick's piles of 30 cards and 70 cards. The grid on the right shows Rick's piles of 40 cards and 60 cards. Shade the grid in the middle to show what happens if Rick put 35 cards in one pile.

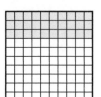 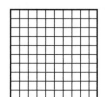

9 Explain how Rick can use the pattern to find the number of cards in the other pile.

_____

_____

_____

10 Describe what happens in addition patterns where the sum stays the same but you change the numbers you add together.

_____

_____

_____

Try It Another Way Work with your group to use the tables to show patterns with addends and sums.

11 Fill in the missing numbers.

Addend	Addend	Sum
20	80	100
30		100
	65	100
	60	100
50		100

12 Fill in the missing numbers.

Addend	Addend	Sum
5	20	25
8		25
10		25
16		25
20		25

Connect ▶ **Ideas About Number Patterns**

13 **Explain** Izzy noticed a pattern in the addition table. She found a diagonal that had all 5s in it. Fill in the table below to show the addends.

	0	1	2	3	4	5
0	0	1	2	3	4	5
1	1	2	3	4	5	6
2	2	3	4	5	6	7
3	3	4	5	6	7	8
4	4	5	6	7	8	9
5	5	6	7	8	9	10

Addend	Addend	Sum
0		5
	4	5
	3	5
	2	5
4		5
5		5

Explain why the 5s form a diagonal line in the addition table.

_____

_____

_____

14 **Examine** Jace counted to 50 by fives. Annabel counted to 50 by tens. What numbers did both Jace and Annabel say? _____

Explain why some of the numbers they said were the same.

_____

_____

15 **Determine** Pat saw an odd number of birds on Monday and an even number of birds on Tuesday. Is the total number of birds he saw odd or even? _____

Explain how you know this, even though you don't know how many birds he saw.

_____

_____

_____

_____

Apply ▶ **Ideas About Number Patterns**

16 Put It Together Look at the multiplication table below.

	0	1	2	3	4	5	6	7	8	9
0	0	0	0	0	0	0	0	0	0	0
1	0	1	2	3	4	5	6	7	8	9
2	0	2	4	6	8					18
3	0		6	9	12	15	18	21	24	27
4	0	4		12		20		28		36
5	0	5		15		25		35		45
6	0	6	12	18	24		36		48	54
7	0	7	14	21	28	35		49		63
8	0				40	48		64		
9	0	9	18		36	45	54	63		81

Part A Fill in the missing numbers.

Part B Describe a pattern you see in the table.

_____

_____

_____

Part C Explain why the pattern works the way it does.

_____

_____

_____

Unit 1
MATH IN ACTION

👥 **Introduction**
SMP1 Make sense
of problems and
persevere in
solving them.

Use Multiplication and Division

Study an Example Problem and Solution

Read this problem involving multiplication and division. Then look at Brandi's solution to this problem.

Seat Set Up

Brandi is planning how to set up seats for a play.

My Notes

- Use between 80 and 100 seats.
- Make 2 seating sections.
- The number of seats in each section can be the same or different.
- Use equal rows of seats in a section.

| Stage |
| Section 1 | Aisle | Section 2 |

Help Brandi set up the chairs.

- Decide the number of chairs to use.
- Tell how many seats to put in each section.
- Tell the number of rows and the number of seats in each row.

Read the sample solution on the next page. Then look at the checklist below. Find and mark parts of the solution that match the checklist.

✏️ Problem-Solving Checklist

- ☐ Tell what is known.
- ☐ Tell what the problem is asking.
- ☐ Show all your work.
- ☐ Show that the solution works.

- **a. Circle** something that is known.
- **b. Underline** something that you need to find.
- **c. Draw a box around** what you do to solve the problem.
- **d. Put a checkmark** next to the part that shows the solution works.

Brandi's Solution

Hi, I'm Brandi. Here's how I solved the problem.

▷ **I know I need a total number of seats between 80 and 100.**

I can find two numbers that add to 80 or 100.

40 + 40 = 80 and 50 + 50 = 100

If I use more than 40 and less than 50 in each section
the total will be correct.

▷ **I need to use numbers that can make equal rows.**

Here are some facts that I know:

4 × 10 = 40

6 × 7 = 42

5 × 9 = 45

I'm making equal rows, so I can use multiplication facts.

▷ **I can choose two of these products.**

If I add the numbers, I should get a number between 80 and 100.

42 + 45 = 87

87 is between 80 and 100.

I have to add the products to make sure the total works.

▷ **I will use 87 chairs.**

6 rows of 7 seats = 42 seats   5 rows of 9 seats = 45 seats

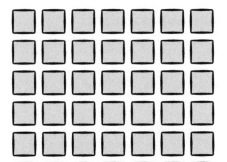   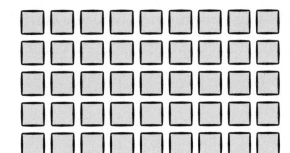

The picture shows my thinking and helps me check my answer.

Try ▶ **Another Approach**

There are many ways to solve problems. Think about how you might solve the Seat Set Up problem in a different way.

Seat Set Up

Brandi is planning how to set up seats for a play.

My Notes

- Use between 80 and 100 seats.
- Make 2 seating sections.
- The number of seats in each section can be the same or different.
- Use equal rows of seats in a section.

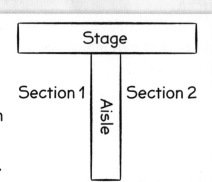

Help Brandi set up the chairs.

- Decide the number of chairs to use.
- Tell how many seats to put in each section.
- Tell the number of rows and the number of seats in each row.

▶ **Plan It** **Answer these questions to help you start thinking about a plan.**

A. What are some numbers that give you a sum between 80 and 100?

_____

_____

B. What are some other facts that you know that could help you solve the problem?

_____

_____

Solve It **Find a different solution for the Seat Set Up problem. Show all your work on a separate sheet of paper.**

You may want to use the problem-solving tips to get started.

Problem-Solving Tips

- **Models** You may want to use . . .
  - an array.
  - equations.

- **Word Bank**

add	multiply	multiplication
array	equal	sum
product	factor	rows

- **Sentence Starters**
  - ________________ a sum of ________________________________
  - There are ________________ in each ________________________

Problem-Solving Checklist

Make sure that you . . .

- ☐ tell what you know.
- ☐ tell what you need to do.
- ☐ show all your work.
- ☐ show that the solution works.

Reflect

Use Mathematical Practices As you work through the problem, discuss these questions with a partner.

- **Use Structure** What kinds of numbers are you able to make equal rows with?
- **Persevere** What is your plan for solving this problem?

Discuss ▸ **Models and Strategies**

Read the problem. Write a solution on a separate sheet of paper. Remember, there can be lots of ways to solve a problem!

Robot Prop

Brandi's play is about space creatures. She wants to make a space robot prop. Brandi has 50 pie plates. She will use the pie plates to make arms and legs for the robot.

My Robot Prop Plan

· Use up to 50 plates.

· Use the same number of plates for each arm.

· Use the same number of plates for each leg.

· Use more plates for each leg than for each arm.

How many pie plates should Brandi use for each leg and each arm?

▶ Plan It and Solve It Find a solution for the Brandi's Robot Prop problem.

Make a plan for Brandi's robot.

- Tell how many plates to use for each arm and leg.
- Tell how many plates you need in all.
- Explain why your plan works.

You may want to use the problem-solving tips to get started.

Problem-Solving Tips

- **Questions**
  - Will you try to use all of the plates?
  - Can you use multiplication facts to find some numbers to try out?

- **Sentence Starters**
  - I can use _____
  - I can add _____

Problem-Solving Checklist

Make sure that you . . .

- ☐ tell what you know.
- ☐ tell what you need to do.
- ☐ show all your work.
- ☐ show that the solution works.

▶ Reflect

Use Mathematical Practices As you work through the problem, discuss these questions with a partner.

- **Use Models** How could a drawing help you find a solution?
- **Make an Argument** How do you know that the numbers you chose work?

**Read the problem. Write a solution on a separate sheet of paper.
Remember, there can be lots of ways to solve a problem!**

Space Creatures

Brandi doesn't know how many space creatures
to have in the play, but she has some ideas.

> **Space Creatures Notes**
>
> The creatures should march out of the
> spaceship in equal groups or in equal rows.
> · There should be more than 20.
> · There should not be more than 30.

How many space creatures should Brandi use?

▶ **Solve It** **Write a plan for Brandi's space creatures.**

- Decide how many space creatures to use.
- Tell how many groups or rows of creatures to use. Also tell how many
  are in each group or row.
- Describe how the space creatures will march out of the spaceship.

▶ **Reflect**

Use Mathematical Practices After you complete the task, choose
one of these questions to discuss with a partner.

- **Use Structure** How did you find numbers that can make equal groups?

- **Make an Argument** How many space creatures did you choose, and why?

Spaceship Prop

Brandi wants to make a spaceship. She will decorate it with silver stars. Brandi estimates that she will need about 180 stars.

The stars come in boxes. Here are the boxes she can choose from:

Box A: 10 stars $2

Box B: 20 stars $3

Box C: 25 stars $4

Box D: 50 stars $5

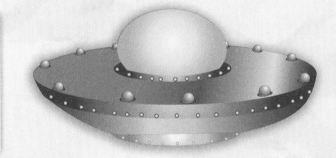

What boxes should Brandi buy?

▶ ## Solve It **Find a way to buy about 180 stars.**

• Tell which boxes and how many of each box Brandi should buy.

• Explain how you know Brandi will get about 180 stars.

• Find the total cost.

▶ ## Reflect

Use Mathematical Practices After you complete the task, choose one of these questions to discuss with a partner.

• **Reason with Numbers** How could estimation help you begin this problem?

• **Use Models** How did you use equations to help you solve the problem?

Solve the problems.

1 Which number makes the equation true?

$$\boxed{} \div 2 = 10$$

A 5

B 8

C 12

D 20

2 Which equation can help Jack find $27 \div 9$?

A $9 - \boxed{} = 27$

B $9 \times \boxed{} = 27$

C $9 \div \boxed{} = 27$

D $9 + \boxed{} = 27$

3 Which equations are true? Circle the letter for all that apply.

A $6 \times 4 \times 2 = 6 \times 2 \times 4$

B $6 \times 4 \times 2 = 6 \times 8$

C $6 \times 8 = (6 \times 2) + (6 \times 4)$

D $6 \times 8 = (6 \times 4) + (6 \times 4)$

E $6 \times 8 = (2 \times 8) + (4 \times 8)$

4 Each classroom in a school has 6 rows of desks with 5 desks in each row. How many desks are in each classroom?

_____ desks

5 Leo had 48 fluid ounces of juice. He measured the juice equally into glasses. Each glass held 6 fluid ounces of juice. How many glasses of juice did Leo have?

_____ glasses of juice

6 Part A Juanita has 24 pencils. She packs boxes with 6 pencils in each box. Fill in the blanks to write a division equation that shows the number of boxes she used.

_____ ÷ _____ = _____

Part B Juanita has 24 markers. She wants to pack them into 8 boxes so that each box has the same number of markers. Write and solve a division equation that shows how many markers Juanita will need to pack into each box.

Solution _____

7 Part A Part of a multiplication table is shown below.

	1	2	3	4	5	6	7	8	9	10
5	5	10	15	20	25	30	35	40	45	50
6	6	12	18	24	30	36	42	48	54	60
7	7	14	21	28	35	42	49	56	63	70

What is the pattern of odd and even products in each row?

_____

_____

_____

_____

Part B Why is the pattern of odd and even numbers in the row for 6 different from the patterns in the other two rows?

_____

_____

_____

_____

Performance Task

Answer the questions and show all your work on separate paper.

Madelyn, William, and Hannah are trying to decide how to display erasers at the school store. The erasers came in 2 packages. Each package has 24 erasers.

William says that they can lay them out in 4 rows with 12 erasers in each row. Hannah thinks that they should lay them out in 7 rows with 7 erasers in each row. Madelyn wants to lay them out in two groups: 3 rows with 6 erasers in each row on one table, and 5 rows with 6 erasers in each row on another table.

Tell whether each person's idea will work and explain why or why not.

Checklist

Did you . . .

☐ write equations to represent the arrangements?

☐ draw diagrams?

☐ use complete sentences?

Reflect

Use Mathematical Practices After you complete the task, choose one of the following questions to answer.

- **Persevere** How did you decide what to do first to solve this problem?

- **Model** What models helped you solve this problem?

Unit 2
Number and Operations in Base Ten

Let's learn about using place value to solve problems.

Real-World Connection Have you ever wanted a faster way to count to 100 while playing hide-and-seek? Count by tens—10, 20, 30, 40, . . . and you will reach 100 in no time! Could you count by tens if you start at 8? Sure, add 10 each time. 8, 18, 28, 38, 48, . . . You might notice the only thing that changes as you add 10 each time is the value of the tens digit.

In This Unit You will learn to round numbers, and add, subtract, and multiply numbers. You will find that understanding place value and knowing the value of each digit in a number can be a big help when solving addition, subtraction, and multiplication problems.

✓ Self Check

Before starting this unit, check off the skills you know below. As you complete each lesson, see how many more you can check off!

I can:	Before this unit	After this unit
use place value to round numbers to the nearest ten and to the nearest hundred, for example: • 315 rounded to the nearest ten is 320. • 826 rounded to the nearest hundred is 800.	☐	☐
use place value to add and subtract, for example: $329 + 148 = (300 + 100) + (20 + 40) + (9 + 8)$ $ = 400 + 60 + 17$ $ = 477$	☐	☐
solve word problems by adding and subtracting using place value.	☐	☐
use place value and grouping to multiply, for example: $6 \times 40 = 6 \times (4 \times 10)$ $ = (6 \times 4) \times 10$ $ = 24 \times 10$ $ = 240$	☐	☐

Use Place Value to Round Numbers

Use What You Know

You know that three-digit numbers are formed by groups of hundreds, tens, and ones. Take a look at this problem.

Look at the number 384. Between which two tens does it fall? Between which two hundreds does it fall? You can show 384 in a place-value chart.

Hundreds	Tens	Ones
3	8	4

a. Including the hundreds, how many tens are in 384? _____

What is the next greatest number of tens? _____

b. How do you write both of these numbers of tens as numerals?

_____

c. Between which two tens does 384 fall? _____

d. How many hundreds are in 384? _____

What is the next greatest number of hundreds? _____

e. How do you write both of these numbers of hundreds as numerals?

_____

f. Between which two hundreds does 384 fall? _____

▷▷ Find Out More

When you **round** a number, you are finding a number that is close to that number. One reason for rounding is to find numbers that are easier to work with. That's why you might want to round three-digit numbers to the nearest ten or hundred. A number line can help you understand how to round.

Rounding to the Nearest Ten

Look at 8, 14, and 5 on the number line.

- Since 8 is closer to 10 than to 0, you round **8** up to **10**.
- 14 is closer to 10 than to 20. Round **14** down to **10**.
- The dot at 5 is exactly halfway between 0 and 10. The rule of rounding 5s is to round up, so round **5** up to **10**.

Rounding to the Nearest Hundred

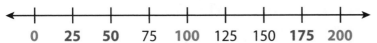

Look at 25, 175, and 50 on the number line.

- Since 25 is closer to 0 than to 100, you round **25** down to **0**.
- 175 is closer to 200 than to 100. Round **175** up to **200**.
- 50 is exactly halfway between 0 and 100. So round **50** up to **100**.

▶ Reflect

1 What is 145 rounded to the nearest ten? What is 145 rounded to the nearest hundred? Explain how you found your answers.

_____

_____

_____

_____

Learn About ▶ **Rounding to the Nearest Ten**

Read the problem below. Then explore different ways to round to the nearest ten.

Ally records the time she spends doing homework. She rounds each time to the nearest ten minutes. If Ally spends 37 minutes on her homework, how does she record this time?

▶ **Picture It** **You can use a hundred chart to help round to the nearest ten.**

37 is between the tens **30** and **40**.

1	2	3	4	5	6	7	8	9	10
11	12	13	14	15	16	17	18	19	20
21	22	23	24	25	26	27	28	29	30
31	32	33	34	35	36	37	38	39	40
41	42	43	44	45	46	47	48	49	50
51	52	53	54	55	56	57	58	59	60
61	62	63	64	65	66	67	68	69	70
71	72	73	74	75	76	77	78	79	80
81	82	83	84	85	86	87	88	89	90
91	92	93	94	95	96	97	98	99	100

▶ **Solve It** **Use what you know about rounding to solve the problem.**

The **halfway** point between **30** and **40** is **35**.

37 is greater than **35**, so round **37** up to **40**.

Ally records the time as 40 minutes.

Connect It Now you can round three-digit numbers to the nearest ten. Try solving a problem like the one on the previous page. Round 943 to the nearest ten.

2 The number 943 is between what two tens? _____

3 What number is halfway between these two tens? _____

4 Is 943 *less than* or *greater than* the halfway number? _____

5 Do you round 943 up or down? _____

6 What is 943 rounded to the nearest ten? _____

7 Explain how to round a number to the nearest ten.

_____

_____

_____

_____

_____

Try It Use what you just learned about rounding to the nearest ten to solve these problems. Show your work on a separate sheet of paper.

8 What is 106 rounded to the nearest ten? _____

9 Round to the nearest ten. What is a number less than 180 that rounds to 180?

_____

_____

What is a number greater than 180 that rounds to 180?

_____

_____

| Learn About > | **Rounding to the Nearest Hundred** |

Read the problem below. Then explore different ways to round to the nearest hundred.

> There are 236 third graders at Huron Elementary School. What is 236 rounded to the nearest hundred?

▶ **Picture It** **Use base-ten blocks to show the number you are rounding.**

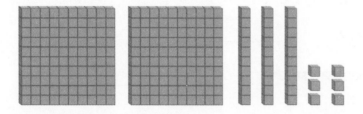

236 has 2 hundreds, so it is between 200 and 300.

The drawing shows that 236 is 2 hundreds + 3 tens + 6 ones.

▶ **Solve It** **Use what you know about rounding to solve the problem.**

There are 10 tens in each hundred. **Halfway** between 0 tens and 10 tens is **5 tens**.

236 has 2 hundreds, **3 tens**, and 6 ones. Since 3 tens is less than 5 tens, round down.

236 rounded to the nearest hundred is 200.

Connect It   Now you can round another three-digit number to the nearest hundred. Try solving a problem like the one on the previous page. Round 358 to the nearest hundred.

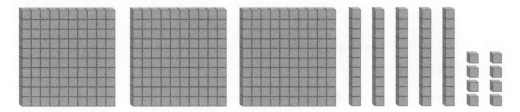

10 The number 358 is between what two hundreds? _____

11 How many tens are in 358? _____

12 What number of tens is halfway between hundreds? _____

13 What is 358 rounded to the nearest hundred? _____

14 Did you round up or round down? Explain how you knew which hundred to round to.

_____

_____

_____

_____

Try It   Use what you just learned about rounding to the nearest hundred to solve these problems. Show your work on a separate sheet of paper.

15 What is 476 rounded to the nearest hundred? _____

16 You are rounding to the nearest hundred. What numbers less than 100 would round to 100?

_____

_____

Practice ▶ **Using Place Value to Round Numbers**

Study the example below. Then solve problems 17–19.

Example

Mr. Watson's sports store has 362 baseballs in stock. What is 362 rounded to the nearest ten?

Look at how you could show your work using base-ten blocks.

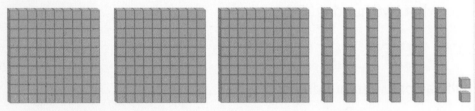

The halfway number is 5 ones. Since 2 ones is less than 5 ones, round down.

Solution 360

The blocks show the number of hundreds, tens, and ones in 362.

 Pair/Share

If the store sells 3 baseballs, does the number of baseballs left still round to 360? Explain.

---

17 The school cafeteria has 879 plates. What is this number rounded to the nearest hundred?

Show your work.

Read the problem carefully. Are you rounding to the nearest ten or hundred?

 Pair/Share

Which digit in the number helps you decide whether to round up or down?

Solution _____

18 Mr. Edwards picked out a TV for $479 and a DVD player for $129. He rounded each price to the nearest $10 to estimate the total cost. What is each price rounded to the nearest $10?

Show your work.

Between what two tens is 479?

Solution _____

 Pair/Share
Why do you think Mr. Edwards rounded the prices to the nearest $10 and not to the nearest $100?

---

19 There are 416 third grade students at Lincoln School. What is the number of third grade students rounded to the nearest hundred?

A 400

B 410

C 420

D 500

Lien chose **C** as the correct answer. How did he get that answer?

How many hundreds and tens are in the number?

_____

_____

_____

_____

Pair/Share
What kinds of mistakes could Lien have made?

Practice Using Place Value to Round Numbers

Solve the problems.

1 Jolon scored 194 points during the basketball season. What is 194 rounded to the nearest hundred?

A 100

B 180

C 190

D 200

2 Round to the nearest ten. Which number will NOT round to 590?

A 596

B 594

C 588

D 585

3 Tell whether each sentence is *True* or *False*.

a. 496 rounded to the nearest 100 is 500.	☐ True	☐ False
b. 496 rounded to the nearest 10 is 500.	☐ True	☐ False
c. 205 rounded to the nearest 10 is 300.	☐ True	☐ False
d. 745 rounded to the nearest 100 is 800.	☐ True	☐ False

4 Which of the following numbers will round to 250 when rounded to the nearest ten? Circle the letter for all that apply.

A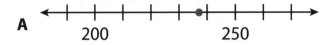

B
Hundreds	Tens	Ones
2	2	6

C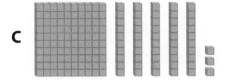

D 259

E 245

5 When rounding to the nearest hundred, what is the least whole number that rounds to 400? What is the greatest whole number that rounds to 400?

Solution _____

_____

_____

6 A total of 778 tickets were sold to a charity event. A newspaper article rounded 778 when it listed the number of tickets sold. Round the number of tickets to the nearest ten and to the nearest hundred. Fill in the blanks to show about how many tickets were sold.

Rounded to the nearest 10, _____ tickets were sold.

Rounded to the nearest 100, _____ tickets were sold.

✓ **Self Check** Go back and see what you can check off on the Self Check on page 69.

Use Place Value to Add and Subtract

🔄 Use What You Know

In this lesson you will add and subtract by breaking apart numbers. Look at the problem below.

Rodney has 147 songs on his MP3 player, and Elaine has 212 songs on her MP3 player. How many songs do Rodney and Elaine have in all?

Rodney's songs:

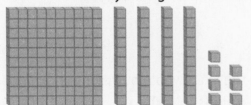

Elaine's songs:

a. 147 can be written as 100 + 40 + 7.

Write 212 in the same way. _____

b. Add the hundreds from both numbers. _____

c. Add the tens from both numbers. _____

d. Add the ones from both numbers. _____

e. Explain how to find the number of songs Rodney and Elaine have in all.

_____

_____

_____

_____

There are different ways to break apart numbers. You can choose the way that works best for the problem you need to solve.

Three ways you can break apart 147 are:

$100 + 40 + 7$ $\qquad$ $100 + 20 + 20 + 7$ $\qquad$ $140 + 7$

Three ways you can break apart 7 are:

$1 + 6$ $\qquad$ $2 + 5$ $\qquad$ $3 + 4$

Breaking apart numbers can make it easier to add and subtract. You can add and subtract hundreds and hundreds, tens and tens, and ones and ones.

Below is one way to find the sum of 147 and 212:

$$147 \longrightarrow 100 + 40 + 7$$
$$212 \longrightarrow 200 + 10 + 2$$
$$\overline{\hphantom{212 \longrightarrow } 300 + 50 + 9}, \text{ or } \mathbf{359}$$

Below is another way to find the sum of 147 and 212:

$$
\begin{array}{r}
147 \\
+\ 212 \\
\hline
9 \\
50 \\
300 \\
\hline
\mathbf{359}
\end{array}
$$

$9 \longleftarrow$ **7** ones + **2** ones = **9** ones
$50 \longleftarrow$ **4** tens + **1** ten = **5** tens
$300 \longleftarrow$ **1** hundred + **2** hundreds = **3** hundreds

▶ Reflect

1 Show how to break apart numbers to add $240 + 130$.

_____

_____

_____

Learn About ▸ **Using Place Value to Add**

Read the addition problem below. Then explore different ways to find sums of three-digit numbers.

> Garcia has 130 trading cards. Mark has 280 trading cards. How many trading cards do Garcia and Mark have together?

▸ **Picture It** **You can use base-ten blocks to help add three-digit numbers.**

This model shows the 130 trading cards Garcia has.

This model shows the 280 trading cards Mark has.

The model below shows the total number of trading cards Garcia and Mark have.

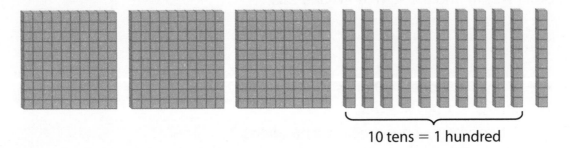

10 tens = 1 hundred

Regroup 11 tens as 1 hundred + 1 ten. Add 4 hundreds + 1 ten = 410.

▸ **Model It** **You can also use place value to help add three-digit numbers.**

$$
\begin{array}{r}
130 \\
+\ 280 \\
\hline
\end{array}
$$

0 ⟶ There are **0 ones** in both numbers.

110 ⟶ 3 tens + 8 tens = **11 tens**, or 1 hundred + 1 ten, or **110**

300 ⟶ 1 hundred + 2 hundreds = **3 hundreds**, or **300**

410

Connect It Now you will solve the problem from the previous page by showing regrouping with digits.

2 Add the ones, 0 + 0. Record the sum in the ones column below the line.

3 Add the tens. How many tens are in the sum?

_____ tens

How do you regroup the tens as hundreds and tens?

_____ hundred and _____ ten

		1	3	0
	+	2	8	0

4 Record the regrouped tens in the addition problem: Write the number of hundreds, regrouped from the tens, in the box above the hundreds column. Then write the number of tens below the line in the tens column.

5 Now add the hundreds. Be sure to include the regrouped hundred in the box. What numbers do you need to add? _____

Record the sum in the hundreds column below the line.

How many trading cards do Garcia and Mark have together? _____ trading cards

6 How could you use this method to add when both tens and ones need to be regrouped? Show this with the problem 158 + 363 at the right.

		1	5	8
	+	3	6	3

Try It Use what you just learned about showing regrouping to find these sums.

7

	1	9	2
+	1	1	4

8

	2	8	4
+	2	5	8

Learn About ▶ **Using Place Value to Subtract**

Read the subtraction problem below. Then explore different ways to find the difference of three-digit numbers.

> Julie recorded the weather for 365 days. It was sunny 186 days. How many days were not sunny?

▶ **Picture It** **You can use base-ten blocks to subtract three-digit numbers.**

This model shows 365 − 186. All the blocks show 365. One ten and one hundred are regrouped. The blocks crossed out show 186.

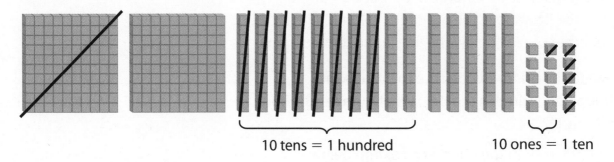

10 tens = 1 hundred   10 ones = 1 ten

Blocks that are left: 1 hundred + 7 tens + 9 ones = 179

▶ **Model It** **You can also use place value to subtract three-digit numbers.**

Write each number as hundreds, tens, and ones. Regroup if you need to.

365 = 3 hundreds + 6 tens + 5 ones
= 2 hundreds + 16 tens + 5 ones
= **2 hundreds + 15 tens + 15 ones**

186 = 1 hundred + 8 tens + 6 ones

Subtract hundreds, tens, and ones.
2 hundreds − 1 hundred = 1 hundred
15 tens − 8 tens = 7 tens
15 ones − 6 ones = 9 ones

Combine these differences.
1 hundred + 7 tens + 9 ones = 179

▶ **Connect It** **Now you will solve the problem from the previous page by first regrouping and then subtracting hundreds, tens, and ones.**

$365 - 186 = \square$

Step 1:	$365 = 300 + 60 + 5$	$186 = 100 + 80 + 6$
Step 2:	$= 200 + 160 + 5$	$= 100 + 80 + 6$
Step 3:	$= 200 + 150 + 15$	$= 100 + 80 + 6$

9 Look at 365 in Step 1. Can you subtract hundreds from hundreds, tens from tens, and ones from ones?

_____

_____

10 Explain the regrouping used to go from Step 1 to Step 2.

_____

Explain the regrouping used to go from Step 2 to Step 3.

_____

11 Subtract each place: $200 - 100 = $ _____ $150 - 80 = $ _____ $15 - 6 = $ _____

Now find what is left by adding the three differences. _____

How many days were not sunny? _____

12 Explain how to subtract three-digit numbers when you need to regroup hundreds and tens.

_____

_____

_____

▶ **Try It** **Use what you just learned about subtraction to solve these problems. Show your work on a separate sheet of paper.**

13   362
       $- 125$

14   425
       $- 289$

Learn About **Adding On to Subtract**

Read the subtraction problem below. Then explore how to find differences by adding on.

Perez has 205 flower seeds. He plants 137 seeds. How many flower seeds does Perez have left?

▶ **Model It** **You can use a number line to add on to find a difference.**

To solve the problem, you can use the subtraction equation $205 - 137 = \square$. You can also solve the problem with the addition equation $137 + \square = 205$. Use a number line to add on to 137 to get to 205.

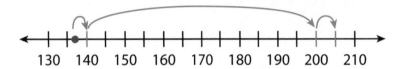

130   140   150   160   170   180   190   200   210

Find the numbers that you add to get to the next number:

$137 + \mathbf{3} = 140$ ⟵ Add on ones to get to the next ten.

$140 + \mathbf{60} = 200$ ⟵ Add on tens to get to the next hundred.

$200 + \mathbf{5} = 205$ ⟵ Add on ones to get to the total, 205.

You added $\mathbf{3} + \mathbf{60} + \mathbf{5}$ to get from 137 to 205.

Connect It Now you can use a place-value chart to record the numbers you add on.

15 Start at 137. What is the next 10? _____
How many ones do you add to get to the next ten? _____

This first number is written in the chart for you.

	Hundreds	Tens	Ones
137			3
140			
200			
205			

16 How many tens do you add to get from 140 to the hundred you need? Write your answer in the chart.

17 Now what do you add to get from 200 to 205? Write your answer in the chart.

18 Write an addition equation to show what you added.

_____

How many flower seeds does Perez have left? _____ seeds

19 Explain how you would add on to find this difference: 202 − 195.

_____

_____

_____

_____

Try It Use what you just learned about adding on using a place-value chart to solve these problems. Show your work on a separate sheet of paper.

20 Edith had $600. She spent $84. How much does Edith have left? _____

21 Juan sent and received 800 text messages. He sent 379 text messages. How many text messages did Juan receive? _____

Practice ▶ **Using Place Value to Add and Subtract**

Study the example below. Then solve problems 22–24.

Example

On Monday, a flower store sold 617 roses. On Tuesday, the store sold 279 roses. How many roses were sold in all on Monday and Tuesday?

Look at how you could show your work by breaking apart 617 and 279.

$$617 + 279 = (600 + 200) + (10 + 70) + (7 + 9)$$
$$= 800 + 80 + 16$$
$$= 896$$

Solution 896 roses

The student broke apart 617 and 219 into hundreds, tens, and ones. That makes it easy to add the two numbers.

 Pair/Share
How else could you solve this problem?

---

22 Diana has 109 magnets. Roger has 56 more magnets than Diana. How many magnets do Diana and Roger have in all?

Show your work.

How many magnets does Roger have?

 Pair/Share
How did you decide which operation to use?

Solution _____

23 Corey works 144 hours a month. He has worked 72 hours so far this month. How many more hours does Corey have to work this month?

Show your work.

Do you need to regroup?

Pair/Share
How can you use adding on to solve this problem?

Solution _____

---

24 Chad practiced batting for 205 minutes this week. Doug practiced batting for 110 minutes. How many more minutes did Chad practice than Doug?

A 90 minutes

B 95 minutes

C 195 minutes

D 315 minutes

Sam chose **D** as the correct answer. How did he get that answer?

To find how many more minutes, should you add or subtract?

_____

_____

_____

_____

Pair/Share
How can you use estimation to see if Sam's answer makes sense?

Practice ▶ **Using Place Value to Add and Subtract**

Solve the problems.

1 Mr. Coleman drove 129 miles on Monday. He drove 78 more miles on Tuesday than on Monday. How many miles did Mr. Coleman drive altogether on Monday and Tuesday?

A 51

B 207

C 285

D 336

2 Which of the following diagrams or solutions represent the difference 354 − 298? Circle the letter for all that apply.

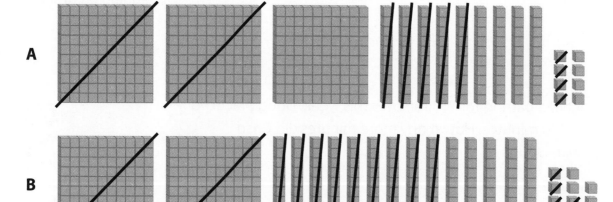

A

B

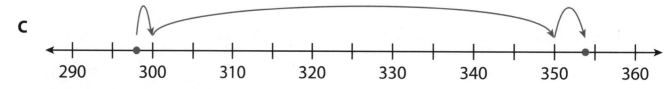

C

D 2 hundreds − 2 hundreds = 0 hundreds
15 tens − 9 tens = 6 tens
14 ones − 8 ones = 6 ones

E 3 hundreds − 2 hundreds = 1 hundred
15 tens − 9 tens = 6 tens
14 ones − 8 ones = 6 ones

3 The sum of the equation below can be written using tens and ones.

68 + 16 = _____?_____ tens and _____?_____ ones.

Select one number from each column to make the equation true.

Tens	Ones
○ 2	○ 4
○ 7	○ 9
○ 8	○ 12
○ 9	○ 14

4 Neke has 308 craft sticks. She buys a package of 625 craft sticks. She uses 245 craft sticks for a project. How many craft sticks does Neke have left?

Show your work.

Answer   Neke has _____ craft sticks left.

5 Fill in the chart to show how many hundreds, tens, and ones are in the number 746.

Number	Hundreds	Tens	Ones
746			

Write a number that meets the following conditions:

- The number must be between 1 and 9.

- When the number is added to 746, the digit in the ones place of the sum is LESS than the ones place of 746.

✔ **Self Check**   **Go back and see what you can check off on the Self Check on page 69.**

Use What You Know

In Lesson 6, you learned multiplication facts. In this lesson, you will learn how to use the facts to help you multiply one-digit numbers by multiples of 10. Take a look at this problem.

There are 4 stacks of books on a table. Each stack has 20 books. How many books are there in all?

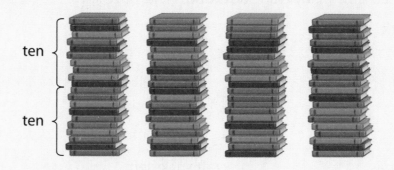

ten

ten

a. How many books are in each stack? _____

b. How many tens are in 20? _____

c. How many groups of 2 tens are there in all the stacks? _____

d. How can you find how many tens there are in all? _____

e. How many tens are there? _____

f. Explain how you can use skip counting to find the total number of books.

_____

_____

_____

_____

▷▷ Find Out More

Multiplication is used to find the total when there are two or more groups with the same number in each group. You have learned some multiplication facts. These facts can help you multiply by tens.

The 4 stacks of 20 books can be shown using base-ten models. You can also show this with the multiplication expression 4 × 20.

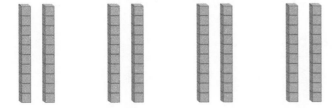

- You can skip count equal groups of 10 or 20 to find the product.

  Skip count by **10** eight times: **10, 20, 30, 40, 50, 60, 70, 80**

  Skip count by **20** four times: **20, 40, 60, 80**

- You can also count on by groups of tens to multiply.

  Count on by groups of 2 tens 4 times to find 4 × 20: 2 tens, 4 tens, 6 tens, 8 tens.

  8 tens is 80.

These two ways to find a product work well when the numbers are not too large. But what if you were looking for the product of 8 × 80? Skip counting and counting on would take time and might be hard to track. This lesson will show you some quicker ways to multiply by tens.

▶ Reflect

1 Explain how you could find the product of 3 × 50.

_____

_____

_____

_____

Learn About Multiplying by Tens

Read the problem below. Then explore different ways to multiply by tens.

A sports store orders 4 boxes of baseball caps. Each box has 40 caps.
How many baseball caps are in all 4 boxes?

▶ **Picture It** **You can use base-ten blocks to help understand the problem.**

4 **boxes** of baseball caps

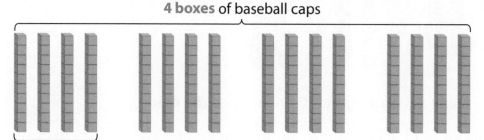

40 **caps** in
each box

4 **groups** of **4 tens** is 4×4 **tens**, or 16 tens.

16 tens is 160.

▶ **Model It** **You can also use factors and grouping to multiply by tens.**

Start with the factors from the problem:	4×40
You can write 40 as 4×10:	$4 \times (4 \times 10)$
You can change the grouping when you multiply:	$(4 \times 4) \times 10$
Multiply 4×4:	16×10

16 tens is 160.

Connect It Now you will solve the problem from the previous page by breaking apart a two-digit number.

Below are three equal multiplication expressions from the previous page.

$$4 \times 40 \qquad\qquad 4 \times 4 \times 10 \qquad\qquad 16 \times 10$$

2 You can break apart 16 into 10 plus another number. Write the number in the blank:

$$16 \times 10 = (10 + \underline{\qquad}) \times 10$$

3 You can multiply both numbers in the parentheses in problem 2 by 10. Write these numbers in the blanks:

$$= (\underline{\qquad} \times 10) + (\underline{\qquad} \times 10)$$

4 Write the products in the blanks:

$$= \underline{\qquad} + \underline{\qquad}$$

5 Add the products and write the sum in the blank:

$$= \underline{\qquad}$$

6 Below are some multiplication equations that you know or that you found products for in this lesson.

$$4 \times 2 = 8 \qquad\qquad 4 \times 4 = 16$$
$$4 \times 2 \times 10 = 80 \qquad\qquad 4 \times 4 \times 10 = 160$$
$$8 \times 10 = 80 \qquad\qquad 16 \times 10 = 160$$

Explain how to find the product of a given number and a multiple of 10.

_____

_____

_____

Try It Use what you just learned to find these products. Show your work on a separate sheet of paper.

7 $60 \times 8 =$ _____

8 $30 \times 7 =$ _____

Practice **Using Place Value to Multiply**

Study the example below. Then solve problems 9–11.

Example

Robin planted 9 rows of flowers. Each row had 30 flowers. How many flowers did Robin plant in all?

Look at how you could show your work by changing the grouping when you multiply.

$$9 \times 30 = 9 \times (3 \times 10)$$
$$= (9 \times 3) \times 10$$
$$= 27 \times 10$$
$$= 270$$

Solution ___270 flowers___

9×30 is 9 groups of 3 tens, or 27 tens, or 270.

Pair/Share
How could you use skip counting to solve this problem? Which way of solving makes more sense?

---

9 Manu drives 50 miles each day. How many miles does he drive in 5 days?

Show your work.

How many groups of 5 tens are there?

Pair/Share
How did you and your partner choose the way to solve this problem?

Solution _____

10 Tanner shoots 90 free throws 6 times a week. How many free throws does she shoot each week?

Show your work.

How can you break apart 90 to multiply by 10?

Pair/Share
How can you check that your answer is correct?

Solution _____

---

11 Raymond can type 40 words each minute. How many words can he type in 8 minutes?

A 32 words

B 48 words

C 320 words

D 360 words

Gina chose **B** as the correct answer. How did she get that answer?

What multiplication fact can you use to solve the problem?

_____

_____

_____

Pair/Share
How can the digit in the ones place help you decide if an answer makes sense?

Lesson 10 Use Place Value to Multiply   **97**

Practice ▶ **Using Place Value to Multiply**

Solve the problems.

1 Jerome ran about 30 yards each time he caught the ball in his last football game. He caught the ball 6 times. About how many yards did Jerome run?

A 5

B 18

C 180

D 200

2 There are 60 toothpicks in a jar. There are 3 jars in 1 box. How many toothpicks are in 2 boxes?

A 120

B 180

C 360

D 480

3 Which multiplication expressions are ways to show 240? Circle the letter for all that apply.

A 40 × 6

B 4 × 60

C 30 × 8

D 80 × 3

E 2 × 40

4 A notebook has 80 sheets of paper. How many sheets of paper do 7 notebooks have?

Answer _____ sheets of paper

5 At a pet store, there are 20 fish in each tank. How many fish are in 8 tanks?

Show your work.

Answer There are _____ fish in 8 tanks.

6 There are 40 nickels in each roll. Tao has 7 rolls of nickels. How many nickels does she have in all?

Show your work.

Answer Tao has _____ nickels.

✓ **Self Check** **Go back and see what you can check off on the Self Check on page 69.**

Study an Example Problem and Solution

Read this problem that uses rounding with addition. Then look at Alex's solution to this problem.

Adopt an Animal

The Wildlife Protectors save endangered animals. Alex helps them raise money. Her goal is to raise at least $750. Alex asks her neighbors to buy adoption kits. Here are her notes.

My Notes

· Two people will spend up to $200.

· Two people will spend about $100.

· Others will spend less than $75.

Adopt an Animal Kits

Tiger
$59 kit
$95 kit
$199 kit

Snowy Owl
$29 kit
$55 kit
$99 kit

Use the information in the notes.
Show what kits and how many of each
Alex can sell to reach her goal. Explain your choices.

Read the sample solution on the next page. Then look at the checklist below. Find and mark parts of the solution that match the checklist.

✏️ **Problem-Solving Checklist**

- ☐ Tell what is known.
- ☐ Tell what the problem is asking.
- ☐ Show all your work.
- ☐ Show that the solution works.

a. Circle something that is known.

b. Underline something that you need to find.

c. Draw a box around what you do to solve the problem.

d. Put a checkmark next to the part that shows the solution works.

Alex's Solution

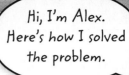

Hi, I'm Alex. Here's how I solved the problem.

▷ **I can round the prices. Then I can estimate how many kits to sell.**

$59 → $60	$95 → $100	$199 → $200
$29 → $30	$55 → $60	$99 → $100

▷ **The 2 people who will spend up to $200 can buy the $199 kits.**
$200 + $200 = $400

▷ **The 2 people who will spend up to $100 can buy the $99 kits. That's about $200 more.**
Now I have $400 + $200, or $600.

I can use rounded numbers first. I can get an idea of what numbers will work before doing all the adding.

▷ **$59 < $75. If 2 people buy $59 kits, I'll have about $120 more.**
Now I have about $600 + $120, or $720.

▷ **$29 < $75. If 2 people buy $29 kits, I'll have about $60 more.**
Now I have about $720 + $60, or $780. This is at least $750.

▷ **Now I can find the actual prices.**
Two kits for $199: $199 + $199 = $398
Two kits for $99: $99 + $99 = $198
Two kits for $59: $59 + $59 = $118
Two kits for $29: $29 + $29 = $58

Each addend is 1 less than the rounded numbers. That means that each actual sum is 2 less than the estimated sum.

$$
\begin{array}{r}
{\scriptstyle 2\,3} \\
\$398 \\
\$198 \\
\$118 \\
+\ \$\ 58 \\
\hline
\$772
\end{array}
$$

$772 > $750, so the plan works.

Try ▶ **Another Approach**

Read this problem that uses rounding with addition. Then look at Alex's solution to this problem.

Adopt an Animal

The Wildlife Protectors save endangered animals. Alex helps them raise money. Her goal is to raise at least $750. Alex asks her neighbors to buy adoption kits. Here are her notes.

My Notes

· Two people will spend up to $200.

· Two people will spend about $100.

· Others will spend less than $75.

Use the information in the notes.
Show what kits and how many of each
Alex can sell to reach her goal. Explain your choices.

▶ **Plan It** **Answer these questions to help you start thinking about a plan.**

A. What kit that costs about $100 was not used in the example problem?

_____

_____

B. What kit that costs about $60 was not used in the example problem?

_____

_____

Solve It **Find a different solution for the Adopt an Animal problem. Show all your work on a separate sheet of paper.**

You may want to use the problem-solving tips to get started.

Problem-Solving Tips

- **Tools** You may want to use . . .
  - mental math.
  - paper and pencil.

- **Word Bank**

round	sum	about
add	estimate	greater than

- **Sentence Starters**
  - I'll round ______________________________
  - ______________ is greater than ______________________

Problem-Solving Checklist

Make sure that you . . .

- ☐ tell what you know.
- ☐ tell what you need to do.
- ☐ show all your work.
- ☐ show that the solution works.

Reflect

Use Mathematical Practices As you work through the problem, discuss these questions with a partner.

- **Be Precise** Why do you have to find actual sums to solve this problem?
- **Reason Mathematically** What addition strategies can you use to solve this problem?

Discuss ▶ **Models and Strategies**

**Read the problem. Write a solution on a separate sheet of paper.
Remember, there can be lots of ways to solve a problem!**

Better Farms

One way to help endangered animals is to make better farms. When land is cleared for farming, it is taken away from wild animals. Alex wants to help farms grow more food so new farms are not needed.

The Wildlife Protectors raise money to buy farming supplies.

Compost: $10 each bag

Wooden Planters: $5 each box

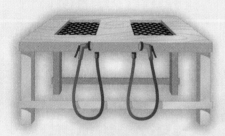

Garden Washing Station: $40

Wooden Raised Bed: $79

Alex wants to know what the money from a $99 animal adoption kit can buy. The kit costs $8 to make. The rest of the money can buy farming supplies. Show Alex what the money from a $99 kit can buy.

©Curriculum Associates, LLC Copying is not permitted.

▶ Plan It and Solve It **Find a solution for the Better Farms problem.**

- Find how much money the sale of one kit makes.
- Find at least two different items that this money can buy.
- Tell how much money is left, if there is any.

You may want to use the problem-solving tips to get started.

Problem-Solving Tips

● **Questions**

- How do you find the amount left after paying for the cost of the kit?
- What items do you think farms need the most?

● **Sentence Starters**

- There is _____ left after _____
- The sale of a $99 kit can buy _____

Problem-Solving Checklist

Make sure that you . . .

- ☐ tell what you know.
- ☐ tell what you need to do.
- ☐ show all your work.
- ☐ show that the solution works.

▶ Reflect

Use Mathematical Practices As you work through the problem, discuss these questions with a partner.

- **Make Sense of Problems** What will you do first? Why?

- **Persevere** What are some different ways that you might solve this problem?

Persevere ▶ **On Your Own**

Read the problem. Write a solution on a separate sheet of paper. Remember, there are many different ways to solve a problem!

Monthly Gifts

People can sign up to make monthly gifts to the Wildlife Protectors. Alex asks people in her town to make monthly gifts. She wants to raise at least $800 in 6 months.

Here are the gift amounts.

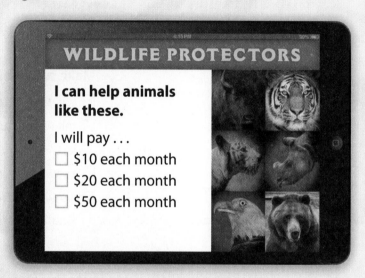

WILDLIFE PROTECTORS

I can help animals like these.

I will pay . . .
☐ $10 each month
☐ $20 each month
☐ $50 each month

How can Alex raise at least $800 in 6 months?

▶ **Solve It** **Help Alex find a way to raise money.**

• Find how much each monthly gift raises in 6 months.

• Then find a way to raise at least $800 in 6 months.

• Tell how you know that your answer works.

▶ **Reflect**

Use Mathematical Practices After you complete the task, choose one of these questions to discuss with a partner.

• **Use Structure** How did you use basic facts to help solve this problem?

• **Reason Mathematically** What computation strategies did you use?

Ticket Sales

Alex works at a zoo. The zoo donates money to the Wildlife Protectors for every ticket sold on Saturday morning. They donate $2 for each children's ticket and $3 for each adult ticket.

Alex looks at ticket records for the past 5 weeks.

Saturday Morning Ticket Sales					
	Week 1	Week 2	Week 3	Week 4	Week 5
Adult Tickets Sold	64	62	59	63	60
Children's Tickets Sold	88	90	89	94	94

Estimate how much money the zoo will donate to the Wildlife Protectors for Week 6.

▶ **Solve It** **Help Alex estimate the donation amount.**

- Find the usual number of adult and children's tickets that are sold on Saturday mornings. Use rounding.
- Then use the ticket numbers to estimate the amount of money that the zoo will donate.

▶ **Reflect**

Use Mathematical Practices After you complete the task, choose one of these questions to discuss with a partner.

- **Make an Argument** Why do the numbers you used make sense with the problem?

- **Be Precise** Can you find an exact answer for this problem? Why or why not?

Solve the problems.

1. A school play ran for three nights. The total attendance at the play for the three nights was 388 people. What is 388 rounded to the nearest hundred?

   A 300

   B 380

   C 390

   D 400

2. At a high school football game, the visiting team had 274 fans. The home team had 173 more fans than the visiting team. How many fans did the home team have?

   A 101

   B 173

   C 347

   D 447

3. Write the difference.

   $703 - 285 =$ _____

4. Which statements are true? Circle the letter for all that apply.

   A 645 rounds to 600 when rounded to the nearest ten.

   B $289 + 543 = 832$

   C $680 - 395 = 315$

   D $4 \times 50 = 200$

5 **Part A** What is 278 rounded to the nearest ten?

Solution _____

Part B Draw a number line from 270 to 280 to show why your answer is correct.

Explain how the number line shows that your answer is correct.

_____

_____

_____

6 **Part A** A school has 7 buses. Each bus has 40 seats. Fill in the missing numbers to find the total number of seats on the 7 buses.

$7 \times 40 = 7$ groups of _____ tens

7 groups of _____ tens = _____ tens

There are _____ seats on the 7 buses.

Part B Another school has 9 buses. Each bus has 50 seats. What is the total number of seats on those 9 buses?

Answer _____ seats

Performance Task

Answer the questions and show all your work on separate paper.

Mr. Gemelli runs the school cafeteria. He needs your help ordering compostable lunch trays and bananas for the students' lunches. He needs to order lunch trays and bananas for lunch next week. Here are Mr. Gemelli's instructions:

"I need 1 tray and 1 banana for each lunch ordered. I usually round the number of lunches for each day to the nearest ten when I order bananas. I think this will give me some extra bananas in case students want more than one. I round the number of lunches for each day to the nearest hundred when I order lunch trays because they are sold in packages of 100."

The table below shows the number of lunches ordered for each day next week.

	Monday	Tuesday	Wednesday	Thursday	Friday
Number of lunches	159	245	113	104	162

Use Mr. Gemelli's guidelines to find the total number of trays and bananas he should order for student lunches for next week. Write a letter to Mr. Gemelli telling him how many of each item he should order and explain how you know.

Reflect

Use Mathematical Practices After you complete the task, choose one of the following questions to answer.

- **Be Precise** How did you decide how to round the numbers in Mr. Gemelli's chart?

- **Reason Mathematically** What strategies did you use to add the numbers in this problem?

Unit 3
Operations and Algebraic Thinking, Part 2

Let's learn about solving one-step and two-step word problems.

Real-World Connection People solve math problems every day. Most problems don't start out looking like $100 ÷ \square = 25$ or $4 × 42 = \square$. Instead, the problems may be more like these:

- A chef has 5 cups of flour to make 3 cakes that each need 2 cups of flour. Does he have enough flour?

- A carpenter might need 80 inches of wood to finish a wall. She can buy wood in 16-inch pieces. How many pieces will she need to buy?

In This Unit You will solve problems in many different ways. You might write an equation or you might draw a picture. You might even solve a problem by talking about it out loud until you find a solution.

✓ Self Check

Before starting this unit, check off the skills you know below. As you complete each lesson, see how many more you can check off!

I can:	Before this unit	After this unit
solve one-step word problems using multiplication or division.	☐	☐
model two-step word problems using addition, subtraction, multiplication, and division.	☐	☐
solve two-step word problems using addition, subtraction, multiplication, and division.	☐	☐

Solve One-Step Word Problems Using Multiplication and Division

🔄 Use What You Know

You have learned about different ways to show multiplication and division. In this lesson, you will learn how to solve multiplication and division word problems. Take a look at this problem.

Write a word problem about the picture at the right.

a. Think of the picture as showing an array. Describe what it shows. _____

_____

b. Now think of the picture as showing equal groups. Describe what it shows. _____

_____

c. Write the fact family that the picture shows. Make sure you use 2 multiplication equations and 2 division equations.

_____

d. Why can the picture be used to describe both multiplication and division?

_____

_____

e. Pick one of the multiplication or division equations you wrote in the fact family. Use this equation to write a word problem about the picture. _____

_____

_____

Sometimes you can write a multiplication equation to help you solve a word problem. Other times you can write either a multiplication or a division equation. Look at the examples below.

Example 1:

There are 6 bananas in each bunch. How many bananas are in 2 bunches?

You can solve this problem using $2 \times 6 = ?$ or $6 \times 2 = ?$.

Example 2:

2 bunches have a total of 12 bananas. Each bunch has the same number of bananas. How many bananas are in each bunch?

You can solve this problem using $2 \times ? = 12$ or $12 \div 2 = ?$.

Example 3:

Each bunch has 6 bananas. If there are 12 bananas, how many bunches are there?

You can solve this problem using $6 \times ? = 12$ or $12 \div 6 = ?$.

▶ Reflect

1 Write a multiplication equation and a division equation that could help you solve the problem below. Then solve the problem.

A hat rack has 2 rows of hooks. Each row has the same number of hooks. The rack has 10 hooks in all. How many hooks are in each row?

_____

_____

_____

Learn About Solving Problems About Equal Groups

Read the problem below. Then explore different ways to solve problems about equal groups.

> A store has 24 saltwater fish. The store has 4 tanks for the fish. Each tank has an equal number of fish. How many fish are in each tank?

▶ **Picture It** You can use a drawing to show and solve problems about equal groups.

Make 4 groups of 1 fish each. Add 1 fish at a time to each group until there are 24 fish.

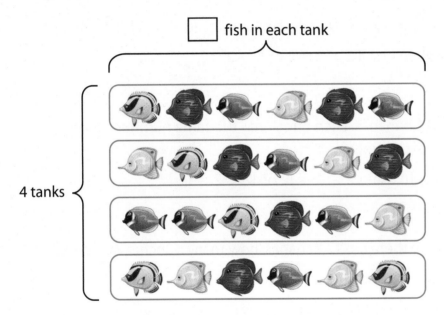

☐ fish in each tank

4 tanks

▶ **Model It** You can also use words to show and solve problems about equal groups.

Make notes about the problem.

24 fish in all. 4 groups, or tanks.

☐ fish in each group.

Use multiplication or division to find the number of fish in each group.

$4 \times \boxed{} = 24$ or

$24 \div 4 = \boxed{}$

Connect It Now you will solve the problem from the previous page.

2 What does 24 in the problem stand for? _____

What does 4 stand for? _____

3 What is the unknown number in the problem? _____

4 Use the letter *F* to stand for the unknown number. Write a division equation that can be used to solve the problem. _____

Write a related multiplication equation. _____

5 What is the solution? Explain how you found your answer.

_____

_____

6 Suppose the problem is changed to the one below.

There are 24 fish. The store manager wants to put 6 fish in each tank. How many tanks will there be?

Write both a multiplication and division equation for it. Then solve the problem.

_____

_____

Try It Use what you just learned about using letters for unknowns to solve these problems. Show your work on a separate piece of paper.

7 Jenna has 30 photos of her friends. She puts 6 photos on each page in her album. How many pages does Jenna use? _____

_____

8 There are 9 drawing kits on a table in the art room. Each kit has 4 pencils. How many pencils are there in all? _____

_____

Learn About Solving Problems About Arrays

Read the problem below. Then explore different ways to solve problems about arrays.

A clothing store uses stacking crates for storing jeans. The manager orders 42 crates. Six crates will fit in one row along the wall. How many rows of crates will there be?

▶ **Picture It** **You can use a drawing to show and solve problems about arrays.**

Use an array. Show a row of 6. Add rows of 6 until you get to 42.

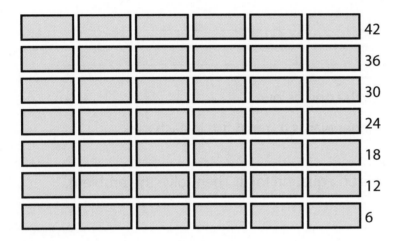

▶ **Model It** **You can also use words to show and solve problems about arrays.**

Make notes about the problem.

42 crates in all.

6 crates in each row.

☐ rows

Use multiplication or division to find the number of rows.

$6 \times \boxed{} = 42$

or

$42 \div 6 = \boxed{}$

Connect It Now you will solve the problem from the previous page.

9 What do the numbers in the problem stand for? _____

_____

_____

10 What is the unknown number in the problem? _____

11 Use the letter R to stand for the unknown number. Write a division equation that can be used to solve the problem. _____

Write a related multiplication equation. _____

12 Show and explain how to solve the problem. _____

_____

_____

_____

13 Explain how you can use an array to solve this problem.

There are 24 crayons in a box. There are 8 crayons in each row.

How many rows of crayons are there?

_____

_____

_____

Try It Use what you just learned about solving array problems to solve these problems. Show your work on a separate piece of paper.

14 Grace's garden has 4 rows of tomatoes with 8 plants in each row. How many tomato plants are in Grace's garden? _____

15 There are 20 children in gym class. The teacher lines up the children in 4 equal rows for warm-up. How many children are in each row?

_____

Learn About Solving Problems About Tiling

Read the problem below. Then explore different ways to solve multiplication and division problems about tiling.

For an art project, Sean pasted colored squares side-by-side with no gaps. He used 48 squares and made 6 rows. Sean used the same number of squares in each row. How many squares did he put in each row?

▶ **Picture It** **You can use a drawing to show and solve problems about tiling.**

Draw a picture. Show 6 rows. Add a square to each row until you get to 48.

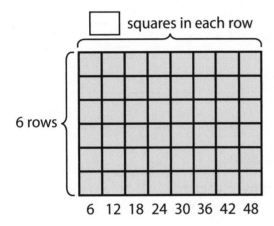

▶ **Model It** **You can also use words to show and solve problems about tiling.**

Make notes about the problem.

48 squares

6 rows

☐ squares in each row.

Use multiplication or division to find the number of squares in each row.

$6 \times$ ☐ $= 48$

or

$48 \div 6 =$ ☐

Connect It Now you will solve the problem from the previous page.

16 What is the unknown in this problem? _____

17 Write a division equation using the letter *T* to stand for the unknown number.

_____

Write a related multiplication equation. _____

18 Show and explain how to solve the problem. _____

_____

19 How could you use the multiplication fact $6 \times 7 = 42$ to find the solution to this problem?

_____

_____

_____

20 Sean changed his mind and decided to use 56 squares. He put them in 7 equal rows. Explain how you could use multiplication and division to find the number of squares in each row.

_____

_____

_____

Try It Use what you just learned about solving problems using tiling to solve these problems. Show your work on a separate sheet of paper.

21 A walkway is made of square patio blocks. There are 2 rows of blocks with 9 blocks in each row. How many blocks are there in all?

_____

22 Michel used 35 tiles to build a patio. He used 5 tiles in each row. How many rows of tiles are there?

_____

Practice ▶ **Solving One-Step Word Problems**

Study the example below. Then solve problems 23–25.

Example

Troy has 18 homework problems to do. He has 3 days to finish the homework. If he does the same number of problems each day, how many problems will he do in a day?

Look at how you could show your work using a drawing.

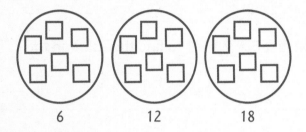

6   12   18

Solution _6 problems each day_

> This problem can be solved using $3 \times ? = 18$ or $18 \div 3 = ?$

 Pair/Share
Which equation did you use and why?

---

23 Mr. Rivera is posting 28 student papers on the bulletin board. He posts the papers in 4 rows, with an equal number of papers in each one. How many papers does Mr. Rivera put in each row?

Show your work.

What does 28 stand for in the problem?

 Pair/Share
Did you multiply or divide to solve the problem?

Solution _____

24 There are 54 players at a baseball clinic. The coach puts them into teams of 9 players. How many teams are there?

Show your work.

What fact do you know that includes both numbers in the problem?

Pair/Share
How can you check that your answer is correct?

Solution _____

---

25 Mai eats 3 servings of fruit each day. How many servings of fruit does she eat in a week? Circle the letter of the correct answer. [1 week = 7 days]

A 10 servings

B 18 servings

C 21 servings

D 24 servings

Harry chose **A** as the correct answer. How did he get that answer?

Should you multiply or divide to solve the problem?

_____

_____

_____

Pair/Share
How did you figure out how Harry got his answer?

Practice ▶ **Solving One-Step Word Problems**

Solve the problems.

1 There are 8 socks in the dryer. How many pairs of socks is this?

A 2

B 4

C 8

D 16

2 Dana forms a rectangle with 15 square sticky notes. She puts 5 notes in each row. How many rows does she make?

A 3

B 5

C 10

D 20

3 Jane has 42 balloons. She gives an equal number of balloons to 6 children. Can each equation be used to find the number of balloons Jane gives each child? Choose *Yes* or *No*.

a. $42 \times 6 = \boxed{}$ ☐ Yes ☐ No

b. $6 \times \boxed{} = 42$ ☐ Yes ☐ No

c. $6 \div \boxed{} = 42$ ☐ Yes ☐ No

d. $42 \div 6 = \boxed{}$ ☐ Yes ☐ No

4 Which problems can be solved using $12 \div 4 = \boxed{}$? Circle the letter for all that apply.

A Brandon has 12 cookies. He gives the same number of cookies to each of his 4 friends. How many cookies does each friend get?

B Zoe has 12 folders. She wants to put 4 papers in each folder. How many papers does she need?

C Michael rides his bike 4 miles a day. How many days will it take him to ride 12 miles?

D Lilah has 12 tomatoes. She always uses 4 tomatoes to make a salad. How many salads can she make?

5 Catrina used 25 square green tiles to form a square in the middle of her kitchen floor. How many rows did she make? How many tiles did she put in each row?

Show your work.

Answer Catrina made _____ rows with _____ tiles in each row.

6 There are 24 different tables to set up for field day. The principal wants the tables set up in equal rows. Should she use 3 rows or 5 rows? Explain.

_____

_____

_____

Show your work.

Answer The principal should use _____ rows.

✓ **Self Check** Go back and see what you can check off on the Self Check on page 111.

Model Two-Step Word Problems Using the Four Operations

Ⓖ Use What You Know

In this lesson, you will learn how to model two-step word problems. You might use any of the four operations—addition, subtraction, multiplication, and division. Take a look at this problem.

> Mr. Orr checks the pantry to see how many granola bars he has. There are 4 full boxes with 8 granola bars in each box. There are also 3 loose granola bars. How many granola bars does Mr. Orr have in all?

a. How many boxes of granola bars are in the pantry? _____

b. How many granola bars are in each box? _____

c. What operation do you use to find how many granola bars there are in all the boxes? Show how to find the total number of bars in all the boxes.

_____

_____

d. How many loose granola bars are in the pantry? _____

e. What operation do you use to combine the number of granola bars in boxes with the number of loose granola bars? Show how to find the total.

_____

_____

When you solve two-step problems, you need to use two **operations**. You might use multiplication and subtraction. You might use addition and division. You might even use addition and addition again!

Before you model the problem, you need to make sense of it. Think about what you are trying to find. Think about what operation fits with each part of the problem. Think about the problem on the previous page.

There are 4 full boxes with 8 granola bars in each box. This sounds like an equal groups problem. You probably have to multiply or divide.

There are also 3 loose granola bars. There are some extras along with the equal groups. You probably have to add or subtract the extras.

You can use different models to solve two-step problems.

• Here is one way to model the problem from the previous page.

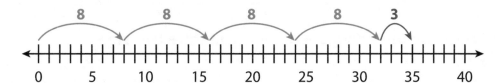

• Here is another way to model it.

4 groups of 8: **4 × 8** = 32

3 more: **32 + 3** = 35

▷ Reflect

1 Explain the operations you would use to solve this problem.

Zan has 5 packages, each with 6 balloons. She opens one package and gives 3 balloons to her brother. How many balloons does Zan have left?

_____

_____

_____

Learn About ▶ **Modeling Problems with Multiplication**

Read the problem below. Then explore different ways to model two-step word problems when one operation is multiplication.

> Anya bought 5 baskets of apples. Each basket had 8 apples. She used 19 apples to make applesauce. How many apples are left?

▶ **Picture It** **You can use a drawing to show and solve two-step word problems.**

▶ **Model It** **You can also use a diagram to show and solve two-step word problems.**

5 groups of 8 is a total of 40.

40
| 8 | 8 | 8 | 8 | 8 |

Anya used **19 apples** and left **the rest**.

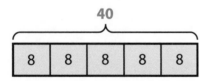

$40 - 19 = \square$

Connect It   Now you will model and solve the problem from the previous page by writing equations with unknowns.

2 How do you find the total number of apples Anya bought?

_____

Let *A* be the total number of apples that Anya bought. Write an equation to show how to find *A*. _____

3 Let *L* be the number of apples that are left after Anya makes applesauce. If you start with *A*, how do you find *L*? Write an equation to show how to find *L*.

_____

4 How can you find the value of *A*? What is the value of *A*? _____

_____

5 Look at the equation you wrote in problem 3. Write the equation using the value of *A* instead of the letter. How many apples are left? _____

_____

6 Explain how you can use equations to model and solve two-step word problems.

_____

_____

_____

Try It   Use what you just learned about modeling problems using equations to solve these problems. Show your work on a separate sheet of paper.

7 Josh had 4 five-dollar bills. Then his grandfather gave him 1 ten-dollar bill. How much money does Josh have now?

_____

8 Vegetable plants are sold in packs of 4. A container holds 2 packs of plants. There are 8 containers on one shelf. How many plants are on the shelf?

_____

Learn About ▶ **Modeling Two-Step Problems with Division**

Read the problem below. Then explore different ways to model two-step word problems when one operation is division.

Sam has a box with 12 cans of paint. There are 3 cans of paint on a table. He puts all of the cans of paint on the table in rows of 5. How many rows of paint cans does Sam make?

▶ **Picture It** **You can use a drawing to show two-step word problems.**

15 cans of paint in rows of 5 cans.

3 cans already on the table.

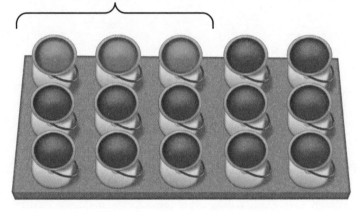

12 cans added to the table.

▶ **Model It** **You can also use words and numbers to model two-step problems.**

12 cans in a box
+ **3** cans on the table
---
15 cans in all

15 cans ÷ 5 cans in each row = ☐ rows

Connect It Now you will model and solve the problem from the previous page by writing equations with unknowns.

9 How do you find the total number of cans of paint that Sam has?

_____

Let *C* be the total number of cans. Write an equation to find *C*. _____

10 How does Sam arrange the paint cans? _____

11 How can you find the number of rows? _____

Let *R* equal the number of rows. Write an equation to find *R* that includes *C* and *R*.

_____

12 How can you find the value of *C*? What is the value of *C*? _____

Write the equation from problem 11 using the value of *C*. How many rows of paint cans does Sam make? _____

13 Explain how you can use multiplication to check that your answer is correct.

_____

_____

_____

Try It Use what you just learned about modeling problems using equations to solve these problems. Show your work on a separate sheet of paper.

14 Rhea does a card trick. She puts 16 cards into 4 equal groups. Then she gives one group of cards to her friend. How many cards does Rhea have left?

_____

15 There are 16 water bottles that are divided equally between 2 teams. Each team has 4 players. Each player gets an equal number of water bottles. How many water bottles does each player get? _____

_____

Practice > **Solving Two-Step Word Problems**

Study the example below. Then solve problems 16–18.

Example

Mrs. Alvarez buys 3 packages of yogurt. Each package has 8 cups. On the way home from the store, her children eat 4 cups of yogurt. How many cups are left?

Look at how you could show your work using a diagram.

3 packages of 8 cups = 24 cups

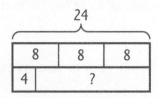

Subtract 4 cups.

$24 - 4 = 20$

Solution <u>There are 20 cups of yogurt left.</u>

The diagram shows 3 packages of 8. The 4 in the diagram stands for the cups of yogurt that were eaten.

 Pair/Share
What equations could you write to solve this problem?

---

16 Jade has an unopened package of 24 beads. She also has 8 beads in a package that is already open. Jade puts all the beads together and divides them into 4 equal groups to share with her friends. How many beads are in each group?

Show your work.

How can you find the total number of beads in both packages?

 Pair/Share
How did you know what operations to use?

Solution _____

©Curriculum Associates, LLC   Copying is not permitted.

17 There are 22 students in Mr. Flynn's class. Today, 2 students are absent. Mr Flynn puts the students that are there into 4 equal groups. How many students are in each group?

Show your work.

> What do you do with the number of students who are absent?

Pair/Share
How can you check that your answer is correct?

Solution _____

---

18 Carmen and Abe act out a math problem. Carmen puts 7 counters each into 3 different cups. Abe takes 3 of the counters. How many counters does Carmen have left? Circle the letter of the correct answer.

A 24

B 21

C 18

D 15

> Should you multiply or divide to find the total number of counters Carmen puts in the cups?

Jim chose **A** as the correct answer. How did he get that answer?

_____

_____

_____

_____

Pair/Share
How did you figure out how Jim got his answer?

Practice ➤ **Solving Two-Step Word Problems**

Solve the problems.

1 Mr. Adkins has 2 packages, each with 6 batteries. He uses 4 of the batteries in a flashlight. How many batteries does he have left?

A 16

B 12

C 10

D 8

2 Ella, James, and Ray's grandmother gave them $24 to divide equally. They spent the money during a 4-day vacation. They spent the same amount of money each day. How much did each person spend each day?

A $1

B $2

C $4

D $8

3 Amir is in charge of getting oranges for today's soccer game. He buys 2 bags with 6 oranges in each bag. He also buys 4 loose oranges.

Which expression can be used to find the number of oranges Amir buys in all? Circle the letter for all that apply.

A $2 \times 6 \times 4$

B $2 + 6 + 4$

C $6 + 6 + 4$

D $2 \times 6 + 4$

E $4 + 2 \times 6$

4 Marisa is keeping track of how many miles she runs. After her run on July 12, she had run a total of 7 miles. If she runs 3 miles each day after that, what is the total number of miles she will have run after her run on July 18?

Answer _____ miles

5 A display of pens has 8 hooks. Each hook can hold 3 packages of pens and there are 3 pens in each package. If the display is completely full, how many pens does it hold?

Show your work.

Answer The display holds _____ pens.

6 Simone is stocking a shelf with bottles of salad dressing. She has one box with 30 bottles and another box with 18 bottles. She can fit 6 bottles in a row on the shelf. How many rows does she make using all the bottles in both boxes?

Show your work.

Answer Simone makes _____ rows of bottles.

✔ Self Check **Go back and see what you can check off on the Self Check on page 111.**

Use What You Know

In this lesson, you will apply what you know to two-step word problems with large numbers. Take a look at this problem.

The Shirt Shack has 438 T-shirts at the end of the day. Then they receive a delivery of new shirts.

- The shirts come in 4 different colors.

- There are 8 shirts of each color.

How many T-shirts does the store have now?

438
T-shirts   +

8 green

8 gray

8 orange

8 purple

a. How can you find how many T-shirts were in the delivery? _____

b. How many T-shirts were in the delivery? _____

c. The store had 438 T-shirts before the delivery. How can you find how many shirts the store has after the delivery? _____

d. Write an equation to show how to find the number of T-shirts the store has after the delivery. _____

e. How many T-shirts will the store have after the delivery? _____

▷▷ Find Out More

Think about the problem on the previous page. You need to find how many shirts the store has after the delivery. Writing an equation could help you. You can use a letter for the unknown number of shirts.

First, find the number of new shirts in the delivery. There were 4 colors of shirts and 8 shirts in each color. The store received **4 × 8** shirts.

The store already had **438** shirts. Add the number of new shirts to 438 to find the total number of T-shirts, **T**.

$$\textbf{Old shirts} + \textbf{New shirts} = \textbf{Total Shirts}$$
$$438 + (4 \times 8) = T$$
$$438 + 32 = T$$
$$470 = T$$

The Shirt Shack now has 470 T-shirts.

Does this answer seem reasonable? You can use estimation or mental math to check.

- **Estimation**

$$438 + 32 = T$$
$$440 + 30 = T \qquad \longleftarrow \text{Round each number to the nearest ten.}$$
$$440 + 30 = 470 \qquad \longleftarrow \text{Add the rounded numbers.}$$

An estimate should be close to the actual number. Sometimes it will be equal to the actual number.

- **Mental math**

$$438 + \textbf{32} = T$$
$$438 + \textbf{2} + \textbf{30} = T \qquad \longleftarrow \text{Rewrite 32 as } 2 + 30.$$
$$440 + 30 = T \qquad \longleftarrow \text{Add 2 and 438.}$$
$$440 + 30 = 470 \qquad \longleftarrow \text{Add 440 and 30.}$$

▶ Reflect

1 Look at the equation $438 + (4 \times 8) = T$ above. Explain why there are parentheses around 4×8.

_____

_____

Learn About ▶ **Solving Two-Step Problems**

Read the problem below. Then explore different ways to model and solve two-step word problems.

Third graders at Brown Elementary School are raising money for the school library.

- The goal is to raise $250.
- They raised $9 each day for 8 days in a row.

How much more money is needed to reach the goal?

▶ **Picture It** You can use a diagram to show a two-step word problem.

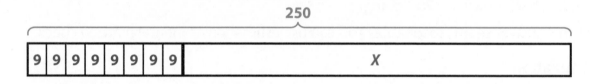

250

| 9 | 9 | 9 | 9 | 9 | 9 | 9 | 9 | X |

▶ **Model It** Use the diagram above to help write an equation for a two-step word problem.

The students raised $9 each day for 8 days. So they have already raised **8 × 9** dollars.

They need a total of **250** dollars. They need to raise *X* more dollars.

The **amount already raised** plus *X* should equal **250**.

Write this as one equation.

$(8 \times 9) + X = 250$

Connect It Now you will model and solve the equation from the previous page.

$(8 \times 9) + X = 250$

$72 + X = 250$

$X = 250 - 72$

$X = 178$

2 What operation is done first? _____ Why? _____

_____

3 Describe in words what $250 = 72 + X$ means. _____

4 Why do you subtract 72 from 250 to find X?

_____

_____

5 What is X and what does it stand for? _____

_____

6 Explain how you can use addition to check your answer. _____

_____

Try It Use what you just learned to solve these two-step word problems. Show your work on a separate sheet of paper.

7 Tim is saving money to buy a pair of hockey skates that cost $289. For the past 6 weeks, he has saved $7 each week. How much money does Tim still need to save?

_____

8 Nima is training for a bike race. During the first three weeks in April she rode a total of 176 miles. During the last week in April, she rode 9 miles each day for 7 days. How many miles in all did Nima ride in April?

_____

Learn About **Estimating Solutions to Word Problems**

Read the problem below. Then explore different ways to estimate solutions to two-step word problems.

A zoo names an elephant Tiny.

- On Saturday, Tiny ate 152 pounds of food.

- On Sunday he ate 12 more pounds of food than he did on Saturday.

How many pounds of food did Tiny eat that weekend?

▶ **Picture It** **You can use a table to show the information in a two-step word problem.**

Amount of Food Tiny Ate	
Saturday	Sunday
152 pounds	152 pounds + 12 pounds

$152 + 152 + 12 = F$

▶ **Model It** **Estimate the solution to the two-step problem.**

- You can round each number to the nearest hundred and then add.

    152 rounds to 200.

    12 rounds to 0.

    $200 + 200 + 0 = 400$

- You can also round each number to the nearest ten and then add.

    152 rounds to 150.

    12 rounds to 10.

    $150 + 150 + 10 = 310$

▶ **Connect It** Now you will model and solve the equation from the previous page.

$$152 + (152 + 12) = F$$
$$152 + 164 = F$$

9 Add the numbers in parentheses. Break the numbers apart to use numbers that are easy to work with: **150 + 2 + 10 + 2 =** _____

10 What is the next step? Explain and show it.

_____

11 How many pounds of food did Tiny eat that weekend? Compare your answer to the estimates on the previous page. Are they close?

_____

_____

12 Do you think your answer is reasonable? Explain why.

_____

_____

13 Explain how estimation is useful when solving two-step equations.

_____

_____

▶ **Try It** Use what you just learned to solve these two-step word problems. Show your work on a separate sheet of paper.

14 Joan earned $136 last week and $215 this week. She used some of her earnings to buy a jacket. Joan had $273 left after buying the jacket. How much did she spend on the jacket? _____

15 A bookstore had 650 copies of a new book. The first day, 281 copies were sold. At the end of the week there were only 43 copies left. How many books were sold between the first day and the end of the week?

_____

Practice ▶ **Solving Two-Step Word Problems**

Study the example below. Then solve problems 16–18.

Example

Bridget is packing strawberries in sandwich bags to sell at her gymnastics meet. She has 140 strawberries, and she makes bags of 5. So far Bridget has packed 105 strawberries. How many more bags of 5 strawberries can Bridget make?

Look at how you could show your work using a diagram.

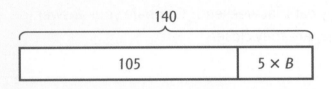

140

| 105 | $5 \times B$ |

$$105 + (5 \times B) = 140$$
$$5 \times B = 140 - 105$$
$$5 \times B = 35$$
$$B = 7$$

Solution ___7 more bags_____

The student uses a diagram to show the 105 strawberries already packed. $5 \times B$ shows how many more bags can be made.

 Pair/Share

Can you write a different equation to solve this problem?

---

16 Students in Miss Kemp's class earn 1 point for each page they read. A student who earns 300 points gets a prize. Elise reads 8 pages a day for 7 days in a row. How many more points does she need to get a prize?

Show your work.

What operation do you use to find how many pages Elise has read?

 Pair/Share

How can you check your answer?

Solution _____

17 Troy scored 945 points playing 3 games of pinball. He scored 312 points in the first game and 356 points in the second game. How many points did Troy score in the third game?

Show your work.

Will you round the numbers to the nearest ten or hundred to estimate?

Solution _____

Pair/Share

Can you solve this problem in a different way?

---

18 In the morning 134 books were checked out from the library. In the afternoon 254 books were checked out and 118 books were checked out in the evening. How many books in all were checked out from the library that day?

A 270

B 388

C 496

D 506

Paolo chose **B** as the correct answer. How did he get that answer?

How can you estimate the answer?

_____

_____

_____

_____

Pair/Share

How can you tell if Paolo's answer is reasonable?

Practice ▶ **Solving Two-Step Word Problems**

Solve the problems.

1 Which equation can NOT be used to solve the problem below?

Rosa and Brett are the only two people in a school election. Rosa got 314 votes in the election. She got 18 more votes than Brett. How many people voted in the election?

A $314 + 314 - 18 = N$

B $N = 314 + 314 - 18$

C $314 - 18 + 314 = N$

D $314 + 314 + 18 = N$

2 George estimated that 800 people voted in the election in problem 1. Which mistake could he have made?

A George rounded 18 down to 10 instead of up to 20.

B George rounded 314 up to 320 instead of down to 310.

C George rounded 314 up to 400 instead of down to 300.

D George rounded 18 up to 100 instead of down to 0.

3 A produce manager unpacks 108 bananas. There are 9 bunches of 4 bananas each. The rest are single bananas.

Which equations can be used to find the number of single bananas, N? Circle the letter for all that apply.

A $N + (9 \times 4) = 108$

B $9 \times 4 = 108 + N$

C $N - (9 \times 4) = 108$

D $108 - (9 \times 4) = N$

E $N + (9 + 4) = 108$

4 A theater sold 379 tickets to a movie. Of those, 192 were children's tickets. The rest were adult tickets. How many fewer adult tickets were sold than children's tickets?

Show your work.

Answer _____ tickets

5 Greg is packing a book order. He has already packed 3 boxes with 5 books in each box. There are 210 books left to pack. How many books are in the whole order?

Show your work.

Answer There are _____ books in the whole order.

6 Gina wants to estimate the total of three bills she has to pay. The bills are for $125, $115, and $138. Gina wants to make sure that she has enough money. She wants the estimate to be greater than the total of the bills. Should she round to the nearest ten or hundred?

Answer Gina should round to the nearest _____ .

Explain your answer.

_____

_____

_____

_____

✔ **Self Check** **Go back and see what you can check off on the Self Check on page 111.**

Unit 3
MATH IN
ACTION

👥 **Introduction**

Use the Four Operations

SMP1 Make sense
of problems and
persevere in
solving them.

Study an Example Problem and Solution

**Read this problem that involves using different operations to solve it.
Then look at Sweet T's solution to this problem.**

Sweet T's Tees

Sweet T wants to buy shirts for his fingerboard team. The team will have
between 8 and 10 members. Everyone should get two different shirts.

- $50 set-up fee to print
- Add $2 to the cost
  of each shirt to print
  on it.

Short Sleeve
$6 each

Long Sleeve
$8 each

Collar
$7 each

Sweet T can spend up to $225 for shirts. It's okay to have money left over.

- Tell what kind of shirts and how many to order.
- Decide whether or not to print on the shirts.
- Give the total cost and amount of money left over.

**Read the sample solution on the next page. Then look at the checklist
below. Find and mark parts of the solution that match the checklist.**

✏️ **Problem-Solving Checklist**

☐ Tell what is known.

☐ Tell what the problem
  is asking.

☐ Show all your work.

☐ Show that the
  solution works.

a. Circle something that is known.

b. Underline something that you need
  to find.

c. Draw a box around what you do to
  solve the problem.

d. Put a checkmark next to the part
  that shows the solution works.

Sweet T's Solution

▷ **I know that there will be 8 to 10 team members.**
I will plan on buying for 9 members. I don't want to have
too many extra shirts.

▷ **I can make a table to show the costs for different kinds of shirts.**
Multiply the price of the shirt by the number to buy.

Type of Shirt	Plain	With Print
Short Sleeve	9 x $6 = $54	9 x $8 = $72
Collar	9 x $7 = $63	9 x $9 = $81
Long Sleeve	9 x $8 = $72	9 x $10 = $90

The table helps me see all of the choices.

▷ **I can find the cost for the two most expensive shirts.**
Cost of shirts: $81 + $90 = $171
Add set-up fee: $171 + $50 = $221
I think this is too close to $225.

▷ **I'll buy . . .**

collar shirts with print:	$ 81
plain short-sleeve shirts:	$ 54
set-up fee:	+ $ 50
total:	$185

I could buy the most expensive shirts. I would rather have money to buy other things.

▷ **I can subtract to find the amount left over.**
$225 – $185 = $40
There will be $40 left over after buying the shirts.

This plan gives the team two different looking shirts.

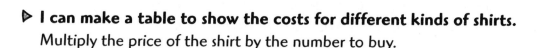

Try ▶ **Another Approach**

There are many ways to solve problems. Think about how you might solve Sweet T's Tees problem in a different way.

Sweet T's Tees

Sweet T wants to buy shirts for his fingerboard team. The team will have between 8 and 10 members. Everyone should get two different shirts.

- $50 set-up fee
- Add $2 to the cost of each to print on shirts.

Short Sleeve **Long Sleeve** **Collar**
$6 each $8 each $7 each

Sweet T can spend up to $225 for shirts. It's okay to have money left over.

- Tell what kind of shirts and how many to order.
- Decide whether or not to print on the shirts.
- Give the total cost and amount of money left over.

▶ **Plan It** **Answer these questions to help you start thinking about a plan.**

A. How many team members will you buy for?

_____

_____

B. Do you want to have any leftover money? If so, about how much?

_____

_____

Solve It Find a different solution for Sweet T's Tees problem. Show all your work on a separate sheet of paper.

You may want to use the problem-solving tips to get started.

Problem-Solving Tips

- **Models**

Type of Shirt	Plain	With Print

- **Word Bank**

add	subtract	multiply
sum	difference	product

- **Sentence Starters**

  • The cost to buy _____

  • I need to multiply _____

Problem-Solving Checklist

Make sure that you . . .

☐ tell what you know.

☐ tell what you need to do.

☐ show all your work.

☐ show that the solution works.

Reflect

Use Mathematical Practices As you work through the problem, discuss these questions with a partner.

• **Reason Mathematically** What are all of the numbers in the problem and what do they mean?

• **Persevere** What is your plan for solving the problem?

Discuss **Models and Strategies**

Read the problem. Write a solution on a separate sheet of paper.
Remember, there can be lots of ways to solve a problem!

Fingerboard Parts

Sweet T wants to have lots of extra fingerboard parts.
He wants members to be able to mix and match parts to make
different boards.

Decks

$8 each

Available in yellow,
red, pink, purple,
orange, and green.

Trucks

$6 for a set of 2

Available in pink,
red, blue, black,
and white.

Wheels

$7 for a set of 4

Available in yellow,
red, blue, black,
and white.

Put the parts together to make your own board!

Sweet T can spend up to $160 on fingerboard parts. What should he buy?

▶ Plan It and Solve It Find a solution for the Fingerboard Parts problem.

- Make a list of the parts to buy. Include the numbers of the different parts and the colors.
- Tell why you chose the parts that you did.
- Find the total cost to buy the parts. Tell how much money is left.

You may want to use the problem-solving tips to get started.

Problem-Solving Tips

- **Questions**
  - How many of each part do you need to make one fingerboard?
  - Do you want to have more of one kind of part? Why?

- **Tools** You may want to use . . .
  - a table.
  - an organized list.

- **Sentence Starters**
  - I would like to have _____
  - I will buy _____

Problem-Solving Checklist

Make sure that you . . .

☐ tell what you know.

☐ tell what you need to do.

☐ show all your work.

☐ show that the solution works.

▶ Reflect

Use Mathematical Practices As you work through the problem, discuss these questions with a partner.

- **Use Models** How can you use equations to help find a solution?

- **Persevere** How can you check that your solution makes sense?

**Read the problem. Write a solution on a separate sheet of paper.
Remember, there are many different ways to solve a problem!**

Skate Park

Sweet T has $80 left after buying items for the team. He wants to buy at least three different items for the skate park he is making. Here are the items Sweet T is looking at.

Table $24   **Bench $15**   **L-Shaped Box $15**

Box $18   **Palette $10**   **Rail $22**

What items should Sweet T buy?

▶ **Solve It** **Tell which items Sweet T should buy.**

- Give the total cost.
- Explain why you chose the items you did.

▶ **Reflect**

Use Mathematical Practices After you complete the task, choose one of these questions to discuss with a partner.

- **Persevere** What steps did you take to get your solution?

- **Use a Model** Which operations did you use to solve the problem?

Grip Tape

Sweet T wants to buy pieces of grip tape for the team. The tape sticks to the deck of the fingerboard to make it less slippery. Sweet T thinks that each of the 9 members of his team needs at least 4 pieces of grip tape.

Grip Tape

1 piece for $1

OR

Buy 5 and get 1 piece free.

How many pieces of grip tape should Sweet T buy?

▶ **Solve It** **Decide how many pieces of grip tape Sweet T should buy for each team member.**

- Tell why you chose this number.
- Tell the total number of pieces needed.
- Find a way to buy groups of 5 or separate pieces to get this total.
- Give the total cost.

▶ **Reflect**

Use Mathematical Practices After you complete the task, choose one of these questions to discuss with a partner.

- **Make an Argument** What reasons did you have for your decision about the number of pieces to buy?

- **Persevere** What was your first step in finding a solution? Why did you start this way?

Solve the problems.

1 A school ordered 36 books for its library. The books came packed in 4 cartons, with an equal number of books in each carton. Which drawing can be used to find the number of books in each carton?

A

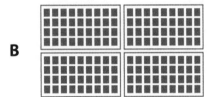

B

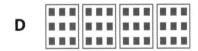

C

D

2 Jessie bought a number of DVDs for $8 each. She also bought a T-shirt for $12. Jessie spent a total of $84. Which equation can be used to find the number of DVDs, *D*, that she bought?

A $(8 \times D) + 12 = 84$

B $8 \times (12 + D) = 84$

C $8 + (12 \times D) = 84$

D $(8 + 12) \times D = 84$

3 Bianca has 40 books. She decides to put them in a bookcase with 6 shelves. She put the same number of books on each shelf and has 4 books left over. In the picture below, draw the number of books she put on one of the shelves.

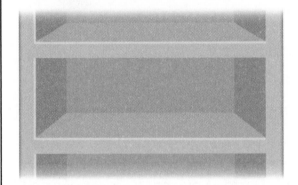

4 Braden worked for 2 hours. Mateo worked for 8 hours. They each earned $10 for every hour they worked. How much more money did Mateo earn than Braden?

$_____ more

5 There are 23 tables in the library. Each table has 4 chairs. Third graders sit in all the chairs at 3 tables. Fourth graders sit in all the chairs at 6 tables. The rest of the chairs are empty.

Part A The letter *C* stands for the number of chairs with students sitting in them. Write an equation that will help you find *C*.

Equation _____

Part B Solve the equation to find the number of chairs with students sitting in them.

Answer _____ chairs with students sitting in them

6 Kanti's school put on three music shows. Kanti sold 289 tickets for the first show, 115 tickets for the second show, and 198 tickets for the third show.

Part A How many tickets did Kanti sell for all three shows?

Show your work.

Answer _____ tickets

Part B Explain how you could estimate to find out if your answer is reasonable.

_____

_____

_____

Performance Task

Answer the questions and show all your work on separate paper.

Mr. Perennial has a vegetable garden. His plants are planted in 6 rows with 5 plants in each row. Each plant needs 2 ounces of fertilizer on the day it is planted. One week later he will use a total of 8 ounces of fertilizer for all of the plants.

Draw a picture of Mr. Perennial's garden. How many total ounces of fertilizer will he need for his garden? Write and solve an equation to find your answer.

Mr. Perennial has two 20-ounce containers of fertilizer. How much more fertilizer does he need to buy? Write and solve an equation to find your answer.

Checklist

Did you . . .

☐ draw a picture?

☐ use an unknown in each equation you wrote?

☐ check your calculations?

▶ Reflect

Use Mathematical Practices After you complete the task, choose one of the following questions to answer.

- **Persevere** Which words helped you decide to use multiplication to solve this problem?

- **Use Structure** How could you find the total number of plants in Mr. Perennial's garden using addition? How could you find the total number of plants using multiplication?

Unit 4
Number and Operations—Fractions

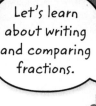

Let's learn about writing and comparing fractions.

Real-World Connection Can you imagine what it would be like if you could only order a whole pizza when you only wanted one slice? What if time was only measured in whole hours because no one knew what to call 45 minutes? Fractions are an important part of your everyday life. If a pizza is cut into 8 equal slices, one slice is $\frac{1}{8}$ of the pizza. Forty-five minutes is $\frac{3}{4}$ of an hour. And one fourth of a dollar is—you guessed it—a quarter!

In This Unit You will write fractions and compare fractions. You will also learn to recognize when two fractions show the same amount.

✔ Self Check

Before starting this unit, check off the skills you know below. As you complete each lesson, see how many more you can check off!

I can:	Before this unit	After this unit
use a fraction to show equal parts of a whole, for example: when a whole has 4 equal parts, each part is $\frac{1}{4}$ of the whole.	☐	☐
use a number line to show fractions, and find a fraction on a number line.	☐	☐
understand equivalent fractions, for example: $\frac{1}{3} = \frac{2}{6}$, because they show the same amount.	☐	☐
find equivalent fractions, for example: fractions equivalent to $\frac{1}{2}$ include $\frac{2}{4}$, $\frac{3}{6}$, and $\frac{4}{8}$.	☐	☐
write whole numbers as fractions, for example: $5 = \frac{5}{1}$ or $\frac{10}{2}$.	☐	☐
compare fractions when they have same-sized wholes using $<$, $>$, and $=$, for example: $\frac{1}{3} > \frac{1}{8}$, $\frac{4}{6} < \frac{5}{6}$, and $\frac{2}{3} = \frac{4}{6}$.	☐	☐

Understand What a Fraction Is

 **Think It Through**

> **How can we describe equal parts?**

Fractions are numbers that tell about equal parts of a whole. A fraction is named by the number of equal parts. One of three equal parts is one third. One of four equal parts is one fourth, and so on. One third and one fourth are fractions.

There are two parts to a fraction. The bottom number is the **denominator**. It tells how many equal parts are in the whole. The top number is the **numerator**. It tells how many equal parts you have.

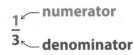

$$\frac{1}{3}$$ numerator / denominator

$$\frac{1 \text{ part shaded}}{3 \text{ equal parts in the whole}}$$

Think Fractions always show equal parts.

To use a fraction to tell about the parts of a whole, all the parts must be the same size. Think about sharing a cake with some friends. You cut the cake into pieces that are the same size so that it is fair.

There are 6 equal parts.

These parts are sixths.

Each part is $\frac{1}{6}$.

All the parts are not the same size.

These parts are not sixths.

✏️ **Circle** the model that shows equal parts.

Think Unit fractions help us understand other fractions.

A **unit fraction** has a 1 in the numerator. $\frac{1}{4}$ is a unit fraction. It names
1 part of a whole that has 4 equal parts.

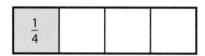

> You can count unit fractions like you count whole numbers. Instead of 1, 2, 3, count $\frac{1}{4}$, $\frac{2}{4}$, $\frac{3}{4}$.

If you know the name of 1 part of the whole, you can count to
name more parts of that whole.

Look at the rectangle below. It has 4 equal parts. Each part is $\frac{1}{4}$.

The rectangle has three parts shaded. Three $\frac{1}{4}$s is $\frac{3}{4}$.

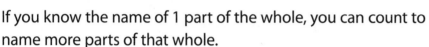

When you count the shaded parts of this rectangle, you say: one fourth,
two fourths, three fourths. Three fourths of the rectangle is shaded.

You can also describe the whole rectangle by counting the number of $\frac{1}{4}$s.

There are four $\frac{1}{4}$s in the rectangle, or $\frac{4}{4}$.

$\frac{1}{4}$	$\frac{1}{4}$	$\frac{1}{4}$	$\frac{1}{4}$

▶ Reflect

1 Mike draws a large rectangle. He wants to color $\frac{3}{8}$ of the rectangle blue.
How many equal parts should he make? What fraction names each part?
How many parts should he color?

_____

_____

_____

Think About ▷ **Describing Parts of a Whole with Fractions**

🔍 **Let's Explore the Idea** You can use models to help you think about fractions.

2 How many equal parts are shown in this model? _____

How many parts are shaded? _____

Write the fraction that names the shaded part. _____

Circle the name for this fraction: one half   one third   one fourth

3 How many equal parts are shown in this model? _____

How many parts are shaded? _____

Write the fraction that names the shaded parts. _____

Circle the name for this fraction: three halves   three thirds   three fourths

First write the unit fraction shown. Then shade the given number of parts. Write the fraction that names the shaded parts.

4

Unit fraction: _____

Shade 2 parts:

What fraction of the square did you shade? _____

5

Unit fraction: _____

Shade 6 parts:

What fraction of the circle did you shade? _____

Write the fraction of the figure that is shaded. The parts in each model are all equal.

6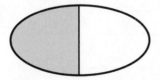

Fraction: _____

7

Fraction: _____

8

Fraction: _____

Let's Talk About It

Solve the problems below as a group.

9 Look at your answers to problems 4 and 5. Explain how you figured out what unit fraction was shown in each model. _____

_____

_____

Explain how you figured out what fractions to write for the parts you shaded.

_____

_____

Do you think you could have shaded the number of parts another way in each model? Explain. _____

_____

_____

10 Look at the rectangle below.

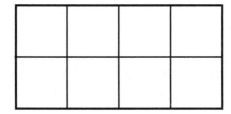

What unit fraction is each part? _____ Now shade $\frac{4}{8}$ of the rectangle.

Try It Another Way Work with your group to use the pictures to draw the figure described.

11 The model below shows $\frac{1}{3}$ of a square. Draw what $\frac{2}{3}$ of the square looks like.

12 The model below shows $\frac{1}{6}$ of a shape. Draw what $\frac{3}{6}$ of the shape could look like.

Connect ▶ **Parts of a Whole with Fractions**

Talk through these problems as a class, then write your answers below.

13 **Create** The part shown below is $\frac{1}{6}$ of a rectangle. Draw a model to show what the whole rectangle might look like.

14 **Explain** Look at the squares below. Each square is divided into equal parts.

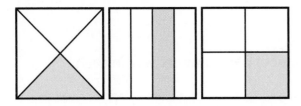

Lynn says each square has the same fraction shaded. Rose says each square has a different fraction shaded. Explain who is correct and why.

_____

_____

_____

15 **Compare** Look at the triangles below. Each triangle is divided into equal parts.

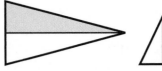

What is the same about the fraction of each model that is shaded?

_____

_____

What is different about the fraction of each model that is shaded?

_____

_____

Ideas About Parts of a Whole with Fractions

16 Put It Together Use what you have learned to complete this task.

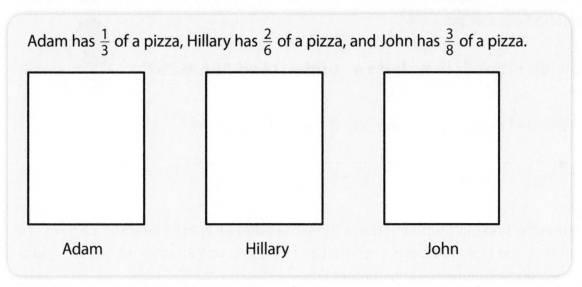

Adam has $\frac{1}{3}$ of a pizza, Hillary has $\frac{2}{6}$ of a pizza, and John has $\frac{3}{8}$ of a pizza.

Adam   Hillary   John

Part A Show the number of equal parts in each pizza. Then shade each pizza to show the fraction each person has.

Part B Circle one of the pizzas. Explain how you knew how many equal parts to show and how many parts to shade.

_____

_____

_____

_____

_____

_____

_____

Think It Through

How do number lines help us understand numbers?

You are used to seeing a number line show whole numbers.

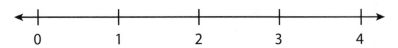

The numbers on this number line are the same distance apart. The distance from one number to the next number is 1 whole. Each time you add another whole, you count another whole number on the number line.

1 whole	1 whole	1 whole	1 whole

```
←—+——————+——————+——————+——————+—→
  0      1      2      3      4
```

Think You can show more than whole numbers on a number line.

Fractions show equal parts of a whole. You can see this on a number line too.

The section between 0 and 1 on a number line shows 1 whole. If you mark this section to show equal parts, it is the same as dividing a whole into equal parts.

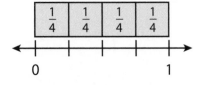

The section between 0 and 1 is marked off into 4 equal parts, so each part shows $\frac{1}{4}$.

> ✏️ **Underline** the sentence that tells why each part of the number line shows $\frac{1}{4}$.

You can count fractions on a number line just like you can count whole numbers.

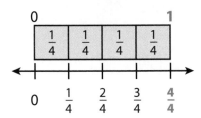

When you count whole numbers, you say 1, 2, 3, 4, . . . When you count fourths, you say $\frac{1}{4}, \frac{2}{4}, \frac{3}{4}, \frac{4}{4}, \ldots$

You can also use number lines to show fractions greater than 1.

To do this, mark off each section between pairs of whole numbers (like 0 and 1 and 1 and 2), into the same number of equal parts. Then count the fractions.

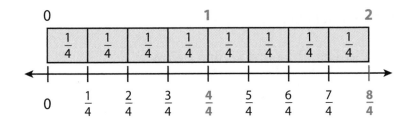

The distance from zero to 2 on the number line can be named as 2, or $\frac{8}{4}$.

▶ Reflect

1 How many $\frac{1}{3}$s or "thirds" are there between 0 and 1 on a number line? How do you know?

_____

_____

_____

_____

_____

Think About **Fractions as Equal Groups on a Number Line**

🔍 **Let's Explore the Idea** **Looking at the number of equal parts helps you think about fractions on a number line.**

2 Look at the section between 0 and 1 on the number line below.

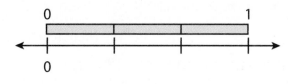

How many equal parts are there? _____

What fraction does each part show? _____

Write the missing labels on the number line.

3 Look at the section between 0 and 1 on the number line below.

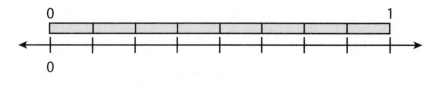

How many equal parts are there? _____

What fraction does each part show? _____

Write the missing labels on the number line.

4 Look at the section between 0 and 1 on the number line below.

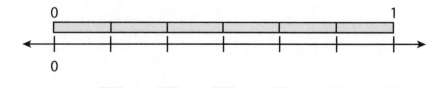

How many equal parts are there? _____

What fraction does each part show? _____

Write the missing labels on the number line.

Let's Talk About It

Solve the problems below as a group.

5 Look at the number lines in problems 2–4. How is showing fractions on a number line like showing fractions using models? _____

_____

6 Look at the sections between the whole numbers on the number line below.

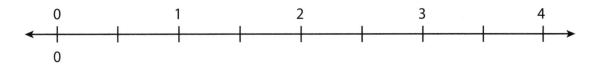

How many equal parts are in each section? _____

What fraction does each part show? _____

Each mark on the number line represents a fraction. What denominator will all the fractions have? _____

Write the missing labels on the number line.

7 Look at the fractions you wrote on the number line above that are greater than 1. What do you notice about the numerator and denominator in each of these fractions? _____

_____

▶ Try It Another Way Work with your group to identify each fraction.

8 Look at the number line below. What fraction is at *A*? _____

9 Look at the number line below. What fraction is at *B*? _____

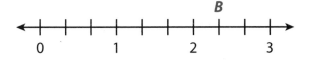

Lesson 15 *Understand* Fractions on a Number Line

Connect ▶ **Ideas About Fractions on a Number Line**

Talk through these problems as a class, then write your answers below.

10 Explain Look at the number line below.

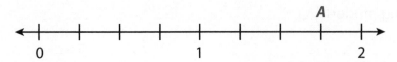

A

0   1   2

Amira says that A is at $\frac{7}{8}$. Is she right? Explain why or why not.

_____

_____

_____

_____

_____

_____

11 Demonstrate Use the number line below to show the fraction $\frac{4}{6}$.

0   1

Explain how you knew where to label $\frac{4}{6}$.

_____

_____

_____

12 Illustrate Use the number line below to show that there are 8 eighths in 1 whole.

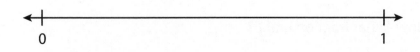

0   1

Ideas About Fractions on a Number Line

13 Put It Together Use what you have learned to complete this task.

> Zara and John are hiking on a trail that is 2 miles long. There are signs to mark each eighth of a mile along the trail.

Part A Draw a number line to show the length of the trail. Then mark the number line off to show where each sign is.

Part B Zara stopped for water at the $\frac{3}{8}$-mile sign. Label the $\frac{3}{8}$ mark on the number line with a *Z* for Zara.

Part C John stopped to rest after $\frac{12}{8}$ miles. Label the $\frac{12}{8}$ mark on the number line with a *J* for John.

Part D Who stopped before the 1-mile mark? Who stopped after the 1-mile mark? Explain how you know.

_____

_____

_____

_____

_____

_____

_____

💭 Think It Through

How can two different fractions be equal?

Two fractions are equal if they name the same amount of the whole. Different fractions that name the same amount of the whole are called **equivalent fractions**.

Look at the circles. The same amount is shaded in each circle. Each circle is divided into a different number of equal parts. So, the fractions used to name the shaded parts are different, $\frac{1}{2}$ and $\frac{2}{4}$, but equivalent.

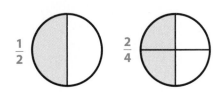

You can also see equivalent fractions using a number line. $\frac{1}{2}$ and $\frac{2}{4}$ are located at the same point on the number line. This shows they are equivalent.

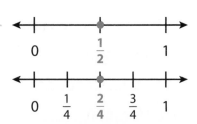

Think To find equivalent fractions, the size of the wholes must be the same.

The two rectangles at the right are the same size. One $\frac{1}{2}$ part is the same size as two $\frac{1}{4}$ parts. So, $\frac{1}{2}$ and $\frac{2}{4}$ are equivalent.

The two rectangles below are not the same size. They show that $\frac{1}{2}$ of a small rectangle is not equivalent to $\frac{2}{4}$ of a large rectangle.

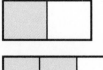

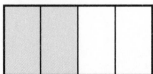

✏️ **Shade** the parts of the first two rectangles to show that $\frac{1}{2}$ and $\frac{2}{4}$ are equivalent.

Think It takes more than one smaller part to equal one bigger part.

Once you make sure the wholes are the same size, look at the size of the parts in each whole to name equivalent fractions.

$\frac{1}{2}$	$\frac{1}{2}$

Each part is $\frac{1}{2}$.

$\frac{1}{4}$	$\frac{1}{4}$	$\frac{1}{4}$	$\frac{1}{4}$

Each part is $\frac{1}{4}$.

Remember,
two $\frac{1}{4}$s are the same as $\frac{2}{4}$,
three $\frac{1}{6}$s are the same as $\frac{3}{6}$,
and four $\frac{1}{8}$s are the same as $\frac{4}{8}$.

To shade the same amount as $\frac{1}{2}$, you need to shade two $\frac{1}{4}$s.

$\frac{1}{2}$	$\frac{1}{2}$

$\frac{1}{4}$	$\frac{1}{4}$	$\frac{1}{4}$	$\frac{1}{4}$

You can also divide the rectangle into different numbers of equal parts to find other fractions that are equivalent to $\frac{1}{2}$.

$\frac{1}{2}$	$\frac{1}{2}$

$\frac{1}{6}$	$\frac{1}{6}$	$\frac{1}{6}$	$\frac{1}{6}$	$\frac{1}{6}$	$\frac{1}{6}$

$\frac{1}{8}$	$\frac{1}{8}$	$\frac{1}{8}$	$\frac{1}{8}$	$\frac{1}{8}$	$\frac{1}{8}$	$\frac{1}{8}$	$\frac{1}{8}$

To shade the same amount as $\frac{1}{2}$, shade three $\frac{1}{6}$s or four $\frac{1}{8}$s.

So, $\frac{1}{2}$ is equivalent to $\frac{2}{4}$, $\frac{3}{6}$, and $\frac{4}{8}$.

▶ Reflect

1 Explain why it takes more $\frac{1}{8}$s than $\frac{1}{4}$s to make a fraction equivalent to $\frac{1}{2}$.

_____

_____

_____

Think About ▶ **Equivalent Fractions**

🔍 **Let's Explore the Idea** Models and number lines are two ways to show equivalent fractions.

2 Count the equal parts in each model at the right. Then write the unit fraction that names the part in each section of both models.

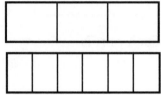

How many $\frac{1}{6}$s does it take to name the same amount as $\frac{1}{3}$? _____

How many $\frac{1}{6}$s does it take to name the same amount as two $\frac{1}{3}$s? _____

3 Fill in the missing fractions on each number line below.

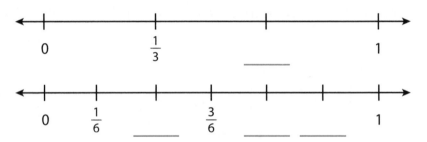

Use the models and number lines above to answer problem 4.

4 Write the equivalent fractions: $\frac{1}{3}$ = _____ $\frac{2}{3}$ = _____

Now try these problems.

5 Fill in the missing fractions on each number line below.

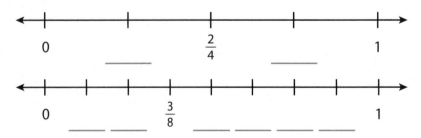

6 Write the equivalent fractions: $\frac{1}{4}$ = _____ $\frac{6}{8}$ = _____

Let's Talk About It

Solve the problems below as a group.

7 You have used models and number lines to find equivalent fractions. How are the two ways alike?

_____

_____

How are the two ways different?

_____

_____

_____

8 Mila thinks $\frac{1}{2}$ is equivalent to $\frac{2}{3}$ and to $\frac{3}{6}$. Label the number lines below and use them to explain whether Mila is correct or not.

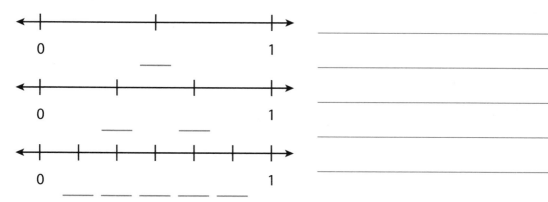

Try It Another Way Work with your group to use the fraction strips to show equivalent fractions.

9 $\frac{2}{3}$ is shaded on one strip. Shade an equivalent amount on the other strip.

$\frac{1}{3}$	$\frac{1}{3}$	$\frac{1}{3}$

$\frac{1}{6}$	$\frac{1}{6}$	$\frac{1}{6}$	$\frac{1}{6}$	$\frac{1}{6}$	$\frac{1}{6}$

What fraction did you shade? _____

10 $\frac{4}{8}$ is shaded on one strip. Shade an equivalent amount on the other strip.

$\frac{1}{8}$	$\frac{1}{8}$	$\frac{1}{8}$	$\frac{1}{8}$	$\frac{1}{8}$	$\frac{1}{8}$	$\frac{1}{8}$	$\frac{1}{8}$

$\frac{1}{6}$	$\frac{1}{6}$	$\frac{1}{6}$	$\frac{1}{6}$	$\frac{1}{6}$	$\frac{1}{6}$

What fraction did you shade? _____

Connect **Ideas About Equivalent Fractions**

Talk through these problems as a class, then write your answers below.

11 Demonstrate Use the fraction strips below to show $\frac{1}{4} = \frac{2}{8}$.

$\frac{1}{4}$	$\frac{1}{4}$	$\frac{1}{4}$	$\frac{1}{4}$

$\frac{1}{8}$	$\frac{1}{8}$	$\frac{1}{8}$	$\frac{1}{8}$	$\frac{1}{8}$	$\frac{1}{8}$	$\frac{1}{8}$	$\frac{1}{8}$

12 Explain Cooper drew the models below. He says they show $\frac{2}{3} = \frac{2}{6}$.

What did Cooper do wrong?

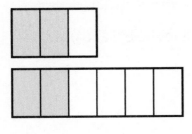

_____

_____

_____

_____

13 Illustrate The number line below is marked to show halves. Draw marks on the number line to show eighths. Above each mark you make, write the fraction it shows.

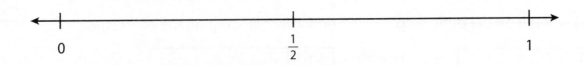

0      $\frac{1}{2}$ 1

Which fraction on the number line above is equivalent to $\frac{1}{2}$? _____

Ideas About Equivalent Fractions

14 Put It Together Use what you have learned to complete this task.

Four friends each ate a part of their own granola bar. All the granola bars were the same size. The table at the right shows what part of a granola bar was eaten by each friend.

Friend	Part of Granola Bar Eaten
Meg	$\frac{4}{6}$
Joe	$\frac{4}{8}$
Beth	$\frac{6}{8}$
Amy	$\frac{2}{3}$

Part A Which two friends ate the same amount of a granola bar? Circle those two names in the table. Draw models to show that your answer is correct.

Meg

Joe

Beth

Amy

Part B Fred also had a granola bar. He divided it into fourths. He ate the same amount as Beth.

Draw a number line to show Beth's granola bar. Label it to show the fraction of the bar she ate. Draw another number line to show Fred's granola bar. Mark it to show how Fred divided his granola bar. Label the fraction of his granola bar Fred ate.

What fraction of his granola bar did Fred eat? _____

Use What You Know

In Lesson 16, you learned that equivalent fractions name the same amount of the whole. In this lesson you will learn more about finding equivalent fractions. Take a look at this problem.

> Izzy's mom baked a cake. She put chocolate frosting on half of the cake and vanilla frosting on half of the cake.
>
>
>
> Then Izzy's mom cut the cake into fourths. What fraction other than $\frac{1}{2}$ names the part of the cake that has chocolate frosting?

a. Look at the picture above. What fraction of the cake has chocolate frosting?

_____

b. How many equal parts should the cake be divided into to show fourths? _____

c. On the picture above, draw lines to divide the cake into fourths. Each fourth should have all chocolate or all vanilla frosting.

d. How many fourths of the cake have chocolate frosting? _____

e. Did the amount of cake with chocolate frosting change? Explain how you know that $\frac{1}{2}$ of the cake is the same amount as $\frac{2}{4}$ of the cake.

_____

_____

_____

In the last lesson, you compared two models to understand equivalent fractions. The models were the same size, but they had a different number of equal parts. You named the fraction shown in one model. Then you looked at the other model to find the fraction that named the same amount.

You can also find equivalent fractions by dividing the same model in different ways. The cake Izzy's mom made already showed $\frac{1}{2}$. You may have drawn lines in one of the ways below to show fourths.

Each of these different ways of making fourths show that $\frac{2}{4}$ of the cake has chocolate frosting.

Remember, you can look at different equal-size parts on a number line to find equivalent fractions. The number line below shows that $\frac{1}{2}$ is equivalent to $\frac{2}{4}$.

▶ Reflect

1 Izzy's mom now wants to cut the cake into eighths. Explain how to figure out how many eighths of the cake have chocolate frosting.

_____

_____

_____

Learn About ▸ Finding Equivalent Fractions

Read the problem below. Then explore different ways to think about equivalent fractions.

> Casen ate $\frac{2}{8}$ of an orange. Trey's orange is the same size. He ate $\frac{1}{4}$ of it.
>
> Show that the two boys ate the same amount of an orange.

▸ **Picture It** **You can use models to help find equivalent fractions.**

This model shows $\frac{2}{8}$.

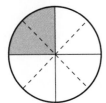

This model shows $\frac{1}{4}$.

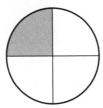

Look at the model of $\frac{2}{8}$. The solid lines divide the circle into fourths. The dashed lines divide each fourth in half to make eighths.

▸ **Model It** **You can also use a number line to help find equivalent fractions.**

This number line shows both fourths and eighths.

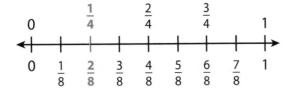

©Curriculum Associates, LLC   Copying is not permitted.

▶ **Connect It** **Now you will solve the problem from the previous page using equations.**

2 Look at the models in *Picture It*. How do you know that $\frac{2}{8}$ of the first model is shaded? _____

3 How do you know that $\frac{1}{4}$ of the second model is shaded? _____

_____

4 Explain how the models show that the fractions $\frac{2}{8}$ and $\frac{1}{4}$ are equivalent.

_____

5 How does the number line in *Model It* show that the fractions $\frac{2}{8}$ and $\frac{1}{4}$ are

equivalent? _____

_____

6 Complete the sentences to show the fractions of the two oranges name the same amount.

Use words: Two eighths is equal to _____.

Use fractions: $\frac{2}{8} =$ _____.

7 Describe two different ways to show two fractions are equivalent. _____

_____

_____

▶ **Try It** **Use what you just learned to solve these problems.**

8 Draw a model to show $\frac{2}{3} = \frac{4}{6}$.

9 Use the number line below. Find a fraction equivalent to $\frac{1}{3}$. Circle the fraction.

$$0 \qquad \frac{1}{3} \qquad \frac{2}{3} \qquad 1$$

Learn About **Writing a Whole Number as a Fraction**

Read the problem below. Then explore different ways to write a whole number as a fraction.

> Kacey used 2 boards of the same size to build a birdhouse. He cut each board into fourths. How can you write the number 2 as a fraction to find how many fourths Kacey divided the boards into?

▶ **Picture It** **You can use models to help you write a whole number as a fraction.**

The fraction strips below show 2 wholes, each divided into fourths.

Each part is $\frac{1}{4}$ of a whole. There are eight $\frac{1}{4}$s in all.

▶ **Model It** **You can use a number line to help you write a whole number as a fraction.**

This number line shows whole numbers on the top and fourths on the bottom.

```
      0               1               2
   ◄──┼───┼───┼───┼───┼───┼───┼───┼──►
      0   1   2   3   4   5   6   7   8
          ─   ─   ─   ─   ─   ─   ─   ─
          4   4   4   4   4   4   4   4
```

Notice that each whole number has an equivalent fraction with a denominator of 4.

▶ **Connect It** **Now you will solve the problem from the previous page using equations.**

10 Look at the models in *Picture It*. How many equal parts are shown in 1 whole?

Explain how you know. _____

_____

_____

11 How many equal parts are shown in 2 wholes? Explain how you know.

_____

_____

12 Complete the sentences to show the fraction that is equivalent to 2.

Use words: Two wholes equals _____.

Use a fraction: 2 = _____.

How many fourths did Kacey cut the boards into? _____

13 Explain how to find a fraction equivalent to a whole number.

_____

_____

_____

▶ **Try It** **Use what you just learned to solve these problems.**

14 Use the model below. Write a fraction equivalent to 3.

15 Draw a model to show $3 = \frac{18}{6}$.

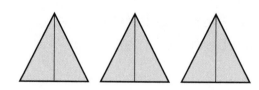

3 = _____

Learn About ▸ Writing a Whole Number as a Fraction

Read the problem. Then explore different ways to write a whole number as a fraction with a denominator of 1.

Justin picked 4 green peppers from his garden. He did not cut them into pieces. How can you write the number of peppers Justin picked as a fraction?

▶ **Picture It You can use models to help you write a whole number as a fraction with a denominator of 1.**

Each circle stands for 1 green pepper.

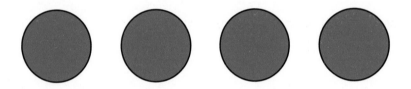

They are not divided into pieces, so each whole has one part.

▶ **Model It You can use a number line to help you write a whole number as a fraction with a denominator of 1.**

This number line shows whole numbers on the top and fractions on the bottom.

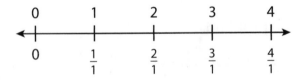

Notice that each whole number has an equivalent fraction. The spaces between whole numbers are not divided into parts. Each whole number has one part, so the denominator of each equivalent fraction is 1.

Connect It Now you will solve the problem from the previous page.

16 Look at the models in *Picture It*. Explain how you know each whole has only 1 part.

_____

17 How many parts do the 4 green peppers make? _____

18 What does the numerator of a fraction show? _____

19 What does the denominator of a fraction show? _____

_____

20 Write a fraction equivalent to 4. Use the fraction below to help you.

21 Explain how to write a whole number as a fraction with a denominator of 1.

_____

_____

_____

Try It Use what you just learned to solve these problems.

22 Use the model below. Write a fraction equivalent to 6.

[ ] [ ] [ ] [ ] [ ] [ ]

6 = _____

23 Draw a model to show $5 = \frac{5}{1}$.

Practice ▶ **Finding Equivalent Fractions**

Study the example below. Then solve problems 24–26.

Example

Caleb and Hannah bought two melons that are the same size. Caleb cut his melon into fourths. Hannah cut her melon into eighths. Hannah ate $\frac{4}{8}$ of her melon. Caleb ate an equal amount of his melon. What fraction of his melon did Caleb eat?

Look at how you could show your work using a model.

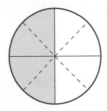

Caleb ate $\frac{2}{4}$ of his melon.

Solution _____

The student used solid lines to show fourths. She used dashed lines to show how to divide fourths to make eighths.

 Pair/Share

How could you solve this problem using a number line?

---

24 Matt says $\frac{3}{3}$ is equivalent to 1. Elisa says $\frac{8}{8}$ is equivalent to 1.

Who is correct?

Show your work.

How many thirds are in 1 whole? How many eighths are in 1 whole?

 Pair/Share

What is another fraction that is equivalent to 1?

Solution _____

25 Write two fractions that are equivalent to 5.

Show your work.

There will be 5 wholes in all. Think about how many parts will be in each whole.

Solution _____

Pair/Share
How did you decide what denominators to use in your fractions?

---

26 Kaia ate $\frac{3}{6}$ of a banana. Zoie ate an equivalent amount. Which fraction shows how much of a banana Zoie ate? Circle the letter of the correct answer.

Find $\frac{3}{6}$ on a number line. What is another fraction that names the same location?

A $\frac{1}{3}$

B $\frac{2}{3}$

C $\frac{5}{8}$

D $\frac{1}{2}$

Landon chose **A** as the correct answer. How did he get that answer?

Pair/Share
Does Landon's answer make sense?

Practice Finding Equivalent Fractions

Solve the problems.

1 Which model below shows a fraction equivalent to $\frac{2}{6}$?

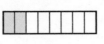

     A   **B**   **C**   **D**

2 Which fraction is equivalent to 3?

A $\frac{3}{1}$

B $\frac{1}{3}$

C $\frac{4}{1}$

D $\frac{6}{3}$

3 Look at point *P* on the number line.

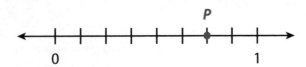

Does the point on the number line show a fraction equivalent to the fraction shown by point *P*? Choose *Yes* or *No* for each number line.

a.    ☐ Yes   ☐ No

b.    ☐ Yes   ☐ No

c. 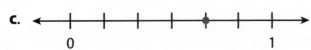   ☐ Yes   ☐ No

4 Does the number marked by the point on the number line represent one whole? Choose *Yes* or *No* for each number line.

a.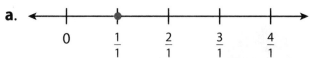

☐ Yes   ☐ No

b.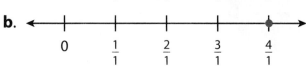

☐ Yes   ☐ No

c.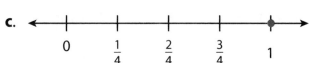

☐ Yes   ☐ No

d.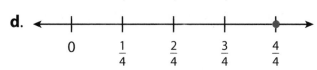

☐ Yes   ☐ No

5 Use the number line below to find a fraction equivalent to 3.

Show your work.

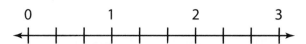

Answer 3 is equivalent to _____.

6 Draw a model to find a fraction equivalent to $\frac{1}{4}$.

Show your work.

Answer $\frac{1}{4}$ is equivalent to _____.

✔ **Self Check** Go back and see what you can check off on the Self Check on page 155.

Understand Comparing Fractions

Think It Through

How do we compare fractions?

When you **compare** two fractions, you figure out if one is more than or less than the other, or if they name the same amount.

Models can help you compare. The models below both help you see that $\frac{1}{4}$ is less than $\frac{2}{4}$.

$\frac{1}{4}$ shaded $\qquad$ $\frac{2}{4}$ shaded

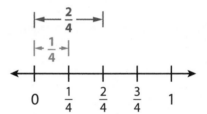

When you use area models to compare fractions, the wholes must be the same size. Look at the models at the right. The wholes are different sizes. They make it look like $\frac{1}{4}$ is greater than $\frac{2}{4}$.

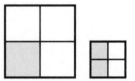

Think You can compare fractions that have the same denominator.

To compare fractions that have the same denominator, think about how many unit fractions it takes to make each of them.

The area models below both show a whole cut into sixths.

> ✏️ **Circle** the model that is less than the other.

$\frac{1}{6}$	$\frac{1}{6}$	$\frac{1}{6}$	$\frac{1}{6}$	$\frac{1}{6}$	$\frac{1}{6}$

$\frac{1}{6}$	$\frac{1}{6}$	$\frac{1}{6}$	$\frac{1}{6}$	$\frac{1}{6}$	$\frac{1}{6}$

It takes **two** $\frac{1}{6}$s to make $\frac{2}{6}$. $\qquad$ It takes **five** $\frac{1}{6}$s to make $\frac{5}{6}$.

$\frac{2}{6}$ is made of fewer unit fractions than $\frac{5}{6}$. So, $\frac{2}{6}$ is less than $\frac{5}{6}$.

Think You can compare fractions that have the same numerators.

To compare fractions that have the same numerators, think about the denominators. The models below show the unit fractions $\frac{1}{3}$ and $\frac{1}{8}$.

Dividing a whole into fractions is like cutting up sheets of paper. The more pieces you cut a sheet into, the smaller each piece is.

The wholes are the same, and the numerators are the same.

So, compare the denominators of $\frac{1}{3}$ and $\frac{1}{8}$. 3 is less than 8, showing that the whole is divided into fewer parts. Since there are fewer parts, each part is bigger. The unit fraction $\frac{1}{3}$ is greater than the unit fraction $\frac{1}{8}$.

Here's another example. Compare $\frac{3}{6}$ and $\frac{3}{4}$.

| $\frac{1}{6}$ | $\frac{1}{6}$ | $\frac{1}{6}$ | | | |

| $\frac{1}{4}$ | $\frac{1}{4}$ | $\frac{1}{4}$ | |

The unit fractions used to make $\frac{3}{6}$ are smaller than the unit fractions used to make $\frac{3}{4}$.

3 smaller parts shade less of the whole than 3 bigger parts. So, $\frac{3}{6}$ is less than $\frac{3}{4}$.

▶ Reflect

1 Explain how you can use unit fractions to help you compare fractions.

_____

_____

_____

_____

_____

Think About Using Models to Compare Fractions

🔍 **Let's Explore the Idea** Use the models to help you compare fractions with the same denominator.

2 Write the fraction shaded below each area model. Circle the fraction that is greater.

3 Write the fraction shaded below the first model. Shade the second model to show a greater fraction. Write the greater fraction.

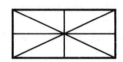

Use the models to help you compare fractions with the same numerator.

4 Write the fraction shaded below each area model. Circle the fraction that is greater.

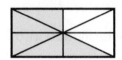

5 Write the fraction shaded below each area model. Circle the fraction that is less.

6 Write the fraction shaded below the first area model. Shade the second area model to show a fraction that is less, but has the same numerator.

Explain how you know the fraction you shaded is the lesser fraction. _____

_____

7 Look at your answers to problems 2 and 3. Explain how to use unit fractions to compare fractions with the same denominator. _____

_____

_____

8 Look at your answers to problems 4 and 5. What do you notice about the numerators and denominators in each pair of fractions? How is this different from the numerators and denominators in the pairs of fractions in problems 2 and 3?

_____

_____

_____

Explain how to use unit fractions to compare fractions with the same numerator.

_____

_____

_____

9 Isaiah is comparing $\frac{3}{8}$ and $\frac{3}{6}$. Both fractions have a numerator of 3. How can he tell which fraction is less? _____

_____

_____

Try It Another Way Work with your group to use the number lines to compare fractions.

10 Look at the fractions on the number lines. Circle the fraction that is less.

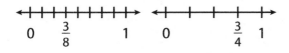

$$0 \quad \frac{3}{8} \quad 1 \qquad 0 \quad \frac{3}{4} \quad 1$$

11 Look at the fractions on the number lines. Circle the fraction that is greater.

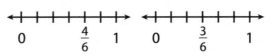

$$0 \quad \frac{4}{6} \quad 1 \qquad 0 \quad \frac{3}{6} \quad 1$$

Connect **Ideas About Comparing Fractions**

Talk through these problem as a class, then write your answers below.

12 Create Draw an area model or number line to show $\frac{5}{8}$. Find a fraction with the same denominator that is less than $\frac{5}{8}$.

Write the fraction you found. Explain how you found it. _____

_____

_____

13 Explain Mario painted $\frac{2}{6}$ of the wall in his bedroom. Mei Lyn painted $\frac{2}{4}$ of a wall in her bedroom. Both walls are the same size. Explain how you know who painted more of their wall. _____

_____

_____

14 Justify Jace and Lianna each baked a loaf of bread. Jace cut his loaf into halves and Lianna cut her loaf into thirds. The models below show their loaves of bread.

Jace says they can use their loaves of bread to show that $\frac{1}{2}$ is less than $\frac{1}{3}$. Lianna says they can't. Who is correct? Explain why. _____

In order to compare your wholes
need to be the same size.

Ideas About Comparing Fractions

15 Put It Together Use what you have learned to complete this task.

Mrs. Ericson made sandwiches for her 4 children. Each sandwich was the same size. After lunch, each child had a different fraction of his or her sandwich left. Matt had $\frac{1}{4}$ left, Elisa had $\frac{3}{8}$ left, Carl had $\frac{3}{4}$ left, and Riley had $\frac{7}{8}$ left.

Part A Use the information above to write a word problem. The problem should be about comparing two fractions with the same numerator.

_____

Part B Use the information above to write a word problem. The problem should be about comparing two fractions with the same denominator.

_____

Part C Choose one of your problems to solve. Circle the problem you chose. Draw a model or number line to help you find the answer.

Explain how you could use unit fractions to think about the problem.

_____

_____

_____

_____

_____

Ⓖ Use What You Know

In Lesson 18, you learned how to compare fractions. In this lesson you will use the symbols <, >, and = to show how fractions compare. Take a look at this problem.

Erica's glass is $\frac{4}{6}$ full. Ethan's glass is $\frac{5}{6}$ full. Compare $\frac{4}{6}$ and $\frac{5}{6}$ using <, >, or =.

Erica's glass ---------- ---------- Ethan's glass

a. The fractions $\frac{4}{6}$ and $\frac{5}{6}$ have the same denominator. What do you need to think about to compare the two fractions? _look at the numerator and see whitch is larger._

b. How many sixths of Erica's glass are filled? __4__

c. How many sixths of Ethan's glass are filled? __5__

d. Compare the number of sixths using <, >, or =.

4 sixths ⬅< 5 sixths

e. Is the amount in Erica's glass less than, greater than, or equal to the amount in Ethan's glass? _has less than ethans_

f. Is the amount in Ethan's glass less than, greater than, or equal to the amount in Erica's glass? _Ericas is Ethans_

You have already learned how to figure out if one fraction is less than, greater than, or equal to another. Now you will compare fractions using the symbols <, >, or =.

< means "less than"   > means "greater than"   = means "equal to"

Think of the < and > symbols as the mouth of an alligator. The alligator's mouth will always be open to eat the greater fraction. Think about the fractions $\frac{1}{2}$ and $\frac{1}{8}$.

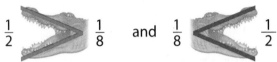

$\frac{1}{2}$ is **greater than** $\frac{1}{8}$ and $\frac{1}{8}$ is **less than** $\frac{1}{2}$.

You can switch the order of the two fractions you compare. If the fractions are not equal, make sure to switch the symbol you are using as well.

Sometimes two fractions are **equivalent**. In those cases, use the symbol =.

$\frac{1}{2} = \frac{4}{8}$ and $\frac{3}{4} = \frac{6}{8}$

▶ **Reflect**

1 Use the symbols > and < to write two statements comparing $\frac{7}{8}$ and $\frac{3}{8}$. Explain how you decided which fraction was greater and which fraction was less.

_____

_____

_____

_____

_____

_____

Learn About ▶ Comparing Fractions Using Symbols

Read the problem below. Then explore different ways to compare fractions.

Compare $\frac{4}{8}$ and $\frac{4}{6}$ using <, >, or =.

▶ **Picture It** **You can use models to help you compare fractions.**

The models show the same-sized wholes.

This model shows $\frac{4}{8}$.   This model shows $\frac{4}{6}$.

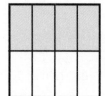   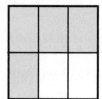

▶ **Model It** **You can also use number lines to help you compare fractions.**

This number line shows $\frac{4}{8}$.

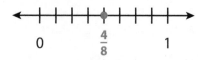   This number line is divided into eighths.

This number line shows $\frac{4}{6}$.

   This number line is divided into sixths.

> **Connect It** **Now you will solve the problem from the previous page.**

2 Look at the models in *Picture It*. How can you use them to compare $\frac{4}{8}$ and $\frac{4}{6}$?

_____

_____

3 Look at the number lines in *Model It*. How can you use them to compare the two fractions?

_____

_____

4 Compare with words: 4 eighths is _____ than 4 sixths.

Compare with a symbol: $\frac{4}{8}$ ◯ $\frac{4}{6}$

5 Now switch the order of the fractions.

Compare with words: 4 sixths is _____ than 4 eighths.

Compare with a symbol: $\frac{4}{6}$ ◯ $\frac{4}{8}$

6 Explain how to use symbols to compare two fractions.

_____

_____

_____

> **Try It** **Use what you just learned about using symbols to compare fractions to solve these problems. Show your work on a separate sheet of paper.**

7 Compare each pair of fractions using $<$, $>$, or $=$.

$\frac{4}{6}$ ◯ $\frac{2}{6}$ $\qquad$ $\frac{2}{4}$ ◯ $\frac{2}{3}$ $\qquad$ $\frac{1}{2}$ ◯ $\frac{1}{2}$

8 Compare each pair of fractions using $<$, $>$, or $=$.

$\frac{3}{4}$ ◯ $\frac{3}{4}$ $\qquad$ $\frac{2}{8}$ ◯ $\frac{2}{2}$ $\qquad$ $\frac{2}{3}$ ◯ $\frac{1}{3}$

Practice ▷ Solving Word Problems with Fractions

Study the example below. Then solve problems 9–11.

Example

Su and Anthony live the same distance from school. Su biked $\frac{3}{4}$ of the way to school in five minutes. Anthony walked $\frac{1}{4}$ of the way to school in five minutes. Who went the greater distance? Compare the fractions using a symbol.

Look at how you could show your work using a number line.

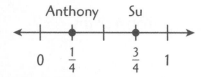

Solution ___Su went the greater distance. $\frac{3}{4} > \frac{1}{4}$___

> The fractions have the same denominator, so they are easy to compare on the same number line.

 Pair/Share
How do you find the greater number on a number line?

---

9 Julia and Mackenzie have the same number of homework problems. Julia has done $\frac{1}{3}$ of her homework. Mackenzie has done $\frac{1}{2}$ of her homework. Which student has done less of her homework? Compare the fractions using a symbol.

Show your work.

> What do you need to think about when you compare fractions that have different denominators?

 Pair/Share
How did you know which fraction was less?

Solution _____

10 David and Rob each got the same-size pack of crackers. David ate $\frac{3}{6}$ of his crackers. Rob ate $\frac{3}{4}$ of his crackers. Who ate more of his crackers? Compare the fractions using a symbol.

Show your work.

I think drawing a model might help. Be sure the wholes are the same size.

Solution

Pair/Share
Which fraction is made of greater unit fractions? How do you know?

---

11 Which fraction goes in the blank to make the comparison true? Circle the letter of the correct answer.

$$\frac{5}{8} < \rule{2cm}{0.4pt}$$

A $\frac{5}{8}$

B $\frac{4}{8}$

C $\frac{6}{8}$

D $\frac{1}{8}$

Blake chose **A** as the correct answer. How did he get that answer?

Is $\frac{5}{8}$ less than or greater than the fraction that goes in the blank?

Pair/Share
Does Blake's answer make sense?

Solve the problems.

1 Which fraction goes in the blank to make the comparison true?

_____ $> \frac{1}{3}$

A $\frac{1}{2}$

B $\frac{1}{3}$

C $\frac{1}{4}$

D $\frac{1}{5}$

2 Shade each model below to show the given fraction. Then use the models to compare the fractions. Complete the statement below the models using <, >, or =.

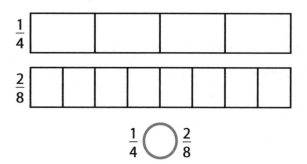

$\frac{1}{4}$ ◯ $\frac{2}{8}$

3 Write a number from the list below in each ☐ to make the statement true.

6   8   1   3   4

$\frac{\square}{8} < \frac{\square}{8}$

4 Look at the comparison below.

$$\underline{\hspace{3cm}} < \frac{3}{4}$$

Tyrone wrote a fraction in the blank to make the comparison true. His fraction had an 8 in the denominator. What fraction could Tyrone have written?

Show your work.

Solution _____

5 Tran and Noah were each given the same amount of clay in art class. Tran divided his clay into 3 equal pieces. He used 2 pieces to make a bowl. Noah divided his clay into 4 equal pieces. He also used 2 pieces to make a bowl. Tran said that he had more clay left over than Noah. Is Tran correct? Explain.

_____

_____

_____

_____

_____

_____

_____

✓ **Self Check** **Go back and see what you can check off on the Self Check on page 155.**

Unit 4
MATH IN
ACTION

👥 **Introduction**
Use Fractions

SMP1 Make sense
of problems and
persevere in
solving them.

Study an Example Problem and Solution

Read this problem involving fractions. Then look at G.O.'s solution to this problem.

The 8-Mile Trail

G.O. is running on The 8-Mile Trail. At the welcome center, he finds trail work plans.

> **Trail Plans**
> · Plant trees along the trail every fraction of a mile.
> · Use a unit fraction greater than $\frac{1}{8}$ but less than $\frac{1}{2}$.

G.O. wants to find how many trees will be planted.

- Name a fraction that is greater than $\frac{1}{8}$ but less than $\frac{1}{2}$.
- Draw a number line from 0 to 8.
- Divide the sections between whole numbers to show your fraction.
- Label each mark with a whole number or fraction.
- Count all the marks from 0 to 8. Tell how many trees will be planted.

Read the sample solution on the next page. Then look at the checklist below. Find and mark parts of the solution that match the checklist.

🖊 **Problem-Solving Checklist**

☐ Tell what is known.

☐ Tell what the problem is asking.

☐ Show all your work.

☐ Show that the solution works.

a. Circle something that is known.

b. Underline something that you need to find.

c. Draw a box around what you do to solve the problem.

d. Put a checkmark next to the part that shows the solution works.

G.O.'s Solution

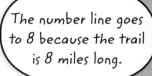

Hi, I'm G.O. Here's how I solved the problem.

▷ **First, I need to find a fraction that is greater than $\frac{1}{8}$ but less than $\frac{1}{2}$.**
I think $\frac{1}{3}$ will work. I can draw same-size models to check.

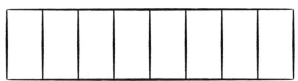

eighths

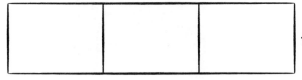

thirds

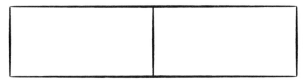

halves

The denominator in $\frac{1}{3}$ tells me there are 3 equal parts.

The $\frac{1}{3}$ parts are bigger than the $\frac{1}{8}$ parts.

The $\frac{1}{3}$ parts are smaller than the $\frac{1}{2}$ parts.

So $\frac{1}{3} > \frac{1}{8}$ and $\frac{1}{3} < \frac{1}{2}$.

▷ **Now I can make a number line.**
I chose thirds, so I'll divide each section between whole numbers into three equal parts.

The number line goes to 8 because the trail is 8 miles long.

▷ **Start at 0 and count the marks.**
There are 25 marks. So 25 trees will be planted.

Try ▶ **Another Approach**

There are many ways to solve problems. Think about how you might solve The 8-Mile Trail problem in a different way.

The 8-Mile Trail

G.O. is running on The 8-Mile Trail. At the welcome center, he finds trail work plans.

> **Trail Plans**
> · Plant trees along the trail every fraction of a mile.
> · Use a unit fraction greater than $\frac{1}{8}$ but less than $\frac{1}{2}$.

G.O. wants to find how many trees will be planted.

- Name a fraction that is greater than $\frac{1}{8}$ but less than $\frac{1}{2}$.

- Draw a number line from 0 to 8.

- Divide the sections between whole numbers to show your fraction.

- Label each mark with a whole number or fraction.

- Count all the marks from 0 to 8. Tell how many trees will be planted.

▶ **Plan It** **Answer these questions to help you start thinking about a plan.**

A. What are some unit fractions greater than $\frac{1}{8}$?

_____

_____

B. Which of these fractions are less than $\frac{1}{2}$?

_____

_____

Solve It Find a different solution for The 8-Mile Trail problem. Show all your work on a separate sheet of paper.

You may want to use the problem-solving tips to get started.

Problem-Solving Tips

- **Models**

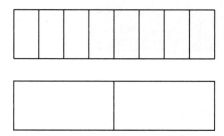

- **Word Bank**

fraction	numerator	less than
equal parts	denominator	greater than

- **Sentence Starters**

- _____ is greater than _____

- The denominator tells me _____

Reflect

Use Mathematical Practices As you work through the problem, discuss these questions with a partner.

- **Use Structure** How can you use the denominators of unit fractions to compare them?

- **Reason Mathematically** How can you think about equal parts to find a unit fraction that is greater than or less than another unit fraction?

Discuss ▶ **Models and Strategies**

Read the problem. Write a solution on a separate sheet of paper.
Remember, there can be lots of ways to solve a problem!

Flower Gardens

G.O. is helping to plant flowers near The 8-Mile Trail.
He will plant two flower gardens at the welcome
center. The gardens are circle shaped.

Here are the plans.

Flower Garden 1

- Divide the circle into
  equal parts. Make
  2, 3, or 4 parts.
- Use a different color
  flower in each part.

Possible Diagrams for Garden 1

Flower Garden 2

- Divide the circle into equal parts.
  Make 6 or 8 parts.
- Use the same color flowers as Garden 1.
- The fraction of Garden 2 that has each
  color flower should be equivalent
  to Garden 1.

Possible Diagrams for Garden 2

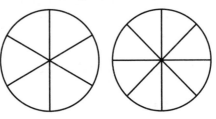

What two circles can G.O. use to draw a diagram of the gardens?

Plan It and Solve It   Find a solution for the Flower Gardens problem.

Use the Flower Gardens Activity Sheet. Follow the directions in the plan.

- Choose two circles that can be used to show equivalent fractions.
- Color the circles or label the sections with color names.
- Write a pair of equivalent fractions. Tell how you know they are equivalent.

You may want to use the problem-solving tips to get started.

Problem-Solving Tips

- **Questions**
  - How many equal parts are shown in the circles?
  - What are some different ways to match up circles to show equivalent fractions?

- **Word Bank**

equivalent fractions	part	size
equal parts	whole	same

Problem-Solving Checklist
Make sure that you . . .
- ☐ tell what you know.
- ☐ tell what you need to do.
- ☐ show all your work.
- ☐ show that the solution works.

Reflect

Use Mathematical Practices As you work through the problem, discuss these questions with a partner.

- **Make an Argument** What are different ways to prove that two fractions are equivalent?

- **Use Models** How can you use the diagrams to help you solve the problem?

Read the problem. Write a solution on a separate sheet of paper.
Remember, there are many different ways to solve a problem!

Drinking Fountains

G.O. talks to a worker along The 8-Mile Trail. The worker is planning where
to put new drinking fountains. Here is what the worker says.

· There will be 4, 6, or 8 drinking fountains.

· The trail will be divided into equal sections.

· One drinking fountain will be placed in the
middle of each section.

Where should the drinking fountains be placed?

▶ **Solve It** **Help G.O. find the locations of the drinking fountains.**

• Decide how many drinking fountains to use.

• Make a diagram of the trail using Drinking Fountains Activity Sheet.

• Divide the rectangle into equal parts. Make the same number
of parts as drinking fountains.

• Write a fraction that names each part.

• Mark with a dot where each fountain will be.

▶ **Reflect**

Use Mathematical Practices After you complete the task, choose
one of these questions to discuss with a partner.

• **Use Tools** What tools did you use to make the equal parts in the diagram?
Tell how you used the tools.

• **Be Precise** What does the diagram show? Describe it to your partner.
Use fractions, whole numbers, and measurement units to describe it.

Trail Signs

G.O. has an idea for signs to be put along The 8-Mile Trail. A sign at each mile marker tells what fraction of the whole trail people have completed.

The sign looks like this. The rectangle will be shaded to show the fraction. The blanks are for the mile number and fraction of the whole trail.

You are at mile _____.

This is _____ of the whole trail.

What would the completed signs look like?

▶ **Solve It** **Help G.O. make drawings of the signs.**

- Use the Trail Signs Activity Sheet to make the drawings.
- Choose four mile numbers along The 8-Mile Trail.
- Draw a sign for each mile number you chose.
- Shade the rectangle and write numbers in the blanks.

▶ **Reflect**

Use Mathematical Practices After you complete the task, choose one of these questions to discuss with a partner

- **Use Models** Look at the shaded models you made. How does each model relate to the words and numbers on the sign?

- **Reason with Numbers** What denominators did you use on your signs? Why?

Solve the problems.

1 Which of these models a fraction that is equivalent to the fraction modeled below?

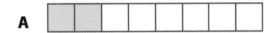

A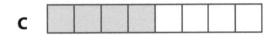

B

C

D

2 Look at the number lines below.

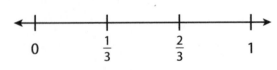

0    $\frac{1}{3}$ $\frac{2}{3}$ 1

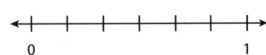

0   1

Which fraction is equivalent to $\frac{1}{3}$?

A $\frac{1}{6}$

B $\frac{2}{6}$

C $\frac{4}{6}$

D $\frac{5}{6}$

3 Fill in each box with the fraction below that names the point on the number line.

$\frac{1}{4}$ $\frac{8}{8}$ $\frac{2}{6}$ $\frac{1}{2}$ $\frac{5}{8}$

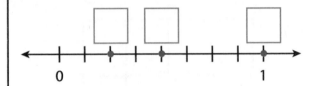

0   1

4 Which fractions are equivalent to 2? Circle the letter for all that apply.

A $\frac{1}{2}$ **D** $\frac{4}{2}$

B $\frac{2}{1}$ **E** $\frac{2}{4}$

C $\frac{2}{2}$

5 Which sentence is NOT true? Circle the letter for all that apply.

A Two fractions cannot be equivalent if they have different denominators.

B A fraction that has the same number in both the numerator and denominator is equal to 1.

C A fraction with the number 1 in the denominator is called a unit fraction.

D All fractions are less than 1.

6 Part A Mark off the number line below to show 4 equal parts. Label each mark you drew with the fraction it shows.

0   1

Part B Look at the number line in Part A. What fraction does each part of the number line show?

Solution _____

7 The pictures below show Mark's backyard and Jamal's backyard. Each boy wants to use $\frac{1}{2}$ of his backyard for a garden.

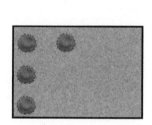

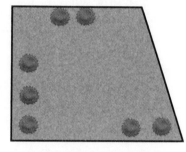

Mark's Backyard   Jamal's Backyard

Will the two gardens be the same size? Explain why or why not.

_____

_____

_____

_____

Performance Task

Answer the questions and show all your work on separate paper.

The owner of the neighborhood pizzeria, **Itsa Pizza**, would like you to draw diagrams to show the different combinations of toppings on 6 pizzas. Each diagram will show a rectangular pizza cut into eight equal-sized pieces. She wants each pizza to be completely covered with toppings with no overlaps.

Use grid paper to draw diagrams of the pizza described below. If the toppings won't fully cover the pizza, add a new topping or change the amounts of the toppings shown. If the instructions list too many toppings, change the amounts of the toppings to make it work.

Checklist
Did you . . .
☐ draw a diagram for each pizza?
☐ show what each letter in your diagram means?
☐ check your calculations?

An example for the Peppers & Roni pizza is shown.

Peppers & Roni	$\frac{1}{2}$ pepper, $\frac{1}{2}$ pepperoni

P	P	P	P
R	R	R	R

P = pepper
R = pepperoni

Deluxe	$\frac{1}{8}$ mushroom, $\frac{3}{8}$ olive, $\frac{1}{4}$ broccoli, $\frac{1}{4}$ sausage
Onion-Roni	$\frac{5}{8}$ pepperoni, $\frac{1}{8}$ onion, $\frac{1}{8}$ sausage
The Itsa Pizza	$\frac{2}{4}$ tomato, $\frac{1}{4}$ olive
Mighty Meaty	$\frac{1}{4}$ sausage, $\frac{4}{8}$ pepperoni, $\frac{2}{4}$ hamburger
The Green Hula	$\frac{3}{4}$ onion, $\frac{3}{3}$ pineapple, $\frac{1}{4}$ broccoli

Reflect

Use Mathematical Practices After you complete the task, choose one of the following questions to answer.

- **Model** How did you decide how much of the pizza to cover with each topping?

- **Reason Mathematically** What are the different fractions listed that show half a pizza?

Unit 5
Measurement and Data

Let's learn about measurement and displaying data in graphs.

Real-World Connection What time does the movie start? How far is it to the basketball court? How much do those apples weigh? How much milk do I need for the pancake recipe? How many tiles do I need to tile that floor? To answer these questions you need to use different types of measurements.

In This Unit You will learn to choose the right kind of measurement for different situations. You will also gather information about groups of items, compare them, and organize the information with graphs.

✓ Self Check

Before starting this unit, check off the skills you know below. As you complete each lesson, see how many more you can check off!

I can:	Before this unit	After this unit
tell and write time on digital clocks and clocks with hands and solve problems about time.	☐	☐
estimate liquid volume and solve problems about liquid volume.	☐	☐
estimate mass and solve problems about mass.	☐	☐
solve problems using picture graphs and bar graphs.	☐	☐
draw picture graphs and bar graphs to show data.	☐	☐
measure lengths and show data on a line plot.	☐	☐
understand area, find areas by multiplying, and add areas.	☐	☐
add to find perimeters, and find shapes with the same perimeter and different areas or the same area and different perimeters.	☐	☐

Use What You Know

In this lesson, you will tell time to the minute. Take a look at this problem.

Lily started reading a book after breakfast at the time shown on the clock.

What time does the clock show?

a. The short hand on the clock shows the hour.
What is the last number the short hand moved past? _____

b. The long hand on the clock shows the minutes.
What is the last number the long hand moved past? _____

c. You can count by fives to help figure out the number of minutes.
Each mark is 1 minute. Every 5 marks there is a number.
If the long hand is exactly on the 6, how many minutes past 8 is it? _____

d. The long hand is 2 small marks past the six. Explain how you can find the time shown on the clock.

_____

_____

_____

_____

_____

Find Out More

It takes **1 hour** for the short **hour hand** to move from one **number** to the next.

It takes **1 minute** for the long **minute hand** to move from one **mark** to the next.

So, it takes **5 minutes** for the **minute hand** to move from one **number** to the next.

Look at the clock at the right. The hour hand has moved **past the 8**, but not to the 9. So, the hour is 8.

The minute hand is between 6 and 7. Here's how to find the number of minutes past 8:00.

- Start at 12.

- Count **five** for each number until you get to the 6: **5, 10, 15, 20, 25, 30**.

- The minute hand is **2 marks** past the 6, so count 2 more than 30: **31, 32**.

When the time is between midnight and noon, the clock shows AM. When the time is between noon and midnight, the clock shows PM. Since Lily is reading the book after breakfast, the time shown is 8:32 AM.

Reflect

1 Sometimes a clock does not have numbers at all. Look at the clock below. It only has small marks and large marks. Explain how you can tell what time this clock shows.

_____

_____

_____

_____

Learn About ▸ Telling Time to the Minute

Read the problem below. Then explore different ways to tell and write time.

Sara sat down to eat lunch at 43 minutes past noon. At what time did Sara sit down to eat lunch?

▶ **Picture It** **You can use a digital clock to show what time it is.**

Noon is 12:00 PM. Sara sat down at 43 minutes past noon.

PM 12:43

The clock shows PM because the time is between noon and midnight.

▶ **Model It** **You can also use the next hour to tell what time it is.**

Sara sat down to eat between 12:00 and 1:00. You can tell the time by saying how many minutes after 12:00. You can also say how many minutes before 1:00.

To count the minutes, you always start at the **12.**

- **Count forward** to find out how many minutes after 12:00.

- **Count backward** from the 12 to find out how many minutes before 1:00.

By counting backward, you can see that **43 minutes after 12:00** describes the same time as **17 minutes before 1:00.**

► **Connect It** **Now you will show the time from the problem on the previous page by drawing the hands on a clock.**

2 Which hand on a clock shows the hour? _____

What two numbers should this hand be between to show the time Sara sat down

to eat? _____

Explain how you know. _____

_____

3 Which hand on a clock shows the minutes? _____

How many minutes should this hand show? _____

4 At what time did Sara sit down to eat? _____

5 Draw the hands on the clock to show
the time Sara sat down to eat.

6 Explain how to tell time to the minute on a clock with hands.

_____

_____

► **Try It** **Use what you just learned to solve these problems.**

7 Write the time in two ways.

_____

_____ minutes before _____

8 It is 7 minutes before 2 PM. Draw the
hands on the clock to show the time.

Write the time. _____

Practice **Telling and Writing Time**

Study the example below. Then solve problems 9–11.

Example

Jen woke up at the time shown on the digital clock below. What time did she wake up? Give your answer in minutes before the next hour.

Look at how you could show your work using a clock.

Solution _18 minutes before 7:00_

The student first drew the hands on a clock. Then she counted backward from the 12 to find the number of minutes before the next hour.

Pair/Share
How else could you solve the problem?

---

9 Ezra started working in the garden at the time shown on the digital clock below.

Draw the hands to show what the time looks like on this clock.

What two numbers is the hour between? What two numbers on the clock is 24 minutes between?

Pair/Share
How did you and your partner know where to draw each hand?

10 Abby's piano lesson started at the time shown on the clock.

Fill in the correct time on the digital clock. Be sure to show whether it is AM or PM.

Pair/Share
What is something else you might be doing at the time shown?

---

11 Luca started cleaning his room at the time shown on the clock.

Which tells the time shown on the clock? Circle the letter of the correct answer.

A 9 minutes before 9:00

B 9 minutes before 10:00

C 11 minutes before 10:00

D 51 minutes before 9:00

Bo chose **D** as the correct answer. How did he get that answer?

Pair/Share
Does Bo's answer make sense?

Practice ▸ **Telling and Writing Time**

Solve the problems.

1 Which pair of clocks shows the same time?

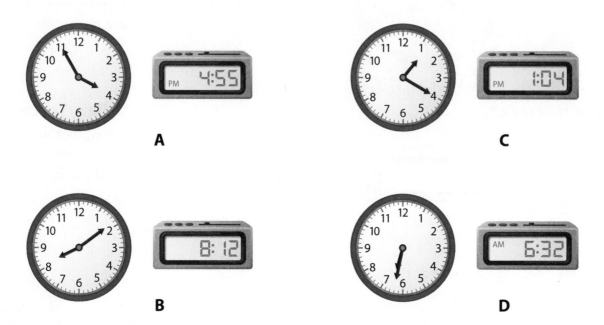

A

C

B

D

2 Which phrases describe the time shown on the clock below? Circle the letter for all that apply.

A 48 minutes after 5:00

B 48 minutes before 5:00

C 48 minutes before 6:00

D 12 minutes before 5:00

E 12 minutes before 6:00

F 12 minutes after 6:00

3 Adam started baseball practice at the time shown on the digital clock below.

Draw the hour and minute hands on the clock below to show the time that Adam started baseball practice.

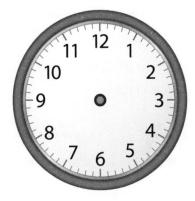

4 Ruby left to go swimming this morning at the time shown on the clock below.

Write the time on the digital clock below. Be sure to mark AM or PM. Then tell the time before the hour. Show your work.

Answer Ruby left _____ minutes before _____ .

✓ **Self Check** **Go back and see what you can check off on the Self Check on page 211.**

 Use What You Know

In Lesson 20, you learned how to tell time to the minute. In this lesson, you use what you learned to solve problems. Take a look at this problem.

Beth left her house at 4:30. She arrived at dance class at 5:05. How long did it take Beth to get from her house to dance class?

a. Draw the hands on the two clocks below to show the two times.

Time Beth Left Her House | **Time Beth Arrived at Dance Class**

b. Look at the first clock. How many minutes before 5:00 is 4:30? _____

c. Look at the second clock. How many minutes after 5:00 is 5:05? _____

d. Explain how you can find the total amount of time it took Beth to get from her house to dance class. _____

_____

_____

_____

_____

▷▷ Find Out More

Elapsed time is the time that has passed between a start time and an end time. Here are three ways you could find elapsed time in this problem.

- You can count by fives on a clock.
  At 4:**30**, the minute hand is on the **6**.
  At 5:**05**, the minute hand is on the **1**.
  It took Beth **35 minutes** to get from her house
  to dance class.

- You can add. Think about the elapsed time as the minutes
  before 5:00 plus the minutes after 5:00.
  4:30 is 30 minutes before 5:00.
  5:05 is 5 minutes after 5:00.
  30 minutes + 5 minutes = **35 minutes**.

- You can also use a number line.
  Each long mark on the number line below shows 5 minutes. Count minutes on the number line just like you would count minutes on a clock.

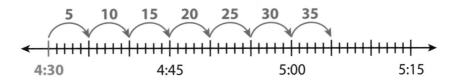

▶ Reflect

1 Elsa started eating lunch at 11:25 and finished at 11:45. Explain how to find how long it took Elsa to eat lunch. _____

_____

_____

_____

_____

Learn About ▷ **Finding the End Time in Word Problems**

Read the problem below. Then explore different ways to find the end time when you know the start time and the amount of elapsed time.

Jenna got home from school at 3:30. She did math homework for 10 minutes. Next she did science homework for 15 minutes. Then she practiced the piano for 22 minutes. What time did Jenna finish?

▶ **Picture It** **You can use a clock to help you find the end time.**

The first clock shows 3:30, because that is when Jenna started her homework. Count **10 minutes** for her math homework, **15 minutes** for her science homework, and **22 minutes** for her piano practice.

The second clock shows the time Jenna finished.

▶ **Model It** **You can also use a number line to help you find the end time.**

The number line below shows times in hours and minutes. Each long mark shows 5 minutes. Each short mark shows 1 minute.

Start at 3:30. Show a jump on the number line for each task. Each jump is equal to the number of minutes it took Jenna to do the task.

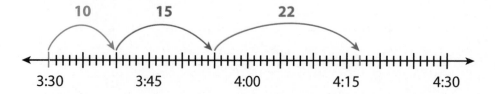

The last jump on the number line shows what time Jenna was finished with all three tasks.

▶ **Connect It** **Now you will find the end time for the problem from the previous page.**

2 Explain how to figure out the total elapsed time from the number of minutes

Jenna spent doing her homework and practicing the piano. _____

_____

3 Explain how you can use the total elapsed time to find Jenna's end time for doing

her homework and practicing the piano. _____

_____

4 What time did Jenna finish? _____ Why is the hour now 4, instead

of 3? _____

_____

5 Explain how to find the end time when you know the start time and the total

elapsed time. _____

_____

_____

_____

▶ **Try It** **Use what you have learned about finding the end time to help you solve these problems. Show your work on a separate sheet of paper.**

6 Nate finished dinner at 7:10. He did dishes for 15 minutes and then took a shower for 10 minutes. Then he read for 15 minutes before he went to bed. What time did Nate go to bed? _____

7 Kari started a phone call to her family at 5:45. She talked to her grandma for 10 minutes, then her grandpa for 5 minutes, and then her cousin for 8 minutes. What time did Kari end the call? _____

5:45   6:00   6:15

Learn About ▶ **Finding the Start Time in Word Problems**

Read the problem below. Then explore different ways to find the start time when you know the end time and the amount of elapsed time.

> Marc's guitar lesson starts at 5:20. It takes Marc 15 minutes to get to his lesson from his house. Before Marc leaves, he has to do chores for 25 minutes. What time should Marc start doing his chores to get to his lesson on time?

▶ **Picture It** **You can use a clock to help you find the start time.**

The clock shows 5:20, because that is when Marc's guitar lesson starts. Count **15 minutes** backward for the time it takes to get to his lesson. Then count **25 minutes** backward for the time it takes him to do his chores.

The second clock shows the time Marc should start doing his chores.

▶ **Model It** **You can also use a number line to help you find the start time.**

The number line below is like the one used for the last problem. It shows times in hours and minutes. Each long mark shows 5 minutes. Each short mark shows 1 minute.

Start at 5:20. Count back the number of minutes it takes Marc to get to his lesson and do his chores.

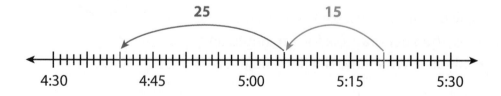

Connect It Now you will find the start time for the problem from the previous page.

8 Explain why the times are counted backward from 5:20 on the clock and on the number line. _____

_____

_____

9 What time should Marc start doing his chores? _____

Why is the number of hours now 4, instead of 5? _____

_____

_____

10 Explain how to find the start time when you know the end time and the elapsed time. _____

_____

_____

_____

Try It Use what you've learned about finding the start time to help you solve these problems. Show your work on a separate sheet of paper.

11 Enrique walked 5 minutes from his grandma's house to the store, stopped at the store for 20 minutes, and then walked 10 minutes from the store to his house. He got to his house at 6:00. What time did he leave his grandma's house? _____

12 Mira finished making fruit slices and sandwiches for lunch at 12:30. She cut up fruit for 10 minutes and made sandwiches for 7 minutes. What time did she start making lunch? _____

12:00   12:15   12:30   12:45   1:00

Practice > **Solving Problems About Time**

Study the example below. Then solve problems 13–15.

Example

Malea's soccer game started at 9:40 and ended at 10:32. How long was Malea's soccer game?

Look at how you could show your work.

9:40 *is* 20 minutes before 10:00.

10:32 *is* 32 minutes after 10:00.

20 + 32 = 52

Solution 52 minutes

The student used what she knew about telling time before and after the hour to find the answer.

 Pair/Share
How else could you have solved this problem?

---

13 Lamar watched his little sister while his mom was busy. He played blocks with her for 15 minutes, peek-a-boo for 5 minutes, and trains for 13 minutes. His mom came back to put his sister down for a nap at 2:15. What time did Lamar start watching his sister?

Show your work.

Do you need to count minutes forward or backward from 2:15 to find the time he started watching his sister?

 Pair/Share
How did you decide how you would solve the problem?

Solution _____

14 Mr. Chen started doing yard work at 10:00. He watered flowers for 6 minutes, weeded his garden for 12 minutes, and trimmed bushes for 27 minutes. What time was Mr. Chen done with his yard work?

Show your work.

I think adding all of the times together first would make this problem easier to solve.

 Pair/Share
Did you need to draw a clock or number line to help you? Why or why not?

Solution _____

15 Carter finished cleaning his room at 11:35. It took him 10 minutes to put all his toys away and 4 minutes to make his bed. What time did Carter start cleaning his room? Circle the letter of the correct answer.

A 11:49

B 11:25

C 11:21

D 10:21

Did Carter start cleaning his room before or after 11:35?

Ann chose **A** as the correct answer. How did she get that answer?

_____

_____

_____

_____

 Pair/Share
Does Ann's answer make sense?

Solve the problems.

1 What is the elapsed time between 1:08 and 1:37?

A 25 minutes   **C** 30 minutes

B 29 minutes   **D** 31 minutes

2 It took Juan 5 minutes to ride his bike to the park, where he played basketball for 25 minutes. Then it took him 5 minutes to ride home again. He got home at 10:10. Which clock shows the time Juan left for the park?

A

C

B

D

3 Patty, Joyce, and Stef leave for school at 7:45. Choose *Yes* or *No* to tell whether each girl can leave for school on time.

a. Patty gets up at 7:10. It takes her 10 minutes to get ready, 7 minutes to pack her lunch, and 15 minutes to eat breakfast. ☐ Yes ☐ No

b. Joyce gets up at 6:50 and exercises for 30 minutes. Then it takes her 20 minutes to get ready and 12 minutes to eat breakfast. ☐ Yes ☐ No

c. Stef gets up at 7:15. It takes her 15 minutes to get ready, 5 minutes to pack her lunch, and 9 minutes to eat breakfast. ☐ Yes ☐ No

4 Joe spent 40 minutes reading a magazine. Which pairs of clocks show possible times that he started and finished reading the magazine? Circle the letter for all that apply.

A

Start:    Finish:

C

Start:    Finish:

B

Start:    Finish:

D

Start: 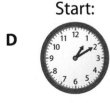   Finish:

5 Mariah played two games of checkers with her brother. The first game took 12 minutes and the second game took 18 minutes. They put the game away at 7:55. What time did they start playing checkers?

Show your work.

Answer   They started playing checkers at _____.

6 Jamal started writing thank-you notes at 5:25. It took him 20 minutes to write them. He also spent some time writing addresses on the envelopes. He finished at 6:00. How long did it take Jamal to write the addresses?

Show your work.

Answer   It took Jamal _____ minutes to write the addresses.

✓ Self Check   **Go back and see what you can check off on the Self Check on page 211.**

Use What You Know

In Lessons 20 and 21, you learned about measuring time using minutes and hours. You can also measure liquid volume. Take a look at this problem.

Zeke has a small bucket and a large bucket. He wants to know how much water each of the two buckets can hold. He has a ruler and a measuring cup. How can Zeke measure the amounts of water each bucket can hold?

a. Think about measuring how tall each bucket is. Explain how you would do this.

_____

_____

b. Does measuring how tall each bucket is help you know how much water each bucket can hold? Explain why or why not. _____

_____

_____

_____

c. What tool can Zeke use to measure the amount of water each bucket can hold?

_____

d. Explain how Zeke can measure the amount of water each bucket can hold.

_____

_____

When you measure how much water is in a bucket, you measure **liquid volume**.

To measure the amount of water each bucket can hold, Zeke must use something that holds liquid, like the measuring cup. He can count how many times he fills the measuring cup and pours it into each bucket until the bucket is full. The total number of measuring cups describes the liquid volume of each bucket.

There are standard units for measuring liquid volume. A **liter** is a standard unit of liquid volume. You can measure the number of liters in a container by using a measuring cup or a liter beaker.

A picture can help you understand about how much liquid 1 liter is. Each of the three pictures below show about 1 liter of liquid.

the amount of water
in a large water bottle

the amount of milk
in 4 small milk cartons

the amount of milk
in $\frac{1}{4}$ of a gallon

▶ Reflect

1 Name one container that definitely holds less than 1 liter, one container that holds about 1 liter, and one container that definitely holds more than 1 liter.

_____

_____

_____

_____

Learn About ▶ **Estimating Liquid Volume**

Read the problem below. Then explore different ways to estimate to solve a word problem about liquid volume.

Kayla will use a liter carton to fill her goldfish's small fish tank. Estimate how many liters of water the fish tank can hold.

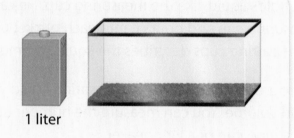

1 liter

▶ **Picture It** **You can use a model to help you estimate.**

You can picture how many liter cartons would fit inside the fish tank.

Front View

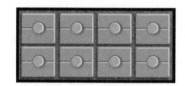

Top View

Count the number of cartons. This is your estimate.

▶ **Model It** **You can model the problem in another way to help you estimate.**

This shows 1 liter of water in the fish tank.

You can think about what fraction of the fish tank is filled when it has 1 liter of water in it.

Connect It Now you will estimate to solve the problem from the previous page.

2 Look at the 1 liter of water shown in the fish tank in *Model It*. Explain how to find the fraction of the fish tank that is filled with water.

_____

_____

_____

3 Explain how you can use this fraction to estimate how many liters of water the fish tank holds.

_____

_____

4 About how many liters of water does the fish tank hold? _____

5 Now look at the picture of the cartons inside the fish tank in *Picture It*. Is your estimate close to the estimate this picture shows? _____

6 Explain how to estimate the number of liters of water it would take to fill a container.

_____

_____

_____

Try It Use the picture of the liter carton and what you just learned to help you estimate the liquid volume of each container.

7

1 liter

_____

8

1 liter

_____

Learn About ▸ Solving Problems About Liquid Volume

Read the problem below. Then explore different ways to solve a word problem about liquid volume.

> Maria has a cooler full of 8 liters of lemonade. She wants to put the lemonade into pitchers to place on the tables at her party. Each pitcher holds 2 liters. How many pitchers will Maria need?

▶ **Picture It** **You can use a model to help you solve the problem.**

The model below shows the lemonade in the cooler. Each mark on the left side of the cooler shows 1 liter. Each full line marks off 2 liter sections.

1 liter { ⎫ 2 liters

▶ **Model It** **You can model the problem in another way to help you solve it.**

Each pitcher holds 2 liters. The pitchers need to hold 8 liters of lemonade in all.

2 liters   2 liters   2 liters   2 liters

Connect It Now you will solve the problem from the previous page using an equation.

9 How does the picture of the cooler in *Picture It* show you how many liters of lemonade are in the cooler? _____

_____

How can you use the picture of the cooler in *Picture It* to figure out how many pitchers are needed to hold all the lemonade? _____

_____

_____

10 What do you need to do to find the number of pitchers Maria needs?

_____

_____

11 Write a division equation using *P* for the unknown in the problem. Then write a related multiplication equation. Then solve the equations.

_____

12 A complete answer has a label with the number, showing what is being counted. Write the answer to the problem, including a label. _____

Explain why it is important to label your answer. _____

_____

_____

Try It Use what you just learned to solve these problems. Show your work on a separate sheet of paper.

13 Ginny's sink was full of 10 liters of water. She drained 4 liters out of it. How much water was left in the sink? _____

14 Ethan has 7 jugs of water. Each jug contains 3 liters. How much water does Ethan have altogether? _____

Practice **Solving Problems About Liquid Volume**

Study the example below. Then solve problems 15–17.

Example

Coach Bond brought 15 liters of water to soccer practice. The players drank 9 liters during practice. How many liters of water are left?

Look at how you could show your work using an equation.

$$15 - 9 = 6$$

The student wrote a subtraction equation because the question asked how much was left.

Solution _____6 liters of water are left._____

Pair/Share
How else could you solve this problem?

---

15 Jack's mom has a 3-liter bottle of liquid laundry soap. Sophie's mom has a 5-liter bottle of liquid laundry soap. They want to combine the two bottles in one big container. How many liters must the big container be able to hold?

Show your work.

How many liters of liquid laundry soap do Jack's mom and Sophie's mom have altogether? The big container must be able to hold that much liquid.

Pair/Share
Use the information in the problem. What question could you ask that would be solved with a subtraction equation?

Solution _____

16 Mary poured the orange juice from a 1-liter bottle into a large container. The large container with the 1 liter of orange juice in it is shown below. Estimate the liquid volume of the large container.

> You could think about how many 1-liter bottles would fit in the large container, or you could look at what fraction of the large container is filled by 1 liter of juice.

Solution _____

 Pair/Share
What strategy did you use to estimate the liquid volume?

---

17 Jason keeps his turtle in a tank that holds 20 liters of water. He keeps his frog in a tank that holds 10 liters of water. How much greater is the volume of the turtle tank than the frog tank? Circle the letter of the correct answer.

A 2 liters

B 10 liters

C 30 liters

D 200 liters

> You need to find out how much more water is in one tank than in the other. How can you do that?

Maya chose **C** as the correct answer. How did she get that answer?

_____

_____

_____

 Pair/Share
Does Maya's answer make sense?

Practice ▶ **Solving Problems About Liquid Volume**

Solve the problems.

1 The pot below contains 1 liter of water.

Which is the best estimate for how much water the pot could hold?

A 2 liters

B 5 liters

C 10 liters

D 20 liters

2 Noah used 8 liters of water to water 4 flower beds. He used the same amount of water on each bed. He used all of the water. How much water did he use on each flower bed?

A 2 liters

B 6 liters

C 12 liters

D 32 liters

3 Susan buys 10 liters of drinking water. If she drinks 1 liter each day, how much water will she have left after one week?

Solution _____

4 Choose all the containers that hold no more than 1 liter.

A kitchen sink

B tube of toothpaste

C baby food jar

D bathtub

E paper cup

5 Molly filled a tub for her dog using a 4-liter bucket. She filled the bucket 6 times. How much water did Molly use to wash her dog?

Show your work.

Answer _____ liters

✓ Self Check   **Go back and see what you can check off on the Self Check on page 211.**

🔄 Use What You Know

In Lesson 22, you learned about measuring liquid volume. You can also measure mass. Take a look at this problem.

Bristol has a measuring cup, a scale, and a bowl. How can she find out how heavy the bowl is?

a. Think about measuring the liquid volume of the bowl. Explain how you could do this. _____

_____

_____

_____

b. What do you know about the bowl if you know its liquid volume? _____

_____

c. What tool can Bristol use to find out how heavy the bowl is?

_____

d. Explain how Bristol could find out how heavy the bowl is. _____

_____

_____

_____

When you describe how heavy something is, you are describing its **mass**. Two units used when measuring mass are **gram** and **kilogram**.

The mass of a paper clip is about 1 gram.

1 kilogram is the same as 1,000 grams. So, an object with a mass of 1 kilogram is about as heavy as 1,000 paper clips.

The mass of a wooden baseball bat or a large hardcover book is also about 1 kilogram.

The picture below shows different types of scales you can use to measure mass.

▶ Reflect

1 Elena's brother says the family dog has a mass of 30 grams. Elena says the dog has a mass of 30 kilograms. Who do you think is correct? Why do you think so?

_____

_____

_____

_____

_____

Learn About ▶ **Estimating Mass**

Read the problem below. Then explore different ways to estimate mass.

Jamie bought a bag of flour at the store. Estimate the mass of the bag of flour.

▶ **Picture It** **You can use models to help you estimate the mass of an object.**

Jamie picked up the two books shown below. Then he picked up the bag of flour. The books and the bag of flour seemed to have about the same mass.

▶ **Model It** **You can also use a balance scale to help you estimate the mass of an object.**

Jamie put the bag of flour on one side of the balance scale and some 1-kilogram and 10-gram weights on the other side.

You can see that it takes about two 1-kilogram weights and three 10-gram weights to balance the scale.

Connect It   Now you will estimate the mass of the bag of flour to solve the problem from the previous page.

2 Look at *Picture It*. Explain why Jamie used books instead of paper clips to help him estimate the mass of the bag of flour. _____

_____

3 The mass of each book is about 1 kilogram. Estimate the mass of the bag of flour. Explain how you did it. _____

_____

_____

4 Look at the balance scale in *Model It*. The two sides of the scale are balanced, so it shows the actual mass of the bag of flour. What is the actual mass of the bag of flour?

_____

Is the estimate you made in problem 3 close to the actual mass? _____

_____

5 Explain how you could estimate the mass of a plastic fork. _____

_____

_____

_____

_____

Try It   Use what you just learned to solve these problems.

6 Would you estimate the mass of a table using grams or kilograms?

_____

7 Would you estimate the mass of a comic book using grams or kilograms?

_____

Learn About > **Solving Word Problems About Mass**

Read the problem below. Then explore different ways to solve a word problem about mass.

Nick has an orange that has a mass of 220 grams and an apple that has a mass of 110 grams. What is the mass of the orange and apple together?

▶ **Picture It** **You can use a balance scale to help you solve the problem.**

The balance scale below shows the mass of the orange.

The balance scale below shows the mass of the apple.

The balance scale below shows the mass of the orange and apple altogether. The orange and apple are on one side of the scale, and the weights are on the other side.

Connect It Now you will use an equation to solve the problem from the previous page.

8 How do you decide which operation to use to solve this problem?

_____

_____

9 Look at the balance scale in *Picture It* that shows the orange and apple together. What does the picture show that could help you solve the problem?

_____

_____

10 Write an equation for the problem. What is the mass of the orange and apple together? _____

11 Explain how you could estimate to know that your answer makes sense.

_____

_____

_____

12 Explain why the label *grams* should be part of your answer to this problem.

_____

_____

_____

Try It Use what you just learned to solve these problems. Show your work on a separate sheet of paper.

13 Jeff had 40 grams of birdseed. He shared it equally among 4 birds. How many grams of birdseed did each bird get? _____

14 Micah's dog has a mass of 23 kilograms. Nate's dog has a mass of 8 kilograms. How much greater is the mass of Micah's dog than the mass of Nate's dog?

_____

Practice ▶ **Solving Word Problems About Mass**

Study the example below. Then solve problems 15–17.

Example

Jen's suitcase has a mass of 2 kilograms when it is empty. After she packed her clothes and shoes for her trip, the suitcase had a mass of 16 kilograms. What is the mass of the clothes and shoes Jen packed in her suitcase?

Look at how you could show your work using an equation.

$$16 - 2 = 14$$

Solution ___14 kilograms___

The student wrote a subtraction equation to find the difference between the mass when the suitcase was empty and the mass when it was full.

 Pair/Share
How else could you solve this problem?

---

15 Ruby's mom buys 4 bags of potatoes. Each bag has a mass of 4 kilograms. What is the total mass of the 4 bags?

Show your work.

There are 4 bags with 4 kilograms of potatoes in each bag. That reminds me of using equal groups.

 Pair/Share
How did you decide which operation to use to solve the problem?

Solution _____

16 Jane has a sandwich and a banana for lunch. The sandwich's mass is 140 grams. The banana's mass is 130 grams. What is the total mass of the sandwich and the banana?

Show your work.

Solution _____

---

17 Brock's dad bought a 10-kilogram bag of rice. Then he divided the rice evenly into 5 smaller bags. How many kilograms of rice did each smaller bag have in it? Circle the letter of the correct answer.

A 2 kilograms

B 5 kilograms

C 15 kilograms

D 50 kilograms

Felicia chose **D** as the correct answer. How did she get that answer?

_____

_____

_____

_____

_____

Practice ▶ Solving Word Problems About Mass

Solve the problems.

1 Which is the best estimate for the mass of a watermelon?

    A 30 kilograms

    B 3 kilograms

    C 30 grams

    D 3 grams

2 Which objects have a mass of about 1 gram? Circle the letter for all that apply.

    A rubber band

    B box of crayons

    C pair of scissors

    D dollar bill

    E library book

3 Mrs. Martin is grocery shopping. Before picking up potatoes, her shopping bag has a mass of 4 kilograms. Then she adds some potatoes to her bag. The scale shows the mass of the potatoes. What is the mass of the bag, in kilograms, after adding the potatoes?

Solution _____

4 When Lara was born, her mass was 3 kilograms. By the time she started third grade, she had gained 24 kilograms. What was Lara's mass at the beginning of third grade?

Show your work.

Answer _____ kilograms

5 Margo's soccer coach brings a large bag of watermelons to practice. The mass of the bag with all the watermelons in it is 12 kilograms.

Explain how you could use estimation to figure out about how many watermelons are in the bag.

_____

_____

_____

Estimate the number of watermelons in the bag. Show your work and explain what you did at each step.

Show your work.

Answer There are about _____ watermelons in the bag.

✔ **Self Check** Go back and see what you can check off on the Self Check on page 211.

Use What You Know

You have had practice modeling and solving word problems. In this lesson, you will use information from graphs to solve word problems. Take a look at this problem.

Ron kept track of the points scored by his teammates during a basketball game. He recorded his data in the picture graph shown below. How many points did each teammate score?

Points Scored During the Game	
Alan	🏀
Cate	🏀 🏀 🏀
Gary	🏀 🏀 🏀 🏀 🏀
Mae	🏀 🏀 🏀 🏀

Key: Each 🏀 stands for 2 points.

a. The sentence at the bottom of the graph tells you that each 🏀 stands for _____ points.

b. There is 1 🏀 next to Alan's name. That means that Alan scored 2 points.

There are 3 🏀 next to Cate's name.

How many points did Cate score? _____ points

c. How many 🏀 are next to Gary's name? _____

d. How many points did Gary score? _____ points

e. Explain how you could find the number of points Mae scored.

_____

▶▶ Find Out More

Look at Ron's **picture graph** on the previous page. The **key** tells you that each 🏀 stands for **2 points**. You can multiply the number of 🏀 by 2 to find the total number of points each student scored.

Student	Number of 🏀	×	Points for each basket	=	Total Number of Points
Alan	1	×	2	=	2
Cate	3	×	2	=	6
Gary	5	×	2	=	10
Mae	4	×	2	=	8

The same basketball data can be shown on a **bar graph**. The bars on the bar graph below show how many points each student scored.

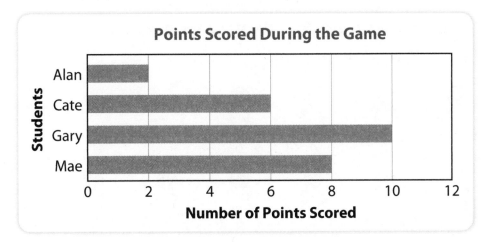

The numbers along the bottom of the bar graph are called the **scale**. The scale marks off equal sections. On this graph each number on the scale is 2 more than the number before it. The scale counts by 2s.

▶ Reflect

1 What would it mean if the symbol for Alan was 🏀? Then how many points would Alan have scored? Explain. _____

_____

_____

Learn About ▶ **Reading and Interpreting Picture Graphs**

Read the problem below. Then explore different ways to answer questions about picture graphs.

Jaime asked students in his school to choose their favorite season. The picture graph shows how students answered. How many more students chose summer than chose winter as their favorite season?

Favorite Season	
Winter	😊 😊 😊 😊
Spring	😊 😊 😊
Summer	😊 😊 😊 😊 😊 😊
Fall	😊 😊 😊 😊 😊

Key: Each 😊 stands for 5 students.

▶ **Picture It** **You can use pictures to understand the problem.**

Remember that each 😊 stands for 5 students.

Winter

Summer

▶ **Model It** **You can also use number lines to help understand the problem.**

Remember that each 😊 stands for **5 students**.

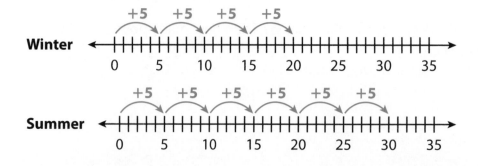

► **Connect It** **Now you will solve the problem from the previous page using equations.**

2 What does the problem ask you to find?

_____

_____

3 Complete the key. Each 😊 stands for _____ students.

4 Complete the table. Find the number of students who chose winter and the number who chose summer.

Favorite Season	Number of 😊	×	Students for each 😊	=	Number of Students
Winter	4	×	5	=	_____
Summer	_____	×	5	=	_____

5 Complete the equation to find how many more students chose summer than chose winter.

$30 - 20 =$ _____

So, _____ more students chose summer than chose winter.

6 Explain why the key is important when you are solving a problem that has a picture graph.

_____

_____

_____

► **Try It** **Use the picture graph on the previous page and what you just learned to solve these problems. Show your work on a separate sheet of paper.**

7 How many students did NOT choose spring or summer? _____

8 How many more students chose spring or fall than chose summer? _____

Learn About **Reading and Interpreting Bar Graphs**

Read the problem below. Then explore different ways to answer questions about a bar graph.

The Hart School wants to build a new playground. The graph shows the number of dollars each grade has raised to build the playground. Grade 3 and Grade 4 together want to raise $300. How much more money must they raise?

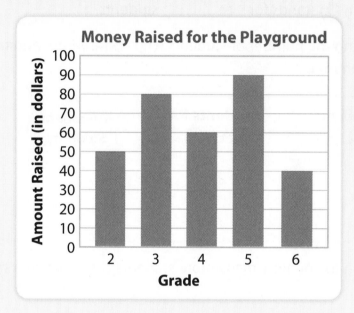

Explain It You can use words to explain how to use the graph to find the number of dollars raised by each grade.

Third Grade

Point to the Grade 3 bar. Find the top of the bar. Follow the line at the top of the bar to the left. Stop at the number on the left side of the graph. This is the number of dollars Grade 3 raised.

Fourth Grade

Point to the Grade 4 bar. Find the top of the bar. Follow the line at the top of the bar to the left. Stop at the number on the left side of the graph. This is the number of dollars Grade 4 raised.

▶ **Connect It** **Now you will solve the problem from the previous page using equations. Use the bar graph on the previous page to answer the questions.**

9 What does each bar on the bar graph show? _____

_____

10 What do the numbers in the scale along the left side of the bar graph stand for?

_____

11 What is the difference between one number on the scale and the next number?

_____

12 Look at the Grade 3 bar. How much money did Grade 3 raise? _____

Look at the Grade 4 bar. How much money Grade 4 raise? _____

13 What operation do you use to find out how much money was raised by

Grade 3 and Grade 4 altogether? _____

How much money did Grade 3 and Grade 4 raise altogether? _____

14 What operation do you use to find out how much more money must be raised in

order for Grade 3 and Grade 4 to together raise $300? _____

How much more money must the two classes raise to raise a total of $300? _____

15 Explain how the numbers in the scale of a bar graph help you to understand what

the bar shows. _____

_____

_____

▶ **Try It** **Use the bar graph on the previous page and what you just learned to solve these problems. Show your work on a separate sheet of paper.**

16 How much money in all have all the grades raised? _____

17 How much more money have Grade 4 and Grade 5 raised altogether than Grade 2

and Grade 3 altogether? _____

| Practice | **Solving Problems Using Scaled Graphs** |

Study the example below. Then solve problems 18–20.

Example

Ms. Santos buys markers for each class. Find how many more markers Ms. Santos buys for Grade 3 than for Grade 2.

Markers for Each Class	
Grade 2	❙ ❙ ❙ ❙
Grade 3	❙ ❙ ❙ ❙ ❙ ❙ ❙
Grade 4	❙ ❙ ❙ ❙ ❙ ❙ ❙ ❙ ❙
Grade 5	❙ ❙ ❙ ❙ ❙

Key: Each ❙ stands for 10 markers.

The student multiplied the number of marker symbols by the number shown in the key. He did this to find the number of markers Ms. Santos bought for each class.

Look at how you could show your work in a table.

Grade	Number of	×	Each ❙ stands for	=	Number of Markers
Grade 3	7	×	10	=	70
Grade 2	4	×	10	=	40

$70 - 40 = 30$

Solution __30 more markers__

Pair/Share

How many more markers does Ms. Santos buy for Grade 4 than Grade 3?

---

18 Use the picture graph above. How many markers did Ms. Santos buy in all?

Show your work.

What steps will you use to solve this problem?

Pair/Share

How else could you solve this problem?

Solution _____

Use the bar graph below to solve problems 19 and 20.

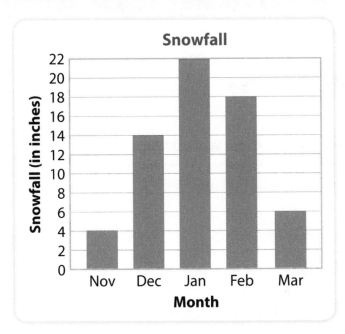

Snowfall

Snowfall (in inches) / Month

19 How much more snow fell in February and March combined than fell in November and December combined?

Show your work.

Pair/Share
What data on the bar graph do you need to solve the problem?

Solution _____

20 Which 2 months have the same amount of snowfall combined as January? Circle the letter of the correct answer.

A February and March

B December and March

C November and December

D November and February

Lara chose **D** as the correct answer. How did she get that answer?

I think the first step is to find the snowfall for January.

Pair/Share
How did you and your partner decide whether to add or subtract?

_____

_____

_____

Lesson 24 Solve Problems Using Scaled Graphs   **257**

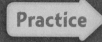

Practice **Solving Problems Using Scaled Graphs**

Solve the problems.

Use the bar graph below to solve problems 1 and 2.

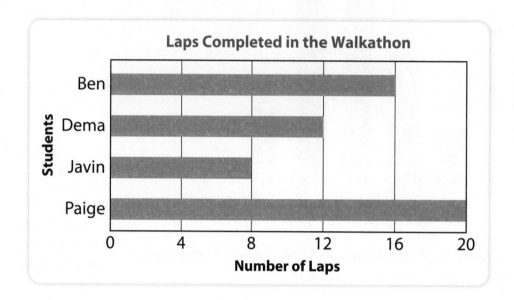

1 The bar graph above shows the number of laps each student completed in a walkathon. How many laps in all did the students complete?

A 4

B 20

C 36

D 56

2 Use the bar graph above. How many more laps did Dema and Paige complete combined than Ben and Javin combined?

Answer _____ laps

Use the picture graph below to solve problems 3 and 4.

Soccer Goals Scored This Season	
Bears	⚽⚽⚽⚽⚽
Cheetahs	⚽⚽
Eagles	⚽⚽⚽⚽⚽
Falcons	⚽⚽⚽⚽⚽⚽⚽
Lions	⚽⚽⚽
Tigers	⚽⚽⚽⚽⚽⚽⚽

Key: Each ⚽ stands for 2 goals.

3 Tell whether each sentence is *True* or *False*.

a. The Eagles scored 10 goals. ☐ True ☐ False

b. The Lions scored 3 goals. ☐ True ☐ False

c. The Tigers scored as many goals as the Bears and the Lions combined. ☐ True ☐ False

d. The Falcons scored 2 more goals than the Eagles. ☐ True ☐ False

4 Name teams that together scored 20 goals.

Show your work.

Solution _____

_____

✓ **Self Check** Go back and see what you can check off on the Self Check on page 211.

Draw Scaled Graphs

Use What You Know

In Lesson 24, you learned to read picture graphs and bar graphs with scales. In this lesson you will learn how to draw these graphs. Take a look at this problem.

> Tess has a game with letter tiles. Each tile shows one of the letters A, C, S, or T. Tess wants to make a picture graph showing the number of tiles with each letter.
>
>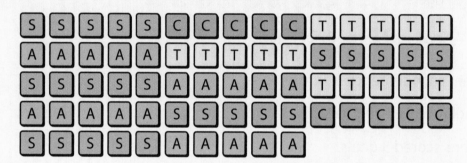

a. How many tiles have the letter A? _____

b. How many tiles have the letter C? _____

c. How many tiles have the letter S? _____

d. How many tiles have the letter T? _____

e. How many tiles are there in all? _____

f. Suppose Tess uses this key: Each ☐ stands for 1 letter tile. How many pictures will she have to draw on the picture graph? _____

g. Explain how Tess could change the key so that she could draw fewer ☐ on her picture graph?

_____

_____

Graphs can help you see and understand a lot of data at once. Tess wants to draw a graph to show the letters on the 70 tiles. That is a lot of data to show!

- Tess makes the picture graph shown at the right. She uses tile symbols to show the data.

  Her key shows each ☐ stands for 5 tiles. 5 is a good choice, because it is easy to show the tile data (20, 10, 25, and 15) as groups of 5.

  Making each symbol stand for more than 1 makes it easier to show data that has a lot of pieces. You can say the picture graph uses a scale of 5.

Letter Tiles	
A	☐ ☐ ☐ ☐
C	☐ ☐
S	☐ ☐ ☐ ☐ ☐
T	☐ ☐ ☐

Key: Each ☐ stands for 5 tiles.

- You can show the same data on a bar graph. The bars on the bar graph show how many tiles there are with each letter. The numbers along the bottom of the bar graph are called the scale. The scale marks off equal sections. This bar graph has a scale of 5.

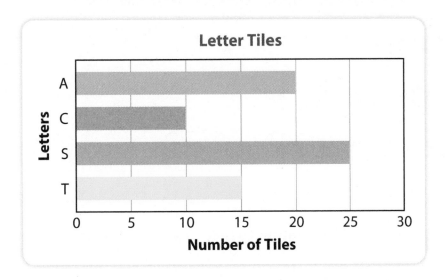

▶ Reflect

1 Describe when you would use a scale greater than 1 for a bar graph.

_____

_____

Learn About ▶ **Drawing a Scaled Picture Graph**

Read the problem below. Then explore how to show data in a picture graph.

Robert records the different bugs he sees. He wants to draw a picture graph using the data in the table. How can Robert make a picture graph?

Bugs Robert Saw	
Type of Bug	**Number of Bugs**
Ant	16
Bee	4
Moth	6
Spider	12

▶ **Picture It** **You can use models to show the data.**

You want to use a scale of 2. Use a 🐛 for each bug. Then draw circles around groups of 2.

Ant 🐛🐛 🐛🐛 🐛🐛 🐛🐛 🐛🐛 🐛🐛 🐛🐛 🐛🐛

Bee 🐛🐛 🐛🐛

Moth 🐛🐛 🐛🐛 🐛🐛

Spider 🐛🐛 🐛🐛 🐛🐛 🐛🐛 🐛🐛 🐛🐛

▶ **Model It** **You can use multiplication to help you show the data.**

Use a **scale of 2**. Now each 🐛 stands for 2 bugs.

$16 \div 2 = 8$	To show 16 ants, use 8 🐛.
$4 \div 2 = 2$	To show 4 bees, use 2 🐛.
$6 \div 2 = 3$	To show 6 moths, use 3 🐛.
$12 \div 2 = 6$	To show 12 spiders, use 6 🐛.

Connect It Now you will solve the problem from the previous page by drawing a picture graph.

2 What is a good title for Robert's picture graph? Write it on the picture graph below.

Complete the key for the picture graph.

Use the data in the table on the previous page and the key to complete the last two rows.

_____								
Ant	🐜	🐜	🐜	🐜	🐜	🐜	🐜	🐜
Bee	🐜	🐜						
_____								
_____								

Key: Each 🐜 stands for _____ bugs.

3 Why does a scale of 2 work better here than a scale of 1?

_____

_____

Try It Use what you just learned to solve this problem. Show your work on a separate sheet of paper.

4 Lin records the number of shells she collects at the beach. Draw a picture graph of Lin's data. Use a scale of 10. Be sure to write a title, a key, and draw symbols to show the data.

Number of Shells Collected	
Saturday	20 shells
Sunday	40 shells
Monday	30 shells
Tuesday	10 shells

_____	

_____

Learn About ▶ Drawing a Scaled Bar Graph

Read the problem below. Then explore different ways to show the data and make a bar graph.

Nan keeps track of how many minutes she practices the guitar each day. She wants to draw a bar graph using the data shown at the right. How can Nan make a bar graph?

Time I Practice Guitar	
Monday	5 minutes
Tuesday	30 minutes
Wednesday	15 minutes
Thursday	25 minutes
Friday	20 minutes

▶ **Picture It** **You can use number lines to help you choose a scale.**

The number line below has a scale of 5. The points on the number line show the number of minutes Nan practices on the different days.

Scale of 5

```
    0   5  10  15  20  25  30  35  40
```

The number line below has a scale of 10. The points on the number line show the number of minutes Nan practices on the different days. Some points fall between the numbers on the scale.

Scale of 10

```
    0      10      20      30      40
```

▶ **Model It** **You can also use multiplication to help you make a bar graph.**

Multiply to find the numbers to write on the bar graph scale. Use a scale of 5.

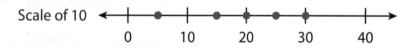

$1 \times 5 = 5$	$2 \times 5 = 10$	$3 \times 5 = 15$	$4 \times 5 = 20$
$5 \times 5 = 25$	$6 \times 5 = 30$	$7 \times 5 = 35$	$8 \times 5 = 40$

The scale numbers will be 5, 10, 15, 20, 25, 30, 35, 40.

Connect It Now you will solve the problem from the previous page by drawing a bar graph.

5 How do you use the scale to help you draw the bars on a bar graph?

_____

6 What is a good title for Nan's bar graph?

Write the title on the graph.

Write the two labels for the graph.

Complete the scale.

Draw the remaining bars on the graph.

7 Do you think a scale of 2 would work as well as a scale of 5 for this graph? Why or why not?

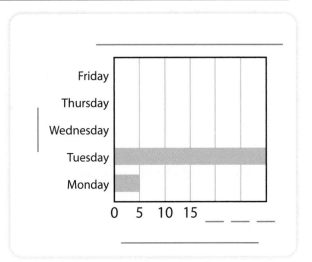

_____

_____

_____

Try It Use what you just learned to solve this problem. Show your work on a separate sheet of paper.

8 The table below shows ways that students get to school.

Draw a bar graph using the data in the table.
Be sure to write a title, choose a scale, label all the parts of the graph, and draw the bars.

Ways We Get to School	
Way We Travel	**Number of Students**
Bicycle	10
Bus	80
Car	40
Walk	20

Practice ▶ **Drawing Scaled Graphs**

Study the example below. Then solve problems 9–11.

Example

Sean asks his classmates to choose their favorite bike color. He records the results in this table. He wants to draw a bar graph of the data. How can he decide what scale to use?

Favorite Bike Colors	
Color	**Number of Classmates**
Blue	12
Green	6
Orange	3
Red	9

Look at how you could show your work using number lines.

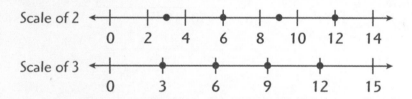

Solution Sean could look at the data and find a scale that will be easy to use with the data. The data are all numbers you say when you skip count by 3, so 3 is a scale that makes sense.

 Are the numbers in the data set numbers you say when you skip count by 2 or skip count by 3?

💬 **Pair/Share**
How could you multiply to solve this problem?

---

9 Complete the bar graph using the data in Sean's table above.

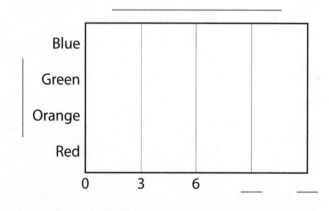

 Remember to write a title on your graph and label all the parts of your graph.

💬 **Pair/Share**
Take a quick look at your graph. How can you tell that it matches the data you used?

10 Students recycled cans for the can drive. Elia recycled 20 cans. Liam recycled 40 cans. Jamal recycled 10 cans. Sara recycled 50 cans. Complete the picture graph of the recycling data.

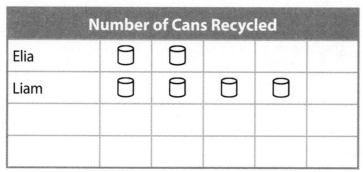

Key: Each stands for 10 cans.

Each ⊖ stands for 10 cans. How many cans should I draw next to Jamal's name?

Pair/Share
How can you use skip counting to check your answer?

---

11 Emilio begins a picture graph of the data in the table below.

Favorite Yogurt Flavor	
Cherry	☺ ☺
Lemon	☺
Strawberry	☺ ☺ ☺ ☺
Vanilla	☺ ☺ ☺

Key:

Favorite Yogurt Flavor	
Yogurt Flavor	**Number of Students**
Cherry	10
Lemon	5
Strawberry	20
Vanilla	15

I think I can compare the data in the table to the data in the graph to figure out the key.

Which key does Emilio use for his picture graph? Circle the letter of the correct answer.

A Each ☺ stands for 1 student.

B Each ☺ stands for 2 students.

C Each ☺ stands for 5 students.

D Each ☺ stands for 10 students.

Vicky chose **C** as the correct answer. How did she get that answer?

_____

_____

_____

Pair/Share
How can you check that Vicky's choice is correct?

Practice ▶ **Drawing Scaled Graphs**

Solve the problems.

Jane makes a bar graph of the number of tickets to the school play she sells each day. Use the bar graph to answer problems 1–3.

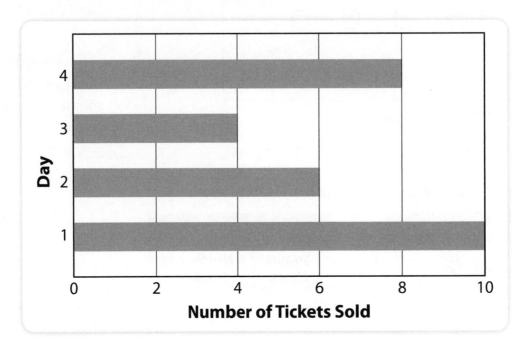

Number of Tickets Sold

1 Tell whether each sentence is *True* or *False*.

a. The scale for Jane's bar graph is 2. ☐ True ☐ False

b. A good title for Jane's bar graph would be "Tickets Sold for Ten Days." ☐ True ☐ False

c. If Jane had used a scale of 3 for her bar graph, she would have written the numbers 3, 6, 9, and 12 on the scale. ☐ True ☐ False

d. If Jane had used a scale of 3 for her bar graph, all of the bars would have ended between the numbers on the scale. ☐ True ☐ False

2 Suppose Jane made a picture graph of her data and used a ticket symbol to represent two tickets sold. How many ticket symbols would she need to draw to show the number of tickets sold on Day 1?

Answer _____ ticket symbols

3 Which set of data does Jane use to make the bar graph?

Tickets Sold				
Day	1	2	3	4
Tickets Sold	4	2	3	5

A

Tickets Sold				
Day	1	2	3	4
Tickets Sold	10	6	4	8

C

Tickets Sold				
Day	1	2	3	4
Tickets Sold	4	8	6	10

B

Tickets Sold				
Day	1	2	3	4
Tickets Sold	8	4	10	6

D

4 The table below shows data for students' favorite games. Choose a scale for the data. Then use your scale and the data to complete the picture graph below.

Favorite Games	
Game	Number of Students
Hopscotch	20
Jump Rope	10
Kickball	50
Tag	30

_____

Key: Each ☺ stands for _____ students.

✓ **Self Check** **Go back and see what you can check off on the Self Check on page 211.**

Measure Length and Plot Data on Line Plots

3.MD.B.4

🔄 Use What You Know

In Lesson 25, you drew picture graphs and bar graphs. In this lesson, you will measure objects and draw line plots. Take a look at this problem.

Rosa is following directions for putting charms on a bracelet. She places her bracelet along the ruler and completes Step 1. What will Rosa's bracelet look like when she is done?

Directions

Step 1: Place a 💜 at 1 inch.

Step 2: Place a ⬛ at $2\frac{1}{2}$ inches.

Step 3: Place a ◆ at $\frac{1}{4}$ inch.

Step 4: Place a ⬤ at $1\frac{3}{4}$ inches.

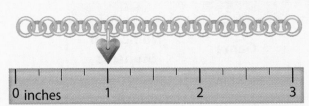

a. Where did Rosa place the 💜 on the bracelet? at _____ inch

b. Where should Rosa place the ⬛ on the bracelet? at _____ inches

c. On a number line, $2\frac{1}{2}$ is between the numbers 2 and _____.

d. Rosa should place the ⬛ on the bracelet between 2 inches and _____ inches.

e. Where should Rosa place the ◆ on the bracelet? at _____ inch

f. On a number line, $\frac{1}{4}$ is between the numbers 0 and _____.

g. Rosa should place the ◆ on the bracelet between 0 inches and _____ inch.

h. Explain how you could find where Rosa should place the ⬤.

_____

_____

▷▷ Find Out More

Look at the bracelet on the previous page. Sometimes the length you need to measure is between the inch marks on a ruler. When that happens, you measure to the nearest fraction of an inch.

A ruler is like a number line. It shows whole numbers. It can also show fractions. The rulers on this page shows half-inch marks and one-fourth-inch marks. Usually the fractions are not labeled on a ruler.

Rosa places the ■ at $2\frac{1}{2}$ inches. That is halfway between 2 inches and 3 inches on the ruler.

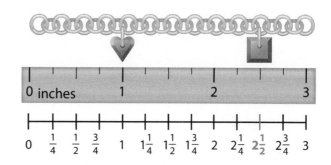

Rosa places the ◆ at $\frac{1}{4}$ inch. That is between 0 and 1 inch. It is closer to the 0 mark. She places the ● at $1\frac{3}{4}$ inches. That is between 1 inch and 2 inches. It is closer to 2 inches.

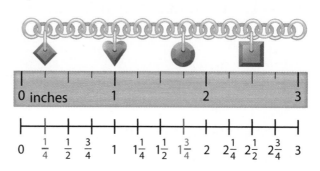

The picture above shows what Rosa's bracelet looks like when she is done.

▶ Reflect

1 Describe how to find the $1\frac{1}{2}$-inch mark on a ruler.

_____

_____

_____

_____

Learn About ▷ Measuring Length

Read the problem below. Then explore different ways of measuring length.

Brian is measuring the lengths of 6 earthworms. The earthworms he collected are shown. How can he find the length of each earthworm?

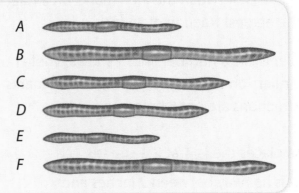

▷ **Picture It** **You can use an inch ruler to help you understand how to measure length.**

This ruler shows half-inch marks. You can measure to the nearest $\frac{1}{2}$ inch.

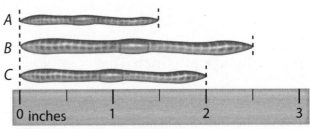

This ruler shows one-fourth-inch marks. You can measure to the nearest $\frac{1}{4}$ inch.

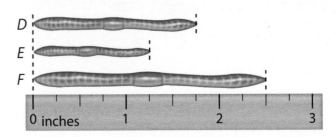

▷ **Model It** **You can use words to describe how to measure length.**

Line up the left end of the earthworm with zero on the ruler.

Look at the other end of the earthworm.

Find the mark on the ruler that is closest to the other end of the worm. You can measure to the nearest inch, $\frac{1}{2}$ inch, or $\frac{1}{4}$ inch.

Connect It   Now you will measure to solve the problem from the previous page.

2 Complete the sentence to describe how you begin to measure earthworm *A*.

I line up the left end of the earthworm with _____ on the ruler.

3 Look at *Picture It*. Is earthworm *A* longer than 1 inch or shorter than 1 inch?

_____

4 The mark on the ruler that is closest to the other end of earthworm *A* is

_____ inches.

5 Earthworm *A* is _____ inches long.

6 Use the rulers in *Picture It* to measure earthworms *B, C, D, E,* and *F*. Write your measurements in the table.

Earthworm Lengths						
Earthworm	*A*	*B*	*C*	*D*	*E*	*F*
Length (in inches)						

7 Explain how you found the length of earthworm *F*.

_____

_____

Try It   Use what you just learned about measuring to solve these problems. Use an inch ruler to measure each earthworm.

8 Brian finds two more worms. He labels them *G* and *H*. What are the lengths of the worms to the nearest $\frac{1}{4}$ inch?

G

H

Worm *G* is _____ inches long.   Worm *H* is _____ inches long.

Learn About ▶ Displaying Data in a Line Plot

Read the problem below. Then explore different ways to display the data.

Brian recorded the lengths of the earthworms in his table. He wants to make a line plot of the measurements. What will Brian's line plot look like?

Earthworm Lengths								
Earthworm	A	B	C	D	E	F	G	H
Length (in inches)	$1\frac{1}{2}$	$2\frac{1}{2}$	2	$1\frac{3}{4}$	$1\frac{1}{4}$	$2\frac{1}{2}$	$1\frac{1}{2}$	$2\frac{3}{4}$

▶ **Model It** **You can use a number line to help you begin to draw the line plot.**

The earthworms are measured to the nearest $\frac{1}{4}$ inch. So, the scale is $\frac{1}{4}$ inch.

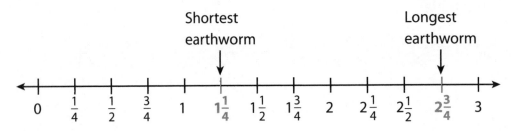

▶ **Model It** **You can use models to help you display the data.**

The table shows how many earthworms there are of each length.

Each **X** stands for 1 earthworm.

$1\frac{1}{4}$ inches	X
$1\frac{1}{2}$ inches	X X
$1\frac{3}{4}$ inches	X
2 inches	X
$2\frac{1}{4}$ inches	
$2\frac{1}{2}$ inches	X X
$2\frac{3}{4}$ inches	X

> **Connect It** Now you will solve the problem from the previous page. Use the data in the table to help you complete the line plot.

9 Complete the scale on the line plot number line below. Use a scale of $\frac{1}{4}$ inch.

Lengths of Earthworms Measured

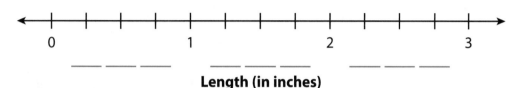

Length (in inches)

10 How many worms did Brian measure? _____

11 There will be an X on the line plot for each earthworm. If two or more earthworms are the same length, the Xs will be drawn one above the other. How many Xs will be on the line plot? _____

12 How many worms are $1\frac{1}{4}$ inches long? _____ Draw that many Xs above $1\frac{1}{4}$.

13 How many worms are $1\frac{1}{2}$ inches long? _____ Draw that many Xs above $1\frac{1}{2}$.

14 Complete the line plot. Make sure to draw an X for each earthworm measurement.

15 Explain what each X on the line plot stands for. _____

_____

> **Try It** Use what you just learned to solve this problem. Draw your line plot on a separate sheet of paper.

16 Draw a line plot of the data in the table. Start by choosing and labeling a scale.

Plant Lengths							
Plant	A	B	C	D	E	F	G	H
Length (in inches)	$6\frac{1}{4}$	$6\frac{1}{2}$	$5\frac{3}{4}$	$6\frac{1}{2}$	$6\frac{3}{4}$	$6\frac{1}{4}$	$5\frac{3}{4}$	$6\frac{1}{2}$

Practice ▸ **Plotting Data on Line Plots**

Study the example below. Then solve problems 17–19.

Example

In science club, Lily measured the length of dragonfly wings. She made a line plot of her data shown below. Then she found one more dragonfly wing.

Measure the wing
to the nearest $\frac{1}{4}$ inch.

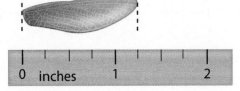

Add the last measurement to Lily's line plot. Which wing length appears most often on the line plot?

Look at how you could show your work using Lily's line plot.

Dragonfly Wings Measured

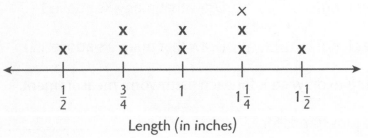

Length (in inches)

Solution $1\frac{1}{4}$ inches

The student lines up one end of the dragonfly wing with 0 on the ruler. Then the student finds the mark on the ruler closest to the other end of the wing.

 Pair/Share
How do you know which wing length appears most often?

---

17 Use the line plot in the example above. How many dragonfly wings are shorter than 1 inch?

What does each X tell me?

 Pair/Share
Describe how you found the answer.

Solution _____

18 Lee measures the lengths of his friends' hands. He records the measurements in the table below. Complete the line plot below using Lee's data.

Hand Lengths						
Person	Arty	Leo	Meg	Olivia	Ruby	Zain
Length (in inches)	$5\frac{1}{2}$	5	$4\frac{3}{4}$	$5\frac{1}{2}$	5	$5\frac{3}{4}$

Hand Lengths

Length (in inches)

---

19 Use a ruler to measure the marker. To the nearest half inch, how long is the marker? Circle the letter of the correct answer.

A 3 inches

B $3\frac{1}{4}$ inches

C $3\frac{1}{2}$ inches

D $4\frac{1}{2}$ inches

Vicky chose **B** as the correct answer. How did she get that answer?

_____

_____

_____

Practice ▶ Plotting Data on Line Plots

Solve the problems.

Use the line plot below to answer problems 1–3.

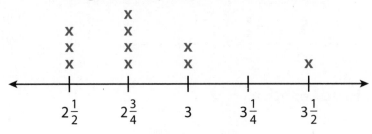

Lengths of Toy Airplanes Measured

Length (in inches)

1 Which set of data was used to make the line plot?

A

Toy Airplane Lengths (in inches)				
$2\frac{1}{2}$	$2\frac{3}{4}$	3	$3\frac{1}{4}$	$3\frac{1}{2}$

B

Toy Airplane Lengths (in inches)				
3	4	2	0	1

C

Toy Airplane Lengths (in inches)				
$2\frac{1}{2}$	$2\frac{1}{2}$	$2\frac{1}{2}$	$2\frac{3}{4}$	$2\frac{3}{4}$
$2\frac{3}{4}$	$2\frac{3}{4}$	3	3	$3\frac{1}{2}$

D

Toy Airplane Lengths (in inches)				
3	4	2	0	1
$2\frac{1}{2}$	$2\frac{3}{4}$	3	$3\frac{1}{4}$	$3\frac{1}{2}$

2 Tell whether each sentence is *True* or *False*.

a. There are four airplanes shown on the line plot.   ☐ True   ☐ False

b. None of the airplanes measures $3\frac{1}{4}$ inches.   ☐ True   ☐ False

c. All of the planes are longer than 2 inches.   ☐ True   ☐ False

d. Exactly three planes measure $2\frac{3}{4}$ inches.   ☐ True   ☐ False

3 How long is the longest airplane measured? _____

4 Use an inch ruler for this problem.

Part A Measure the leaves to the nearest one-fourth inch. Record the lengths in the table.

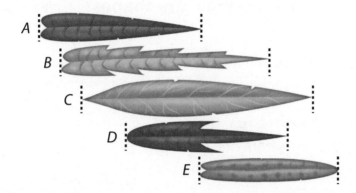

Leaf Lengths					
Leaf	A	B	C	D	E
Length (in inches)					

Part B Complete the line plot below using the measurements you recorded in the table.

Leaf Lengths

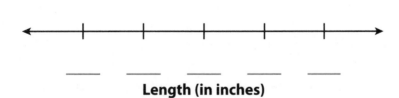

Length (in inches)

✓ Self Check Go back and see what you can check off on the Self Check on page 211.

Think It Through

What are some ways that we measure shapes?

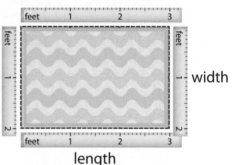

Think about different ways you can measure a rug that has the shape of a rectangle.

You can measure the length of the rug. The length tells how long the rug is from one end to the other. The rug at the right is 3 feet long.

You can also measure the width of the rug. The width tells how wide the rug is from one side to the other. The rug at the right is 2 feet wide.

Think **When you measure area, you measure both length and width.**

Suppose you want to know the area of the rug. What you want to know is how much floor the rug covers. **Area** is the amount of space a shape covers.

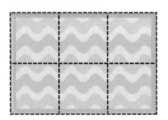

🖊 **Underline** the sentence that tells what area is.

You can use a measuring tape to find out how long the rug is and to find out how wide it is. But that won't tell you how much of the floor the rug covers. You want to know about the space between the sides of the rug.

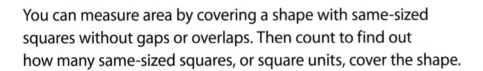

Think Area is the amount of space a shape covers.

You measure area in **square units**.

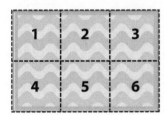 This square has an area of 1 square unit.

You can measure area by covering a shape with same-sized squares without gaps or overlaps. Then count to find out how many same-sized squares, or square units, cover the shape.

When I measure area, I make sure the square units line up with the edges of the shape. I also make sure the squares do not overlap or have gaps between them.

| 1 | 2 | 3 |
| 4 | 5 | 6 |

The rug is covered by 6 square units with no gaps or overlaps. So, the area of the rug is 6 square units.

▶ Reflect

1 Explain how you use square units to find the area of a shape.

_____

_____

_____

_____

Think About ▶ **Area Using Different Square Units**

🔍 **Let's Explore the Idea** You find area by measuring and counting square units.

2 Use an inch ruler to measure the length and width of one square unit in Square A.

The square unit is _____ inch long and _____ inch wide.

So, 1 square unit has an area of _____ square inch.

Square A

3 Count the square units in Square A to find the area.

The area of Square A is _____ square inches.

4 Use a centimeter ruler to measure the length and width of one square unit in Rectangle B.

1 square unit

The square unit is _____ centimeter long and _____ centimeter wide.

So, 1 square unit has an area of

_____ square centimeter.

Rectangle B

5 Count the square units in Rectangle B to find the area.

The area of Rectangle B is

_____ square centimeters.

6 Suppose Square A is divided into smaller-sized square units. Can you also count these square units to describe the area of Square A? _____

1 square unit

7 Does the size of the square unit that is used to cover a shape make a difference in how you find the area? Explain.

_____

_____

Let's Talk About It
Solve the problems below as a group.

8 How is finding the area of the Square *A* in square inches like finding the area of Rectangle *B* in square centimeters? _____

_____

9 If you found the area of Square *A* in square centimeters, do you think the number of square centimeters would be greater or less than the number of square inches you found for its area? Explain. _____

_____

_____

10 Suppose you were measuring the area of a door. Would you need more square feet or more square inches to cover the door? Why? _____

_____

_____

11 Number each square unit in the shapes below. Count the square units to find the area.

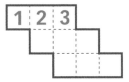

Area = _____ square units   Area = _____ square units

Try It Another Way Work with your group to find the area of each shape.

12

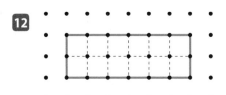

Area = _____ square units

13

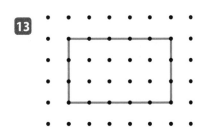

Area = _____ square units

Connect **Ideas About Finding Area**

Talk through these problems as a class, then write your answers below.

14 Compare Find the area of each shape below.

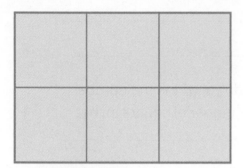

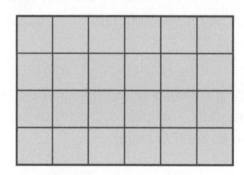

Each [ ] has an area of 1 square unit.

Each [ ] has an area of 1 square centimeter.

Area = _____

Area = _____

15 Examine Anna counted the units in this rectangle. She said the area of the rectangle is 12 square units. What did Anna do wrong?

1	2	3
4	5	6
7	8	9
10	11	12

_____

_____

16 Relate Think about how you could find the area of this shape.

First draw the square units.

Then number the square units to find the area of the shape.

Area = _____ square units

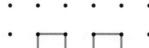
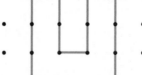

Ideas About Finding Area

17 Put It Together Use what you have learned to complete the task. Use a centimeter ruler.

Part A Draw a rectangle with an area of 8 square centimeters.

Part B Draw another rectangle with an area greater than 8 square centimeters.

Part C How did you know how to draw a rectangle with an area that is greater than 8 square centimeters?

_____

_____

_____

Use What You Know

In Lesson 27, you learned to find the area of a rectangle by counting the number of square units that cover the rectangle. In this lesson you will learn how you can multiply to find the area. Take a look at this problem.

Jenny wants to find the area of the rectangle at the right. But some ink spilled on it. How can she find the area if she cannot count all of the square units?

Area of ▢ = 1 square unit.

a. How many rows are in the rectangle? _____ rows

How many square units are in each row? _____ square units

b. Multiply to find the number of square units that cover the rectangle.

3 rows of 5 square units ⟶ 3 × 5 = _____ square units

c. How many columns are in the rectangle? _____ columns

How many square units are in each column? _____ square units

d. Multiply to find the number of square units that cover the rectangle.

5 columns of 3 square units ⟶ 5 × 3 = _____ square units

e. How many square units long is the rectangle? _____ square units

How many square units wide is the rectangle? _____ square units

f. Explain how you could find the area using the length and the width of the rectangle. _____

_____

You can measure the area of a shape by counting the number of square units that cover it. Sometimes the square units in rectangles are not shown, like in Jenny's rectangle. Other times, there are too many square units to count. There is another way to find the area of a rectangle.

You can multiply the number of rows by the number of columns to find the number of square units in the rectangle. There are 3 rows of square units in the rectangle. There are 5 columns of square units.

3 rows × 5 columns ⟶ 3 × 5 = 15, so there are 15 square units.

5 columns × 3 rows ⟶ 5 × 3 = 15, so there are 15 square units.

Now think about the length and the width of Jenny's rectangle.

- The rectangle is **5 squares long**.
  Each square is 1 unit long.
  So, the length of the rectangle is 5 units.

- The rectangle is **3 squares wide**.
  Each square is 1 unit wide.
  So, the width of the rectangle is 3 units.

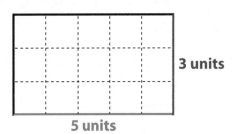

3 units

5 units

You can multiply the length by the width to find the area of the rectangle. It is just like multiplying the number of columns by the number of rows in an array.

5 units × **3 units** = 15 square units

The area of Jenny's rectangle is 15 square units.

▶ Reflect

1 What are some real-life examples of objects that are rectangles and made of square tiles in rows and columns?

_____

_____

_____

Learn About ▸ **Multiplying to Find Area**

Read the problem below. Then explore different ways to multiply to find area.

What is the area of the rectangle?

2 centimeters

4 centimeters

▶ **Picture It** **You can use models to help you multiply to find area.**

The model below shows the rectangle covered by 1-centimeter squares.

Area of ☐ = 1 square centimeter.

▶ **Model It** **You can also use words to help you multiply to find area.**

The length of the rectangle is **4 centimeters**.
Using 1-centimeter squares,
4 squares will fill a row.

The width of the rectangle is **2 centimeters**.
Using 1-centimeter squares,
2 squares will fill a column.

Connect It Now you will solve the problem from the previous page using multiplication.

2 How many 1-centimeter squares fit along the length of the rectangle? _____

What is the length of the rectangle? _____ centimeters

3 How many 1-centimeter squares fit along the width of the rectangle? _____

What is the width of the rectangle? _____ centimeters

4 What does the problem ask you to find? _____

5 The unit of measurement for the length and width of the rectangle is centimeters. What is the unit of measurement for the area? _____

6 Complete the equation below to find the area of the rectangle.

length	×	width	=	area
_____ centimeters	×	_____ centimeters	=	_____ square centimeters

7 The area of the rectangle is _____ square centimeters.

8 Explain how you multiply to find the area of a rectangle. _____

_____

Try It Use what you just learned about multiplying to find area to solve these problems. Show your work on a separate sheet of paper.

9 What is the area of the square?

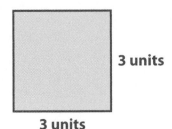

3 units

3 units

_____

10 A rectangle has a length of 8 inches and a width of 6 inches.

What is the area of the rectangle?

_____

Learn About ▶ **Solving Word Problems About Area**

Read the problem below. Then explore different ways to multiply to find area in a word problem.

> Tyler's bedroom is 9 feet wide and 9 feet long. Suki's bedroom is 8 feet wide and 10 feet long. Who has the bedroom with the greater area?

▶ **Picture It** **You can use models to help you multiply to find area.**

The models below show the length and width of Tyler's and Suki's bedrooms.

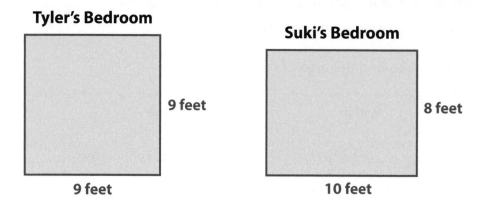

Tyler's Bedroom

9 feet

9 feet

Suki's Bedroom

8 feet

10 feet

▶ **Model It** **You can also use words to help you multiply to find area.**

Use words to describe the measurements of each bedroom.

Tyler's room:

The length of the room is 9 feet.
The width of the room is 9 feet.

Suki's room:

The length of the room is 10 feet.
The width of the room is 8 feet.

► **Connect It** **Now you will solve the problem from the previous page using multiplication.**

11 What does the problem ask you to find? _____

_____

12 What units are used to measure the length and width of the bedrooms? _____

13 What unit should you use to record the area of each bedroom?

_____

14 Complete the equation below to find the area of Tyler's bedroom.

length	×	width	=	area
_____ feet	×	_____ feet	=	_____ square feet

The area of the Tyler's bedroom is _____ square feet.

15 Complete the equation below to find the area of Suki's bedroom.

length	×	width	=	area
_____ feet	×	_____ feet	=	_____ square feet

The area of the Suki's bedroom is _____ square feet.

16 So, _____ has the bedroom with the greater area.

17 Explain how you know that the area of Tyler's bedroom must have the label "square feet." _____

_____

► **Try It** **Use what you just learned about multiplying to find area to solve this problem. Show your work on a separate sheet of paper.**

18 Fran found the area of a rectangle by multiplying 5 units × 4 units. Draw Fran's rectangle. Label the length and width. What is the area of the rectangle?

_____

Practice ▶ **Multiplying to Find Area**

Study the example below. Then solve problems 19–21.

Example

Ms. Cruz is putting a carpet in the living room. The length and width of the room is shown below. How many square feet of carpet does Ms. Cruz need to cover the floor?

Living Room

8 feet

9 feet

Look at how you could show your work using multiplication.

length	×	width	=	area
9 feet	×	8 feet	=	72 square feet

Solution _72 square feet_

The student multiplies the length by the width to find the area.

 Pair/Share
How else could you solve this problem?

---

19 Marcia finds the area of a square. The length of one side of the square is 5 centimeters. What is the area of the square?

Show your work.

The sides of a square are all the same length.

 Pair/Share
How did you and your partner solve this problem?

Solution _____

20 Ms. Clark is building a patio that is 4 yards long and 3 yards wide. She has enough bricks to cover an area of 14 square yards. Does Ms. Clark have enough bricks to build the patio? Explain.

Show your work.

I think there are at least two different steps you need to do to solve this problem.

Solution _____

_____

Pair/Share
How could you use a picture to solve this problem?

---

21 What is the area of the rectangle shown below? Circle the letter of the correct answer.

7 meters

5 meters   **5 meters**

7 meters

To find the area of the rectangle, do you add or multiply?

A   35 square meters

B   24 square meters

C   12 square meters

D   7 square meters

Bobby chose **B** as the correct answer. How did he get that answer?

_____

_____

_____

Pair/Share
Do you need the measure of each side of the rectangle labeled to solve the problem? Why or why not?

Practice ▶ Multiplying to Find Area

Solve the problems.

1 Mr. Frank is putting tile on the bathroom wall. The model shows the length and width of the wall. How many square feet of tile does he need to cover the wall?

A 49 square feet

B 42 square feet

C 26 square feet

D 13 square feet

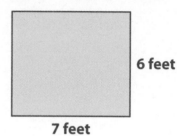

6 feet

7 feet

2 Which shape below has an area of 12 square feet?

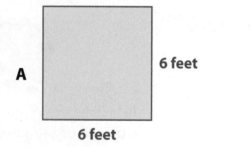

A

6 feet

6 feet

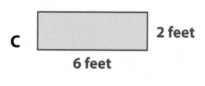

C

2 feet

6 feet

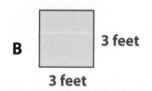

B

3 feet

3 feet

D

2 feet

4 feet

3 The area of a driveway is 24 square yards. What could be the length and width of the driveway? Circle the letter for all that apply.

A Length: 8 yards, Width: 4 yards

B Length: 4 yards, Width: 6 yards

C Length: 3 yards, Width: 6 yards

D Length: 6 yards, Width: 4 yards

E Length: 8 yards, Width: 3 yards

4 Rita is making a quilt. It is made with 45 square blocks of fabric and is 9 blocks long.

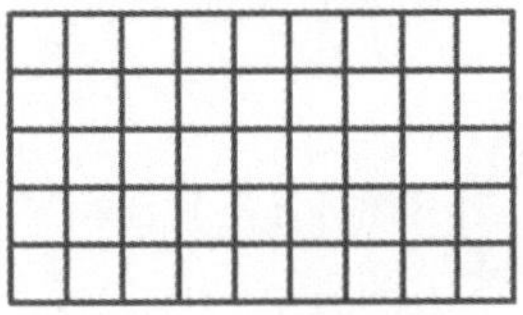

9 blocks long

? blocks wide

Complete the equation below to show how many blocks wide the quilt is. Use numbers from the ones listed below.

| 4 | 5 | 6 | 9 | 45 |

_____ × _____ = _____

5 Kayla draws the rectangle shown below.

2 units

12 units

Part A What is the area of Kayla's rectangle?

Answer _____ square units

Part B James draws a rectangle that has the same area as Kayla's rectangle, but a different length and width. What is a possible length and width for James' rectangle?

Solution _____

_____

✔ Self Check Go back and see what you can check off on the Self Check on page 211.

Use What You Know

In Lesson 28, you learned how to count squares and use multiplication to find the areas of rectangles with whole-number sides. Now look at this problem.

Ana makes a poster that is 3 feet long and 2 feet wide. Raul makes a poster that is 3 feet long and 1 foot wide. They hang the posters on their classroom wall, as shown at the right.

What is the total area of the wall covered by the posters?

a. How many 1-foot squares cover Ana's poster? _____

b. What is the area of Ana's poster? _____

c. Three 1-foot squares cover Raul's poster. What is the area of his poster?

_____

d. Explain how you can find the area of the wall covered by both posters.

_____

_____

_____

_____

▷▷ Find Out More

You can use multiplication to find the area of a rectangle. Sometimes two rectangles can be combined to make a larger shape.

Think about the posters from the problem on the previous page. Both posters are placed on the same wall. You need to find out how much wall is covered by the posters.

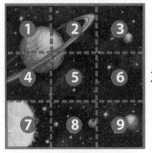

3 feet

3 feet

- One way to find the total area is to think of the two posters as one large poster. Then multiply the side lengths to find the area.

    3 feet × 3 feet = 9 square feet

- Another way is to add the areas of the two posters together.

3 feet

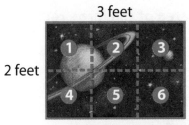

2 feet

3 feet × 2 feet = 6 square feet

1 foot

3 feet

3 feet × 1 foot = 3 square feet

    6 square feet + 3 square feet = 9 square feet

Using either method, 9 square feet of the wall will be covered by the posters.

▷ Reflect

1 Describe how you can find the area of the shape shown.

2 in.

2 in.   1 in.

_____

_____

_____

_____

_____

Learn About ▶ Finding Area of Combined Rectangles

Read the problem below. Then explore different ways to multiply to find area.

Mrs. Chang's vegetable garden is shown at the right. It is shaped like a rectangle. She grows tomatoes in one part. She grows corn in the other part.

What is the area of the garden?

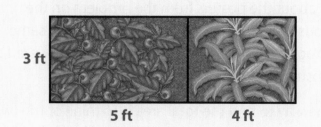

3 ft

5 ft　　　4 ft

▶ **Picture It** **You can find the area of a large rectangle by splitting it into 2 smaller rectangles and using square units to find the area of each small rectangle. Then add the two areas to find the area of the large rectangle.**

Tomatoes　　　Corn

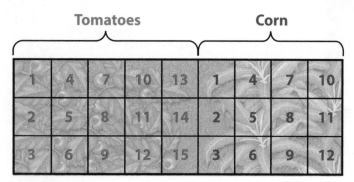

Each square unit has an area of 1 square foot.

15 square units + **12 square units** = 27 square units

▶ **Model It** **You can find the area of a rectangle by multiplying the length by the width.**

The length of the rectangle is **5 feet** + **4 feet**, or **9 feet**.

The width of the rectangle is **3 feet**.

$$9 \times 3 = 27$$

The area is 27 square feet.

3 ft

5 ft　　　4 ft

► **Connect It** **Now you will solve the problem from the previous page using two multiplication facts.**

2 Look at *Model It*. The equation 9 × 3 = 27 is used to find the area. Explain what each factor stands for in the equation.

_____

3 The picture of the garden in *Model It* shows the length broken into two lesser numbers. What are these two numbers? _____

4 You can use these numbers to find the areas of the two parts of the garden.

3 × _____ = _____   3 × _____ = _____

5 You can add the areas of the two garden parts to find the area of the whole garden.

_____ + _____ = 27   The area of the garden is _____ square feet.

6 Explain how you can find the area of a rectangle by adding the areas of the two smaller rectangles it is made from. _____

_____

_____

► **Try It** **Use what you just learned to solve these problems. Show your work on a separate sheet of paper.**

7 What is the area of the figure at the right?

_____

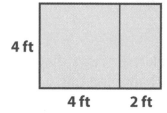

4 ft

4 ft   2 ft

8 How many 1-meter squares will it take to cover the figure at the right?

_____

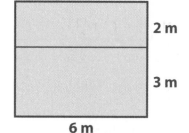

2 m

3 m

6 m

Learn About ▶ Finding Area of Non-Rectangular Shapes

Read the problem below. Then explore different ways to find areas of shapes that are not rectangles.

Elsa used 1-inch-square tiles to build the shape shown at the right.

What is the area of Elsa's shape?

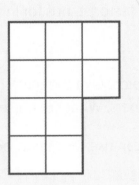

▶ **Picture It** **You can find the area of a shape by counting the number of square units that cover the shape.**

There are 10 square units. Each square unit has an area of 1 square inch.

1	2	3
4	5	6
7	8	
9	10	

▶ **Model It** **You can find the area of a shape by breaking it apart into smaller shapes.**

One Way:

You can break apart Elsa's shape into two smaller shapes like this:

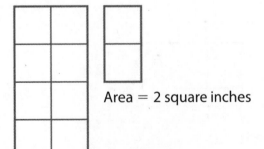

Area = 2 square inches

Area = 8 square inches

Another Way:

You can break apart Elsa's shape into two different smaller shapes like this:

Area = 6 square inches

Area = 4 square inches

Connect It Solve the problem from the previous page using multiplication and addition.

9 *Model It* shows two ways to break apart Elsa's shape. Look at the first way. For each smaller shape, write a multiplication equation to show its area.

_____ × _____ = _____   _____ × _____ = _____

Write an addition equation to show the total area of Elsa's shape.

_____ + _____ = _____

The total area of Elsa's shape is _____ square inches.

10 Look at the second way to break apart Elsa's shape. For each smaller shape, write a multiplication equation to show its area.

_____ × _____ = _____   _____ × _____ = _____

Write an addition equation to show the total area of Elsa's shape.

_____ + _____ = _____

The total area of Elsa's shape is _____ square inches.

How does this total area compare to the total area you found in problem 9?

_____

11 Mike breaks apart a shape into two smaller shapes. Rick breaks the same shape apart into two different shapes. Explain how you know that the total area of Mike's two shapes is the same as the total area of Rick's two shapes. _____

_____

_____

Try It Use what you just learned about adding areas to solve these problems. Show your work on a separate sheet of paper.

12 What is the total area of the shape below?

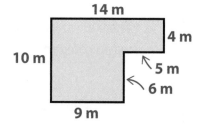

13 What is the area of the shape below?

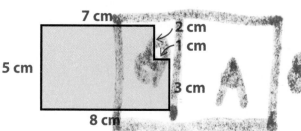

_____

Practice ▶ **Solving Area Problems**

Study the example below. Then solve problems 14–16.

Example

Miguel drew this shape in his notebook.

What is the area of Miguel's shape?

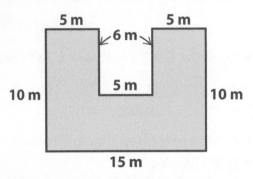

The student broke apart the shape into 3 smaller rectangles and then added the areas of these shapes to find the area of Miguel's shape.

Look at how you could show your work by breaking apart the shape into three rectangles.

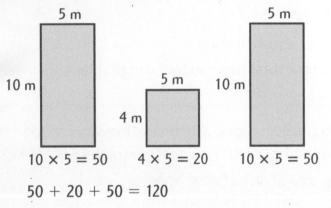

$10 \times 5 = 50$ $4 \times 5 = 20$ $10 \times 5 = 50$

$50 + 20 + 50 = 120$

Solution ___120 square meters_____

Pair/Share
What is another way you can break apart the shape?

---

14 What is the area of the shape below?

$A = 3 \times 3 = 9$ $9 + 6 = 15$
$B = 2 \times 3 = 6$

There are at least two ways I could solve this.

Pair/Share
Compare the way you and your partner solved the problem.

Solution _____

15 Seth used 1-inch-square tiles to build the shape shown below.

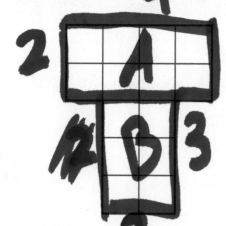

$A = 2 \times 4 = 8$

$B = 3 \times 2 = 6$

$8 + 6 = 14$

How can counting help you solve this problem?

What is the total area of Seth's shape?

Solution _____ $8 + 6 = 14$ _____

Pair/Share
How else could you solve this problem?

---

16 Kale drew a model of a birdhouse.

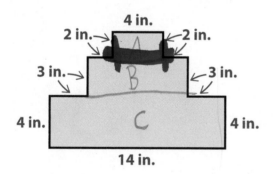

4 in.
2 in. → ← 2 in.
A
3 in. → B ← 3 in.
4 in.   C   4 in.
14 in.

$A = 2 \times 4 = 8$

$B = 3 \times 8 = 24$

$C = 14 \times 4 = 56$

Is area the distance around a shape or the amount of space the shape covers?

$8 + 24 + 56 = 88$

What is the total area of the birdhouse? Circle the letter of the correct answer.

A 46 inches

C 88 inches

B 46 square inches

D 88 square inches

Sue chose **C** as the correct answer. How did she get that answer?

_____

_____

_____

_____

Pair/Share
Does Sue's answer make sense?

Practice ▶ Solving Area Problems

Solve the problems.

1 Mrs. Ambrose drew the model below of her new patio and rock garden.

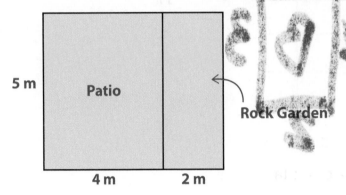

What is the total area of Mrs. Ambrose's new patio and rock garden?

A 22 meters

C 30 meters

B 22 square meters

D 30 square meters

2 At the right are two rectangles that are joined together.

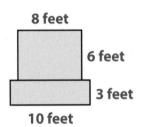

Choose *Yes* or *No* to tell whether joining the rectangle shown to the two rectangles above would make a shape that has an area of 98 square feet.

a.

8 feet
3 feet

☐ Yes ☐ No

b.
10 feet
2 feet

☐ Yes ☐ No

c.
5 feet
4 feet

☐ Yes ☐ No

d.
9 feet
2 feet

☐ Yes ☐ No

3 Find the missing measurements in the shape below. Then break apart the shape into two rectangles to find its area.

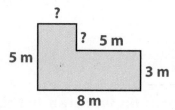

Answer The area is _____ square meters.

4 Opal drew this model of a picnic table.

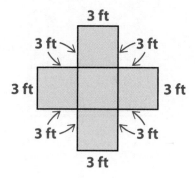

What is the total area of the picnic table?

Show your work.

Answer The total area of the picnic table is _____ square feet.

✔ Self Check   Go back and see what you can check off on the Self Check on page 211.

Connect Area and Perimeter

Use What You Know

In Lessons 27–29, you learned about finding area. In this lesson you will learn how to find the perimeter of shapes. Take a look at this problem.

Claire ran along the edges of the soccer field at school. She ran around the whole field one time. How far did Claire run?

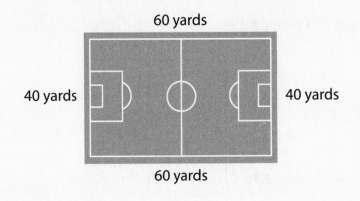

60 yards

40 yards   40 yards

60 yards

a. How many sides does the soccer field have? _____

b. How many long sides are there? _____

How long are the long sides? _____

c. How many short sides are there? _____

How long are the short sides? _____

d. Explain how you could use these numbers to figure out how far Claire ran.

_____

_____

You have already learned about finding the area of shapes. Area tells the amount of space a shape covers. In the soccer field, the shaded part, the white lines, and the black border are all included in the area of the field.

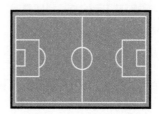

Perimeter is the distance around a shape. The red line around the soccer field shows the perimeter of the field.

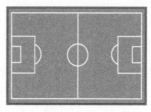

You can find the perimeter of a shape by adding the lengths of all the sides.

60 + 40 + 60 + 40 = 200

The perimeter of the soccer field is 200 yards.

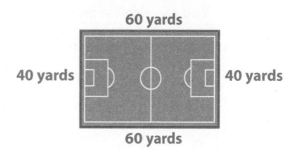

▶ Reflect

1 Richard wants to put a fence around his backyard. Does he need to find the area or the perimeter of his backyard? What measurements does he need to find to figure out how much fence he needs? _____

_____

_____

_____

_____

| Learn About | **Finding the Missing Side Length** |

Read the problem below. Then explore how to find a missing side length when you know the perimeter.

Willis made an L-shaped pen for his pet rabbit.

- The pen has 6 sides.

- The perimeter is 10 meters.

- The lengths of five of the sides are 1 meter, 3 meters, 2 meters, 1 meter, and 1 meter.

What is the length of the sixth side?

▶ **Picture It** **You can draw a model to help understand the problem.**

The L-shaped figure below shows the shape of the rabbit pen. The side lengths you know are labeled.

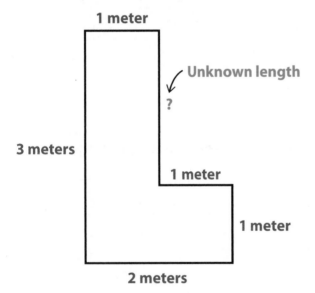

The perimeter of the pen is 10 meters.

©Curriculum Associates, LLC Copying is not permitted.

Connect It   Now you will solve the problem from the previous page using an equation.

2 Explain how you would find the perimeter of the shape if you knew all of the side lengths. _____

_____

3 You know the perimeter is 10 meters. Explain how you could figure out the unknown side length. _____

_____

_____

4 Write an equation to find the missing side length. Use a ? for the number you do not know. _____

5 What is the length of the sixth side? _____

6 Explain how an addition equation can help you find the perimeter of a shape.

_____

_____

Try It   Use what you just learned about perimeter to solve these problems. Show your work on a separate sheet of paper.

7 Jordan has a kite with four sides. Two of the sides are 8 inches long. Two of the sides are 12 inches long. What is the perimeter of the kite? _____

8 The perimeter of the shape at the right is 18 feet. What is the unknown side length?

_____

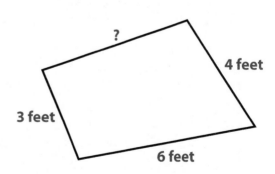

Learn About › Same Area and Different Perimeter

Read the problem below. Then explore different ways to find rectangles with the same area and different perimeters.

Emma drew the rectangle at the right. What other rectangles have the same area, but different perimeters?

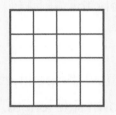

▶ Picture It You can use drawings to help you find rectangles with the same area and different perimeters.

The area of Emma's rectangle is 16 square units. Below are two other rectangles that also have an area of 16 square units.

You can also turn these rectangles on their sides. You would have a rectangle 1 unit wide and 16 units tall and another rectangle 2 units wide and 8 units tall.

▶ Model It You can use a table to help you find rectangles with the same area and different perimeters.

You can make a table showing the measurements of rectangles that have an area of 16 square units. The rectangle Emma drew is circled.

Length	Width	Area	Perimeter
16 units	1 unit	16 square units	34 units
8 units	2 units	16 square units	20 units
4 units	4 units	16 square units	16 units
2 units	8 units	16 square units	20 units
1 unit	16 units	16 square units	34 units

Connect It Now think about how the problem was solved on the previous page.

9 Look at *Picture It*. How can you tell the two rectangles shown have the same area as Emma's rectangle?

_____

_____

10 To find other rectangles with an area of 16 square units, think of multiplication facts with a product of 16. What are the multiplication facts that have a product of 16? _____

Look at the table in *Model It*. Where do you see the factors and products of the multiplication facts you wrote? _____

_____

11 Can two rectangles have the same area but have different perimeters? How do you know? _____

_____

_____

Try It Use what you just learned about area and perimeter to solve these problems. Show your work on a separate sheet of paper.

12 Look at the rectangle below. Draw a rectangle that has the same area but different side lengths.

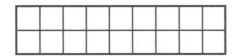

13 Look at the rectangle you drew for problem 12. Is its perimeter the same, greater than, or less than the perimeter of the rectangle shown? _____

Read the problem below. Then explore different ways to find rectangles with the same perimeter and different areas.

Kai drew the rectangle below. What other rectangles have the same perimeter, but different areas?

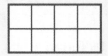

▶ **Picture It** **You can use drawings to help you find rectangles with the same perimeter and different areas.**

The perimeter of Kai's rectangle is 12 units. All of the rectangles below have a perimeter of 12 units.

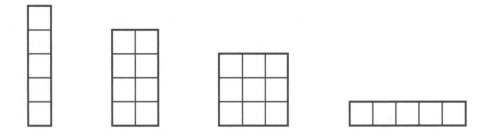

▶ **Model It** **You can use a table to help you find rectangles with the same perimeter and different areas.**

The table below shows the measurements of rectangles that have a perimeter of 12 units. The rectangle Kai drew is circled.

Length	Width	Area	Perimeter
1 unit	5 units	5 square units	12 units
2 units	4 units	8 square units	12 units
3 units	3 units	9 square units	12 units
4 units	2 units	8 square units	12 units
5 units	1 unit	5 square units	12 units

▶ **Connect It** **Now think about how the problem was solved on the previous page.**

14 Look at the table in *Model It*. What do you notice about the sum of the length and the width of each rectangle? _____

How does the sum of the length and width compare to the perimeter?

_____

15 All of the rectangles have the same perimeter as Kai's rectangle. Only one has the same area as Kai's rectangle. What else is the same about that rectangle and Kai's rectangle? _____

_____

_____

16 Can two rectangles have the same perimeter but have different areas? How do you know? _____

_____

_____

▶ **Try It** **Use what you just learned about perimeter and area to solve these problems. Show your work on a separate sheet of paper.**

17 Look at the rectangle below. Draw a rectangle that has the same perimeter but different side lengths.

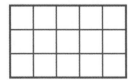

18 Look at the rectangle you drew for problem 17. Is its area the same, greater than, or less than the area of the rectangle shown? _____

Practice ▶ **Solving Problems About Area and Perimeter**

Study the example below. Then solve problems 19–21.

Example

Look at the rectangle below. Draw a rectangle that has the same perimeter but a different area.

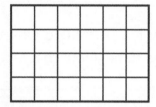

Look at how you could show your work using a drawing.

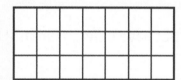

The perimeter of the rectangle is 20 units, and the area is 24 square units. The rectangle the student draws needs to have a perimeter of 20 units, too.

💬 **Pair/Share**
What other rectangles could you draw?

---

19 Jared's dad built a square deck in his backyard. One side of the deck is 10 feet long. What is the perimeter of the deck?

Show your work.

The sides of a square are all the same length. How many sides do you need to add together to find the perimeter?

💬 **Pair/Share**
What equation could you write to find the perimeter?

Solution _____

20 Look at the rectangle below. Draw a rectangle that has the same area but a different perimeter.

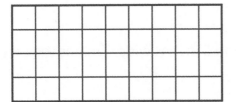

The area is 4 units × 9 units, or 36 square units. What numbers, other than 4 and 9, are factors of 36?

Show your work.

Pair/Share

What other rectangle would have the same area and the same perimeter?

---

21 The perimeter of the shape below is 12 centimeters.

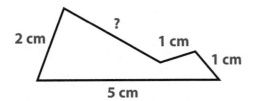

2 cm   ?   1 cm   1 cm   5 cm

What is the unknown side length? Circle the letter of the correct answer.

A   2 cm

B   3 cm

C   4 cm

D   9 cm

Rose chose **D** as the correct answer. How did she get that answer?

You could write an equation with a ? for the missing number to show the perimeter.

_____

_____

_____

_____

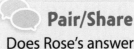

Pair/Share

Does Rose's answer make sense?

Solve the problems.

1 Su drew a rectangle that is 6 inches long and 5 inches wide. What is the perimeter of the rectangle?

A 11 inches

C 22 inches

B 17 inches

D 30 inches

2 Rachel has 20 feet of fencing to put around a rectangular section of her lawn. The fencing must go around the perimeter of the rectangular section with no overlap.

Choose *Yes* or *No* to tell whether Rachel has exactly enough fencing for each rectangular section shown. The area of each ☐ is 1 square foot.

a. ☐ Yes   ☐ No

b. ☐ Yes   ☐ No

c. ☐ Yes   ☐ No

d. ☐ Yes   ☐ No

3 Which of the following is an example of perimeter? Circle the letter for all that apply.

A grass covering a backyard

B the border around a picture

C carpet in a room

D the fence around a park

E the amount of water in a swimming pool

4 Look at the rectangle below. The area of each ☐ is 1 square unit.

Part A Find the perimeter and area of the rectangle.

Perimeter: _____ units   Area: _____ square units

Part B Use the grid to draw a rectangle that has the same perimeter but a different area than the rectangle in Part A. Write the perimeter and area of your new rectangle.

Perimeter: _____ units   Area: _____ square units

Part C Use the grid to draw a rectangle that has the same area but a different perimeter than the rectangle in Part A. Write the perimeter and area of your new rectangle.

Perimeter: _____ units   Area: _____ square units

✔ **Self Check**   **Go back and see what you can check off on the Self Check on page 211.**

Study an Example Problem and Solution

Read this problem involving measurements. Then look at Max's solution to this problem.

Max's Snacks

Max has his laptop and binder in his backpack. He also wants to pack lots of snacks. He can pack snacks with a mass of up to 1,000 grams. That way, the backpack isn't too heavy.

Snack Choices

orange – 95 g

bag of cookies – 424 g

granola bar – 22 g

banana – 124 g

giant sandwich – 365 g

box of crackers – 338 g

apple – 142 g

bag of almonds – 42 g

peanut butter – 345 g

Choose snack items Max can pack. You may use an item more than once. Give the total mass of the snacks. Show that your solution works.

Read the sample solution on the next page. Then look at the checklist below. Find and mark parts of the solution that match the checklist.

✏️ Problem-Solving Checklist

- ☐ Tell what is known.
- ☐ Tell what the problem is asking.
- ☐ Show all your work.
- ☐ Show that the solution works.

- **a. Circle** something that is known.
- **b. Underline** something that you need to find.
- **c. Draw a box around** what you do to solve the problem.
- **d. Put a checkmark** next to the part that shows the solution works.

Max's Solution

▷ **I know the mass of each snack.**
I will pick my favorite snacks and add the masses.

▷ **I really want my giant**
sandwich and an apple.

$$\begin{array}{r} 365 \\ +\ 142 \\ \hline 7 \\ 100 \\ +\ 400 \\ \hline 507 \end{array}$$ sandwich
apple

I can still add about 500 more
grams of food.

507 is about 500
and 500 + 500 is
1,000.

▷ **I love peanut butter**
and bananas.

$$\begin{array}{r} 345 \\ +\ 124 \\ \hline 469 \end{array}$$ peanut butter
banana

▷ **I can add to see what the**
total is for all 4 items.

$$\begin{array}{r} 507 \\ +\ 469 \\ \hline 16 \\ 60 \\ +\ 900 \\ \hline 976 \end{array}$$

▷ **Add up to see how much is left.**
976 + 4 is 980 and 20 more is 1,000.
So I have 24 grams left.

▷ **It looks like I still have**
room for a granola bar.

$$\begin{array}{r} 976 \\ +\ 22 \\ \hline 998 \end{array}$$ granola bar

I like that
I got so close to
1,000 grams.

▷ **The total is 2 grams less than 1,000.** I can't pack anything else.
I'll pack a sandwich, an apple, a banana, peanut butter, and a
granola bar.

Try Another Approach

There are many ways to solve problems. Think about how you might solve Max's Snacks problem in a different way.

Max's Snacks

Max has his laptop and binder in his backpack. He also wants to pack lots of snacks. He can pack snacks with a mass of up to 1,000 grams. That way, the backpack isn't too heavy.

Snack Choices

orange – 95 g

box of crackers – 338 g

bag of cookies – 424 g

apple – 142 g

granola bar – 22 g

bag of almonds – 42 g

banana – 124 g

peanut butter – 345 g

giant sandwich – 365 g

Choose snack items Max can pack. You may use an item more than once. Give the total mass of the snacks. Show that your solution works.

▶ Plan It Answer these questions to help you start thinking about a plan.

A. Could you solve the problem by starting with 1,000 grams? Explain.

_____

_____

B. Do you want lots of lighter snacks or a few heavier snacks?

_____

_____

Solve It Find a different solution for Max's Snacks problem. Show all your work on a separate sheet of paper.

You may want to use the problem-solving tips to get started.

Problem-Solving Tips

- **Models**

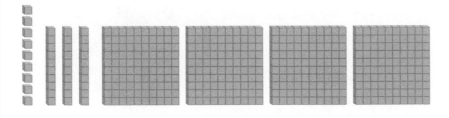

- **Word Bank**

add	sum	mass
subtract	difference	grams

- **Sentence Starters**
  - I can start with _____
  - I want to pack _____

Problem-Solving Checklist
Make sure that you . . .
- ☐ tell what you know.
- ☐ tell what you need to do.
- ☐ show all your work.
- ☐ show that the solution works.

Reflect
Use Mathematical Practices Choose one of these questions to discuss with a partner.

- **Reason Mathematically** What strategies can you use to add or subtract?

- **Persevere** What are some different ways that you could start your solution?

Discuss ▶ Models and Strategies

**Read the problem. Write a solution on a separate sheet of paper.
Remember, there can be lots of ways to solve a problem!**

Max's Snack Mix

Max is making his favorite snack mix. He will share it with friends. He doesn't remember the exact amount of each ingredient. He writes down what he does remember.

Recipe
Nut and Honey Snack Mix

Ingredients
- Honey and Oat cereal
- peanuts
- raisins
- peanut butter
- butter

Snack Mix Notes

- The ingredients are all measured in grams.
- The ingredient with the greatest mass is peanuts.
- Use less than 50 grams of cereal.
- Use less than 100 grams of peanut butter.
- The amount of peanut butter is about double the amount of butter.
- The total mass of all ingredients is about 500 grams.

How much of each ingredient should Max use in his snack mix?

Plan It and Solve It   Find a solution for Max's Snack Mix problem.

Write a recipe for Max's Snack Mix. Be sure to include:

- the amount of each ingredient to use and how you decided each amount.
- the total mass of the snack mix Max will make.

You may want to use the problem-solving tips to get started.

Problem-Solving Tips

- ### Questions
  - How could you use estimation in your solution?
  - What numbers could you use that are easy to work with?

- ### Sentence Starters
  - I can start with _____
  - The mass of the peanuts _____

Problem-Solving Checklist
Make sure that you . . .
- ☐ tell what you know.
- ☐ tell what you need to do.
- ☐ show all your work.
- ☐ show that the solution works.

Reflect

Use Mathematical Practices   Choose one of these questions to discuss with a partner.

- **Make Sense of Problems**   How is this like other problems you have solved in this lesson? How is it different?

- **Make an Argument**   How can you be sure that your solution works with all the information Max wrote down?

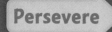
Read the problem. Write a solution on a separate sheet of paper.
Remember, there are many different ways to solve a problem!

Soup Snacks

Max plans to make tomato soup. His recipe makes 24 liters of soup.
He will freeze the soup in containers. Then he'll have plenty of
soup snacks ready to go.

Max wants to buy some 1-liter containers for the soup. He can buy
different packages of 1-liter containers.

- package of 4 containers
- package of 5 containers
- package of 6 containers

What packages should Max buy?

▶ **Solve It** **Tell Max what packages to buy.**

- Tell how many containers Max needs.
- Tell which packages Max should buy.
- Tell how many of each package he should buy.
- Show why your solution gives the exact number of containers Max needs.

▶ **Reflect**

Use Mathematical Practices Choose one of these questions
to discuss with a partner

- **Reason Mathematically** How can you tell by looking at the numbers
  if a package will work or not?

- **Use Models** How did you use basic facts to find a solution?

Rectangular Snack Trays

At the community center Max meets an artist who weaves trays. Max asks the artist to make two snack trays for him. Max's ideas are shown below.

My Ideas

· Each tray is shaped like a rectangle.

· Both trays have the same area.

· The perimeter of each tray is different.

· The area of each tray is less than 100 square inches.

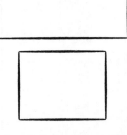

What size trays can Max ask the artist to make?

▶ **Solve It** **Help Max decide what size trays to ask for.**

• Choose an area that is less than 100 square inches.

• Show two different ways to make this area.

• Find the perimeter of each rectangle and show that they are different.

▶ **Reflect**

Use Mathematical Practices Choose one of these questions to discuss with a partner.

• **Persevere** How did you choose the number you used for the area?

• **Be Precise** How did you check that your solution was correct?

Solve the problems.

1 The bar graph shows the number of people who ate lunch at Bob's Diner each day for three days.

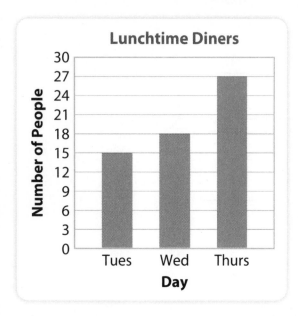

How many more people ate lunch at Bob's Diner on Thursday than on Tuesday?

A 12 people   **C** 27 people

B 15 people   **D** 30 people

2 Which of the following would you measure in kilograms? Circle the letter for all that apply.

A a person's mass

B the height of a tree

C the time it takes to drive to school

D the area of a garden

E the perimeter of a picture

3 Use the diagram below. Which statement is true? Circle the letter for all that apply.

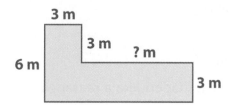

A If ? is 8, the perimeter is 23 meters.

B If ? is 9, the perimeter is 36 meters.

C If ? is 8, the area is 42 square meters.

D If ? is 9, the area is 45 square meters.

E If ? is 10, the area is 39 square meters.

4 Angelica left home at 7:48. It took her 27 minutes to get to school. Draw hour and minute hands on the clock below to show what time she arrived at school.

5 Mark has 15 red balloons, 12 green balloons, 9 blue balloons, and 18 yellow balloons.

Part A Suppose you are going to draw a picture graph of the data for balloon colors. Why might you want each picture to stand for more than 1 balloon?

_____

_____

Part B Draw a picture graph to show Mark's data of balloon colors.

6 The lengths of ten strings are shown in the table.

| Length (in.) | 4 | $4\frac{1}{4}$ | $4\frac{1}{4}$ | $4\frac{3}{4}$ | $4\frac{1}{2}$ | $4\frac{1}{4}$ | $4\frac{1}{4}$ | $4\frac{1}{2}$ | $4\frac{3}{4}$ | 5 |

Part A Draw a line plot to show the lengths of the strings.

Part B What is the length of the greatest number of strings?

Answer _____ inches

Performance Task

Answer the questions and show all your work on separate paper.

Dan is planning to build a square porch attached to the side of his house. After the porch is built, he would like to cover it with 1-foot square tiles. The diagram below shows the measurements of the porch and the lawn where he plans to build. How many tiles will he need to cover the porch?

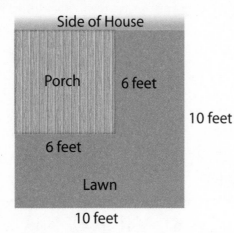

After Dan bought all of the tiles he needed, he changed his mind about the size of the porch. How could he change the length and width of the porch, but still use the same number of tiles? Explain how you found your answer. Then draw a new model for Dan's porch showing the new length and width.

Reflect

Use Mathematical Practices After you complete the task, choose one of the following questions to answer.

• **Persevere** Is this problem mainly about area or perimeter? Explain how you know.

• **Argue and Critique** How did you justify the measurements you chose?

Unit 6
Geometry

Let's learn about describing and comparing shapes.

Real-World Connection Have you ever tried to describe the shape of something when you are talking to a friend? You might say, "It's sort of like a square." This doesn't give your friend many details about the shape. Does this mean that the shape has four sides? Are all of the sides the same length? You might have said, "The shape has four sides and they are all the same length." This still describes more than one kind of shape.

In This Unit You will learn to recognize many four-sided shapes and describe how they are alike and how they are different. You will also use what you know about area and fractions to divide shapes into equal parts.

✔ Self Check

Before starting this unit, check off the skills you know below. As you complete each lesson, see how many more you can check off!

I can:	Before this unit	After this unit
describe shapes, compare them, and put them in groups that tell how they are alike, for example: by the number of sides or by whether they have square corners.	☐	☐
compare quadrilaterals and put them in groups based on their attributes, for example: all four sides are the same length or there are 2 pairs of parallel sides.	☐	☐
divide rectangles into equal parts and name the parts using fractions.	☐	☐

Understand Properties of Shapes

💭 Think It Through

How do sides and angles help you to name shapes?

You can count the sides. The shape at the right has 3 sides.

You can count the angles. This shape has 3 angles.

A shape with 3 sides and 3 angles is a triangle.

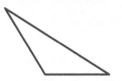

Think   What are other ways to describe the sides of shapes?

- Some shapes have *sides with all different lengths*.

> ✏️ **Measure** the sides of this shape. Use a centimeter ruler. Write the side lengths on the shape.

- Some shapes have *two or more sides that are the same length*.

  Sides *A* and *B* of the triangle at the right are the same length. Side *C* is a different length than sides *A* and *B*.

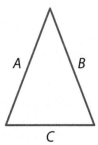

- Shapes can have *all sides the same length*.

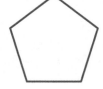

- Shapes can have *opposite sides that are the same length*.

  Sides *A* and *C* of the rectangle at the right are the same length. Sides *B* and *D* are the same length.

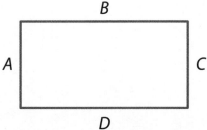

Think What are other ways to describe the angles of shapes?

Angles that look like the corners of a square can be called square corners.

- Shapes can have *all* square corners.

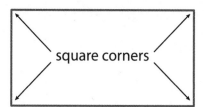

square corners

Shapes that are not squares can have square corners, too.

- Shapes can have *some* square corners.

This triangle has 1 square corner.

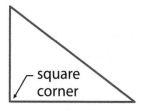

square corner

A **pentagon** is a shape with 5 sides and 5 angles. This pentagon has 2 square corners.

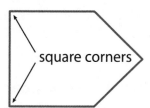

square corners

- Shapes can have *no* square corners.

Reflect

1 What are some ways you can describe shapes?

_____

_____

_____

_____

Think About **Comparing Shapes**

🔍 **Let's Explore the Idea** You can compare shapes and put them in groups. The groups tell how the shapes are alike. Use the two red shapes to answer problems 2–5.

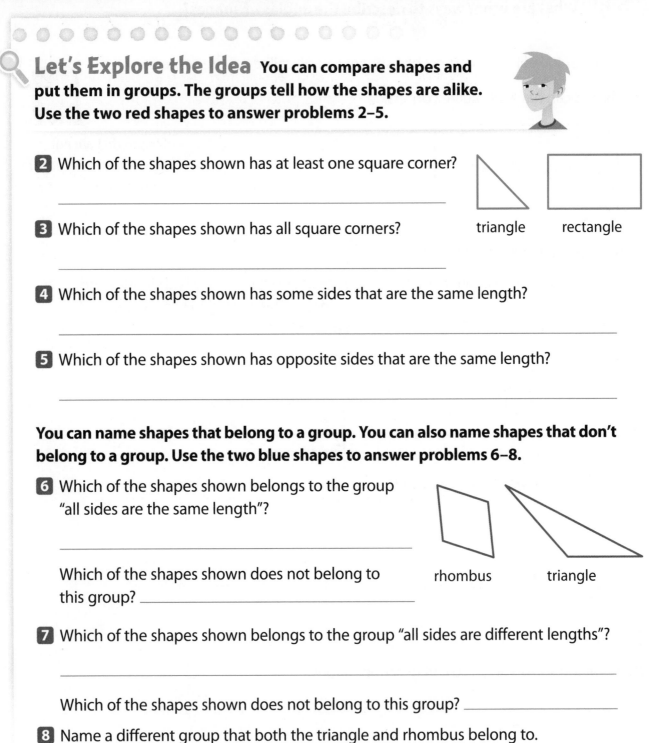

2 Which of the shapes shown has at least one square corner?

_____

3 Which of the shapes shown has all square corners?

_____

4 Which of the shapes shown has some sides that are the same length?

_____

5 Which of the shapes shown has opposite sides that are the same length?

_____

triangle   rectangle

You can name shapes that belong to a group. You can also name shapes that don't belong to a group. Use the two blue shapes to answer problems 6–8.

6 Which of the shapes shown belongs to the group "all sides are the same length"?

_____

Which of the shapes shown does not belong to this group? _____

rhombus   triangle

7 Which of the shapes shown belongs to the group "all sides are different lengths"?

_____

Which of the shapes shown does not belong to this group? _____

8 Name a different group that both the triangle and rhombus belong to.

_____

Solve the problems below as a group.

9 Look at the two triangles shown on the previous page. Draw one triangle in each box below. Describe the sides and angles of each triangle in as many ways as you can.

_____   _____

_____   _____

_____   _____

10 Describe two groups that both triangles belong to.

_____

Try It Another Way   Work with your group to fill in a Venn diagram.

11 A **Venn diagram** helps you to sort things into groups. Shapes that belong in different groups go in the left or right part of the Venn diagram. Shapes that belong in both groups go in the middle part. Draw a shape to match each description.

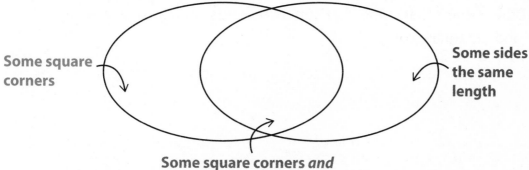

Some square corners

Some sides the same length

Some square corners _and_ some sides the same length

Connect ▶ **Ideas About Comparing Shapes**

Talk through these problems as a class, then write your answers below.

12 Compare Think about how the shapes below are alike and different. You can use a ruler to measure the sides.

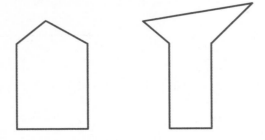

Write two ways in which these shapes are alike.

_____

_____

Write two ways in which these shapes are different.

_____

_____

13 Explain Gwen says that all rectangles belong in the group "some square corners." Li says that all rectangles belong in the group "all square corners." Who is correct? Explain.

_____

_____

14 Illustrate Draw a shape that belongs to both of these groups: "all sides are the same length" and "no square corners."

Apply Ideas About Comparing Shapes

15 Put It Together Use what you have learned to complete this task.

Part A Think about the ways you grouped shapes in this lesson. Think of two different ways you can put shapes into groups. Describe each group on the lines below.

Group 1: _____

Group 2: _____

Draw one shape that belongs to Group 1. Draw another shape that does not belong to Group 1.

Belongs: | **Does not belong:**

Explain why each shape does or does not belong to the group.

_____

_____

Draw one shape that belongs to Group 2. Draw another shape that does not belong to Group 2.

Belongs: | **Does not belong:**

Explain why each shape does or does not belong to the group.

_____

_____

Part B Is there a shape that belongs to both Group 1 and Group 2? Either draw a shape that belongs to both groups, or explain why there is no shape that belongs to both groups.

Classify Quadrilaterals

Use What You Know

In Lesson 31, you compared shapes and put them into groups. In this lesson, you will learn how to group quadrilaterals. Take a look at this problem.

A rhombus is one kind of quadrilateral. A rectangle is another kind of quadrilateral. How are a rhombus and a rectangle the same? How are they different?

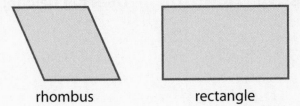

rhombus   rectangle

a. Which of the two shapes has 4 sides and 4 angles?

_____

b. Which of the two shapes has 2 pairs of sides that are the same length?

_____

c. Which of the two shapes has 4 sides that are the same length?

_____

d. Which of the two shapes has 4 square corners? _____

e. How are the rhombus and the rectangle shown above alike? How are they different?

_____

_____

_____

_____

A **quadrilateral** is any shape with 4 sides and 4 angles.

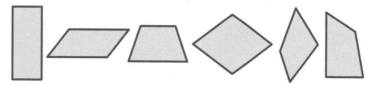

You can name quadrilaterals using their attributes. An **attribute** is a way to describe a shape, like number of sides, or length of sides. One attribute is "4 sides." Another attribute is "at least 1 square corner."

- A quadrilateral is a **parallelogram** if it has 2 pairs of parallel sides and 2 pairs of sides that are the same length. Sides are **parallel** if they are always the same distance apart.

  These are parallelograms: These are not parallelograms:

  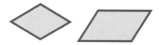 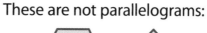

- A quadrilateral is a **rectangle** if it has 4 square corners. A rectangle also has 2 pairs of parallel sides and 2 pairs of sides that are the same length.

  These are rectangles: These are not rectangles:

- A quadrilateral is a **rhombus** if it has 2 pairs of parallel sides and 4 sides that are all the same length.

  These are rhombuses: These are not rhombuses:

    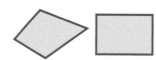

▶ Reflect

1 A square is a quadrilateral. Explain what a square is by writing about its sides and its corners.

_____

_____

Learn About ▶ ## Comparing Quadrilaterals

Read the problem below. Then explore different ways to compare quadrilaterals.

> Is a square a rectangle?
>
> Is a rectangle a square?

▶ **Picture It** **You can use a drawing to compare quadrilaterals.**

All quadrilaterals have 4 sides and 4 angles.

4 square corners
2 pairs of parallel sides
4 sides the same length

4 square corners
2 pairs of parallel sides
2 pairs of sides the same length

▶ **Model It** **You can use a table to compare quadrilaterals.**

Shape	4 sides 4 angles	4 square corners	2 pairs of parallel sides	2 pairs of sides that are the same length	4 sides that are the same length
Square	✓	✓	✓	✓	✓
Rectangle	✓	✓	✓	✓	sometimes

Connect It Now you will solve the problem from the previous page by comparing attributes.

2 What is an attribute of a square that is NOT an attribute of every rectangle?

_____

3 Does every rectangle have all the attributes of a square? _____

4 Does every square have all the attributes of a rectangle? _____

5 Is every square a rectangle? Explain why or why not.

_____

_____

6 Is every rectangle a square? Explain why or why not.

_____

_____

Try It Use what you just learned about comparing quadrilaterals to solve these problems. Show your work on a separate sheet of paper.

7 Circle all the quadrilaterals below that are squares.

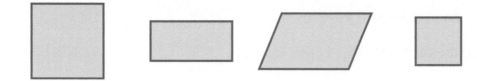

8 Circle all the quadrilaterals below that are rectangles.

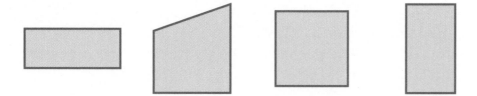

Learn About ▶ Naming and Drawing Quadrilaterals

Read the problem below. Then explore different ways to name and draw quadrilaterals.

> I have a quadrilateral. It has 4 sides that are all the same length. It does not have any square corners. What is the name of my shape?

▶ **Model It** **You can make a model to help name a quadrilateral.**

Cut 4 strips of paper all the same length. Arrange them to look like a quadrilateral. Make sure there are no square corners.

It does not have any square corners, so it is not a square.

▶ **Solve It** **You can make a list of the attributes to help you name a quadrilateral.**

Look at the model above. Think about everything you know about this shape.

- It is a quadrilateral, so it has 4 sides and 4 angles.

- It has 4 sides that are all the same length.

- It does not have any square corners, so it is not a square.

Using this list of attributes, you know that the shape is a rhombus.

Connect It Now you will solve a problem like the one on the previous page. Name the shape shown below.

9 Write the number of sides and angles the shape has. _____ sides _____ angles

10 Does the shape have parallel sides? _____

11 Does the shape have square corners? _____

12 Does the shape have 2 pairs of sides the same length? _____

13 Is the shape a quadrilateral? Explain why or why not.

_____

_____

14 Is the shape a parallelogram? Is it a rectangle? Is it a square? Explain.

_____

_____

_____

_____

Try It Use what you just learned about naming quadrilaterals to solve these problems. Show your work on a separate sheet of paper.

15 Circle all the quadrilaterals below that have 2 pairs of sides the same length, but are NOT rectangles.

16 Draw a quadrilateral that has at least 1 square corner, but is NOT a rectangle.

Practice ▶ **Classifying Quadrilaterals**

Study the example below. Then solve problems 17–19.

Example

A patio has 2 pairs of parallel sides and 2 pairs of sides that are the same length. There are 4 square corners. What shape is the patio?

Look at how you could show your work using a model.

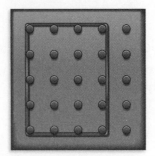

Solution ___The patio is a rectangle._____

> The student used a geoboard to model the shape. Now you can see what the shape looks like.

💬 **Pair/Share**
How else could you model the shape?

---

17 Draw a quadrilateral that has no sides the same length, no parallel sides, and no square corners.

Show your work.

> The shape you draw will not be a rectangle or a square. It will not be a parallelogram or a rhombus.

💬 **Pair/Share**
What is a different shape you can draw to solve the problem?

18 Friona cut along the dashed line shown on the shape below. She knows that she made two quadrilaterals.

It may help to list the attributes of a parallelogram.

Is either of Friona's quadrilaterals a parallelogram? Explain why or why not.

Solution _____

_____

Pair/Share
List the attributes of each of Friona's quadrilaterals.

19 Which shape is NOT a rectangle? Circle the letter of the correct answer.

A

C

What are the attributes of each shape?

B

D

Ari chose **A** as the correct answer. How did he get that answer?

_____

_____

_____

Pair/Share
What are four ways to name the shape Ari chose?

Lesson 32 Classify Quadrilaterals   **343**

Practice ⟩ **Classifying Quadrilaterals**

Solve the problems.

1 A rhombus must have all of these attributes except which one?

A 4 sides that are the same length

B 2 pairs of parallel sides

C 4 square corners

D 4 sides and 4 angles

2 Which of these shape names can NOT be used to name the shape below?

A quadrilateral

C rhombus

B parallelogram

D rectangle

3 Tell whether each sentence is *True* or *False*.

a. All rhombuses are quadrilaterals.   ☐ True   ☐ False

b. All rectangles are squares.   ☐ True   ☐ False

c. All parallelograms are rectangles.   ☐ True   ☐ False

d. All quadrilaterals are parallelograms.   ☐ True   ☐ False

e. All squares are rhombuses.   ☐ True   ☐ False

©Curriculum Associates, LLC   Copying is not permitted.

4 What is the BEST name that describes all the shapes below? _____

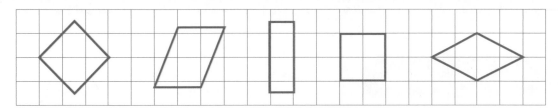

5 Use the grid below. Draw a quadrilateral that belongs to at least two of these groups: parallelogram, rectangle, or square. Explain why your shape belongs to these groups.

Show your work.

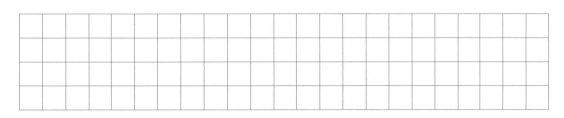

Solution _____

_____

_____

6 Use the grid below. Draw a quadrilateral that does not belong to any of these groups: parallelogram, rectangle, or square. Explain why your shape does not belong to any of these groups.

Show your work.

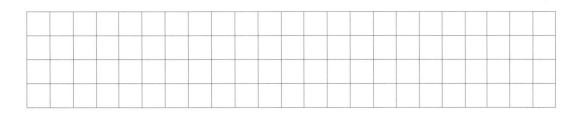

Solution _____

_____

_____

✔ **Self Check** **Go back and see what you can check off on the Self Check on page 329.**

Divide Shapes into Parts with Equal Areas

Ⓖ Use What You Know

You have learned about equal parts of shapes and finding area. In this lesson you will learn how to form and break apart rectangles into squares of equal area.

Students at Memorial School painted square tiles. The tiles were put together to make designs on the office walls. Each design is a rectangle made from 12 tiles. What are some different rectangles that can be made using the 12 tiles?

a. What if you put the tiles in rows that each have 3 tiles? How many rows could you make with 12 tiles? _____ Draw squares in this rectangle to show what this looks like.

b. Imagine you turned the rectangle on its side. Now how many rows does the rectangle have? _____ How many tiles are in each row? _____ Draw squares in this rectangle to show what this looks like.

c. There are other ways to make rectangles with 12 squares. Explain how you would find the other ways. On a separate piece of paper, make drawings to show what the rectangles look like.

_____

_____

_____

_____

On the previous page you formed different rectangles using the same-sized squares. You can also break apart a rectangle to show parts that are all the same size. Each rectangle below is broken into equal parts. Each part is a fraction of the whole area.

The shaded parts of each rectangle below cover $\frac{1}{4}$ of the whole area of the rectangle.

The first two rectangles show 1 out of 4 equal parts shaded. The other two rectangles show 2 out of 8 equal parts shaded.

All shaded areas are equal in size even though the shapes of the parts and the number of parts are different.

If there is more than 1 part shaded, the shaded parts do not need to be next to each other. Each rectangle at the right also shows $\frac{1}{4}$ shaded.

Reflect

1 If you divide a rectangle into 6 same-sized squares, are the areas of the squares equal? What do you know about the area of each square compared to the area of the whole rectangle?

_____

_____

 **Learn About** Dividing Rectangles into Equal Parts

Read the problem. Then explore one way to divide a rectangle.

Brett's art teacher asks him to fold a sheet of paper 4 times and then color $\frac{1}{4}$ of the paper red. His folds are shown below. How could Brett color his paper?

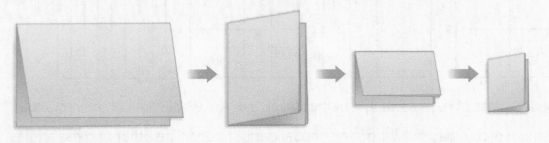

▶ **Model It** You can act out the problem and make a model.

Fold a piece of paper in half 4 times. This is what the paper looks like when you unfold it.

▶ **Solve It** You can use the model to solve the problem.

Count the rows. Count the parts in each row.

There are 4 rows of 4 parts.

Use multiplication to check that there are 16 parts in all.

$4 \times 4 = 16$

Connect It Now you will solve the problem from the previous page.

2 How many rows are on Brett's paper? _____

3 Brett colors 1 row of his paper. What fraction of the whole paper is 1 row? Explain.

_____

_____

4 Did Bret color $\frac{1}{4}$ of the paper? _____

5 How else could Brett have colored $\frac{1}{4}$ of the paper?

_____

_____

6 To color $\frac{1}{4}$ of the paper red, does Brett have to color 4 parts that are next to each other? Explain.

_____

_____

_____

Try It Use what you just learned about dividing rectangles to solve these problems. Show your work on a separate sheet of paper.

7 Divide this rectangle into 8 equal parts. What fraction of the whole rectangle is each part? _____

8 Draw the rectangle from problem 7. Show a different way to divide it into 8 equal parts. What fraction of the whole rectangle is each part?

_____

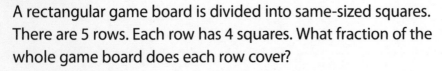

Practice **Dividing Shapes into Equal Parts**

Study the example below. Then solve problems 9–11.

Example

A rectangular game board is divided into same-sized squares. There are 5 rows. Each row has 4 squares. What fraction of the whole game board does each row cover?

Look at how you could show your work using a model.

1 row out of 5 rows is $\frac{1}{5}$.

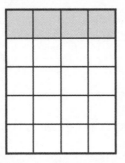

Solution Each row covers $\frac{1}{5}$ of the whole game board.

The student used a grid to make a model of the game board.

Pair/Share
How could you solve the problem without using a model?

---

9 Kevin has a rectangular garden. He wants to divide it into 12 equal sections. Show one way to do this. How many rows are there? How many sections are in each row?

Show your work.

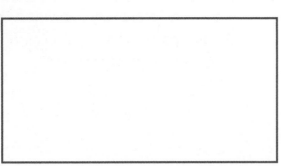

Solution _____

Can you use multiplication or division facts to help?

Pair/Share
What is a different way to divide the garden into 12 equal sections?

10 Shade $\frac{1}{3}$ of the rectangle below. How many same-sized squares cover $\frac{1}{3}$ of the rectangle?

Show your work.

Remember that $\frac{1}{3}$ means 1 out of 3 equal parts.

Answer _____ squares

Pair/Share
What fraction of the whole rectangle is 1 row?

---

11 A rectangle is divided into 2 rows. Each row is divided into 6 same-sized squares. What fraction of the whole rectangle is each square? Circle the letter of the correct answer.

A $\frac{1}{2}$

B $\frac{1}{3}$

C $\frac{1}{6}$

D $\frac{1}{12}$

Ben chose **A** as the correct answer. How did he get that answer?

How many squares are in the whole rectangle?

_____

_____

_____

_____

Pair/Share
What do you think Ben was thinking when he got this answer?

Lesson 33 Divide Shapes into Parts with Equal Areas   **351**

Practice ▶ **Dividing Shapes into Equal Parts**

Solve the problems.

1 A rectangle is divided into 15 same-sized squares. How many squares cover $\frac{1}{3}$ of the rectangle?

A 3 squares

C 6 squares

B 5 squares

D 10 squares

2 A rectangle is divided into same-sized squares. One row covers $\frac{1}{8}$ of the whole rectangle. There are 3 squares in each row. How many squares are in the whole rectangle?

A 8 squares

C 24 squares

B 18 squares

D 32 squares

3 A teacher plans to divide a rectangular bulletin board into equal parts. The teacher wants to make 1 part for each of 36 students. Choose *Yes* or *No* to tell whether the plan will make 1 part for each student.

a. Make 4 rows of 9 parts. ☐ Yes ☐ No

b. Make 6 rows of 6 parts. ☐ Yes ☐ No

c. Make 8 rows of 4 parts. ☐ Yes ☐ No

d. Make 3 rows of 12 parts. ☐ Yes ☐ No

e. Make 7 rows of 5 parts. ☐ Yes ☐ No

4 Shade $\frac{6}{8}$ of the rectangle below.

5 Mark is tiling a square floor. The model below shows how much of the floor he has covered. How many tiles are needed to cover the whole floor?

Show your work. Use a ruler.

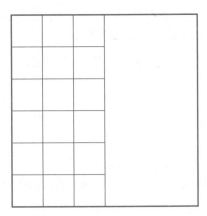

Answer _____ tiles

6 The rectangles below are all the same size. Dani wants to shade $\frac{1}{3}$ of each rectangle. Use the 3 rectangles below to show 3 different ways to shade $\frac{1}{3}$.

      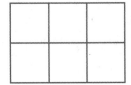

How many squares do you need to shade to cover $\frac{1}{3}$ of one of the rectangles?

Answer _____ squares

✓ **Self Check** **Go back and see what you can check off on the Self Check on page 329.**

Study an Example Problem and Solution

Read this problem about shapes. Then look at Bella's solution to this problem.

Paper Shapes

Bella recycles colored paper and wrapping paper. She cuts the paper into different shapes. She saves the shapes for crafts. Sometimes she looks for pieces with certain kinds of sides. Sometimes she looks for shapes with certain kinds of angles. Bella needs to sort the shapes shown below.

Show a way to sort all of the shapes. You can group shapes by their sides or by their angles. Make at least two groups. Be sure every shape belongs to at least one group. Put each shape into every group it fits in.

Read the sample solution on the next page. Then look at the checklist below. Find and mark parts of the solution that match the checklist.

✏️ **Problem-Solving Checklist**

☐ Tell what is known.

☐ Tell what the problem is asking.

☐ Show all your work.

☐ Show that the solution works.

a. **Circle** something that is known.

b. **Underline** something that you need to find.

c. **Draw a box around** what you do to solve the problem.

d. **Put a checkmark** next to the part that shows the solution works.

Bella's Solution

▷ **I see some shapes with . . .**

· 3 sides and 4 sides and 5 sides and 6 sides.

· sides that are the same length.

· sides that are all different.

▷ **I also see shapes with . . .**

· 3 angles and 4 angles and 5 angles and 6 angles.

· square corners.

· no square corners.

First I looked at what kinds of shapes there are.

▷ **I will sort the shapes into two groups.**

I will make one group of shapes that have some sides the same length.

I will make one group of shapes with no square corners.

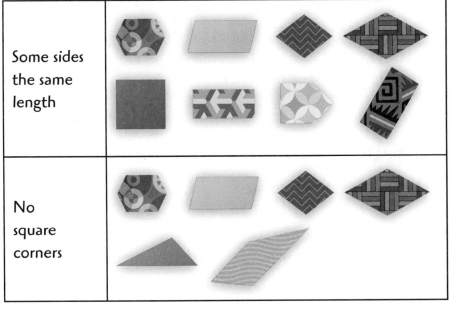

Some sides the same length	
No square corners	

A table is a good way to show groups.

8 shapes are in one group.

6 shapes are in the other group.

4 shapes are in both groups.

All of the shapes are used at least once.

Try ▶ Another Approach

Some problems have more than one answer. Think about how to find a different answer for the Paper Shapes problem.

Paper Shapes

Bella recycles colored paper and wrapping paper. She cuts the paper into different shapes. She saves the shapes for crafts. Sometimes she looks for pieces with certain kinds of sides. Sometimes she looks for shapes with certain kinds of angles. Bella needs to sort the shapes shown below.

Show a way to sort all of the shapes. You can group shapes by their sides or by their angles. Make at least two groups. Be sure every shape belongs to at least one group. Put each shape into every group it fits in.

▶ **Plan It** **Answer these questions to help you start thinking about a plan.**

A. What are some of the different groups you could use?

_____

_____

B. How could a shape be in two groups?

_____

_____

Solve It Find a different solution for the Paper Shapes problem. Show all your work on a separate sheet of paper.

You may want to use the problem-solving tips to get started.

Reflect

Use Mathematical Practices Choose one of these questions to discuss with a partner.

- **Use Tools** What tools could help you tell about the sides and angles of the shapes?

- **Be Precise** What are some of the different words you can use to name the shapes in this problem?

Discuss **Models and Strategies**

Read the problem. Write a solution on a separate sheet of paper.
Remember, there can be lots of ways to solve a problem!

Cut Squares

Bella has some square pieces of paper that are all the same size. She plans to cut each square into equal parts. Then she will sort the parts by shape.

Here are Bella's notes about how she wants to cut the squares.

> **My Notes**
> · Cut each square into the same number of equal parts.
> · Make 4 or more equal parts from each square.
> · Each square should be cut into equal parts that look
>   different than the equal parts from the other squares.

How should Bella cut her squares?

Plan It and Solve It Find a solution for the Cut Squares problem.

Help Bella decide how to cut the squares.

- Pick a number of equal parts.
- Divide the four squares into that number of equal parts in different ways.
- Write the fraction that can be used to name one equal part.
- List all of the shape names that can be used to describe the equal parts for each square.

You may want to use the problem-solving tips to get started.

Reflect

On Mathematical Practices Choose one of these questions to discuss with a partner.

- **Use Tools** What tools can you use to draw the equal parts? How can you use these tools?

- **Critique Reasoning** Tell your partner how you named your shapes. Do you agree with each other? Tell why or why not.

> Persevere > **On Your Own**

Read the problems. Write a solution on a separate sheet of paper. Remember, there are many different ways to solve a problem!

Quadrilateral Envelopes

Bella has so many paper quadrilaterals! She sorts them and keeps them in envelopes. Bella labels each envelope with the name of a shape.

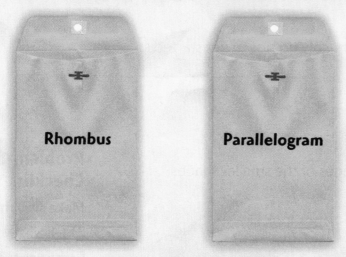

List the attributes of each shape on its envelope. Draw a shape Bella could put in each envelope. Then draw a shape that is close to that shape, but that Bella could not put in the envelope.

▶ **Solve It** **Help Bella label her envelopes.**

For each envelope . . .

• list the attributes of the shape.

• make a drawing of the shape.

• make a drawing that is close to that shape but is not that shape. Explain why it is not right.

▶ **Reflect**

Use Mathematical Practices Choose one of these questions to discuss with a partner.

• **Be Precise** How can you explain to your partner how to tell if a shape is a parallelogram or a rhombus?

• **Make an Argument** Why are the two shapes you drew close but not right?

Bella's Show

Bella is making a show about mosaic art. She uses small square pieces of paper to make colorful designs. At the show, people can enter a mosaic design contest. Here are the rules for the contest.

Design 1
- Use up to 48 squares.
- Put the squares in equal rows.

Design 2
- Use the same number of squares as Design 1.
- Put the squares in a different number of equal rows.

What are two designs you could enter in the contest?

▶ **Solve It** **Enter Bella's mosaic contest.**

Follow Bella's rules to make two different drawings.
- Choose a number of squares to use.
- Make two drawings.
- Write multiplication equations to show the number of rows, the number of squares in each row, and the total number of squares.

▶ **Reflect**

Use Mathematical Practices Choose one of these questions to discuss with a partner.

- **Reason Mathematically** How did you choose the number of squares to use?

- **Use a Model** How does each equation you wrote relate to the design?

Solve the problems.

1 Which shape has the greatest number of square corners?

A

B

C

D

2 Which quadrilateral has 4 sides that are the same length and 4 angles that are NOT square corners?

A

B

C

D

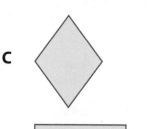

3 Which name describes the shape below? Circle the letter for all that apply.

A quadrilateral

B parallelogram

C rectangle

D rhombus

E square

4 Which rectangle shows $\frac{1}{3}$ shaded? Circle the letter for all that apply.

A

B

C

D

5 Sort the following four shapes according to the descriptions in the boxes below. Draw the shape in each box it belongs. You can use a ruler.

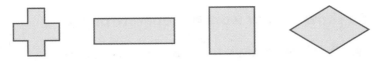

Has at least 1 square corner	Is a parallelogram	All sides the same length

6 **Part A** The rectangle below is divided into equal parts.

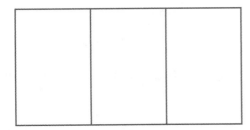

What fraction of the whole rectangle is each part?

_____

Part B Use a ruler to draw a square. Divide the square into equal parts so that each part is $\frac{1}{8}$ of the area of the square.

Performance Task

Answer the questions and show all your work on separate paper.

Read each riddle below. Use the clues to draw the shape or shapes you think they describe. Name the shapes when possible. A riddle may have more than one answer.

1. "I'm a four-sided shape. What could I be?"

2. "I'm a four-sided shape. I have two pairs of parallel sides. What could I be?"

3. "I'm a four-sided shape. I have two pairs of parallel sides. All of my sides are the same length. What could I be?"

4. "I'm a four-sided shape. I have two pairs of parallel sides. All of my sides are the same length. I have four square corners. What could I be?"

Checklist

Did you . . .

☐ write at least 3 clues for each chosen shape?

☐ use vocabulary from the unit?

☐ draw all the shapes possible for each riddle?

Choose two of the shapes below. Write a riddle for each shape. Use vocabulary from the unit. Each riddle should have at least three clues.

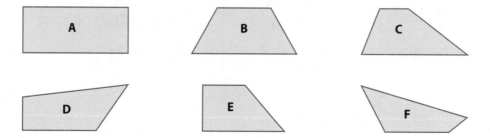

Choose a partner and read the clues for one of your shapes out loud. Have your partner draw the shape he thinks the clues describe. Does your partner's drawing match the shape you chose? Explain how the shape you chose and the shape your partner drew can be different, even if your partner did not make a mistake.

Reflect

Use Mathematical Practices After you complete the task, choose one of the following questions to answer.

- **Be Precise** List all of the geometry words you used to write your clues. What does each word mean?

- **Use Tools** What tools could you use to make accurate drawings of your shapes? Why would you need each of these tools?

Glossary

AM morning, or the time from midnight until noon.

add to combine, or find the total of two or more quantities.

addend a number being added.

analog clock a clock with an hour hand and minute hand.

angle one of the corners where two sides of a shape meet.

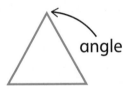

area the amount of space inside a closed, two-dimensional figure. Area is measured in square units such as square centimeters.

array a set of objects grouped in equal rows and equal columns.

☆ ☆ ☆ ☆ ☆
☆ ☆ ☆ ☆ ☆
☆ ☆ ☆ ☆ ☆

associative property of addition
Changing the grouping of three or more addends does not change the sum.

$$(2 + 3) + 4 = 2 + (3 + 4)$$

associative property of multiplication
Changing the grouping of three or more factors does not change the product.

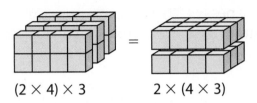

$$(2 \times 4) \times 3 \qquad 2 \times (4 \times 3)$$

attribute a characteristic of an object. One attribute of a shape is how many sides it has.

bar graph a graph that uses bars to show data.

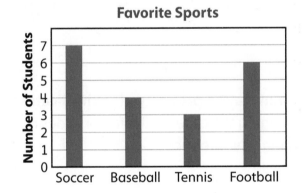

Favorite Sports

capacity the amount of liquid a container can hold. Capacity is measured in the same units as liquid volume.

cent the smallest unit of money in the U.S. One penny is one cent.

Glossary

centimeter (cm) a unit of length in the metric system. Your little finger is about 1 centimeter across. 100 centimeters is equivalent to 1 meter.

column a top-to-bottom line of objects in an array.

commutative property of addition Changing the order of the addends does not change the sum.

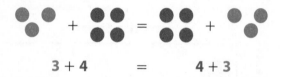

$$3 + 4 \quad = \quad 4 + 3$$

commutative property of multiplication Changing the order of the factors does not change the product.

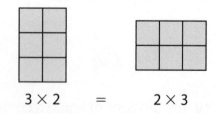

$$3 \times 2 \quad = \quad 2 \times 3$$

compare to decide if one number is greater than (>), less than (<), or equal to (=) another number.

customary system the measurement system used most often in the United States. It measures length in inches, feet, and yards.

data information, often numerical information such as a list of measurements.

denominator the number below the line in a fraction. It tells how many equal parts are in the whole.

$$\frac{2}{3} \longleftarrow \text{denominator}$$

difference the result of subtraction.

digit a symbol used to write numbers. The digits are 0, 1, 2, 3, 4, 5, 6, 7, 8, and 9.

digital clock a clock that uses digits to display the time.

dime a coin with a value of 10 cents.

dimension length in one direction. A figure may have one, two, or three dimensions.

distributive property When one of the factors of a product is written as a sum, multiplying each addend by the other factor before adding does not change the product.

$$2 \times (3 + 6) = (2 \times 3) + (2 \times 6)$$

divide to separate into equal groups.

dividend the number that is divided in a division problem.

divisor the number you divide by in a division problem.

dollar a unit of money with a value of 100 cents.

elapsed time the time that has passed between a start time and an end time.

equal (=) having the same value, same size, or same amount.

equation a mathematical statement that uses an equal sign (=) to show that two expressions have the same value.

equivalent fractions two or more fractions that have the same value. They name the same part of a whole and the same point on a number line.

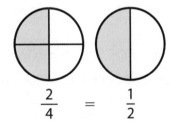

$$\frac{2}{4} = \frac{1}{2}$$

estimate (noun) a close guess made using math thinking.

estimate (verb) to make a close guess based on math thinking.

even number a whole number that ends in the digit 0, 2, 4, 6, or 8. An even number of objects can be divided into two equal groups.

expression numbers or unknown numbers combined with operation symbols. For example, $5 + a$ or 3×6.

fact family a group of related math facts that all use the same numbers. The group of facts shows the relationship between addition and subtraction, or between multiplication and division.

$$5 \times 4 = 20$$
$$4 \times 5 = 20$$
$$20 \div 4 = 5$$
$$20 \div 5 = 4$$

factor a number that is multiplied.

foot (ft) a unit of length in the customary system. One foot is equivalent to 12 inches.

fourths the parts formed when a whole is divided into four equal parts.

fraction a number that names equal parts of a whole; a fraction names a point on the number line.

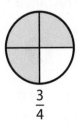

$$\frac{3}{4}$$

Glossary

gram (g) a unit of mass in the metric system. A paper clip has a mass of about 1 gram. 1,000 grams is equivalent to 1 kilogram.

greater than symbol (>) a symbol used to compare two numbers. It shows that the first number has a higher value than the second.

halves the parts formed when a whole is divided into two equal parts.

hexagon a flat shape with exactly six sides and six angles.

hour (h) a unit of time. One hour is equivalent to 60 minutes.

hour hand the shorter hand on the clock. It shows hours.

inch (in.) a unit of length in the customary system. A quarter is about 1 inch across. Twelve inches is equivalent to 1 foot.

key (on a picture graph) the part of a picture graph that tells what each symbol represents.

kilogram (kg) a unit of mass in the metric system. One kilogram is equivalent to 1,000 grams.

length a measurement that tells the distance from one point to another, or how long something is.

less than symbol (<) a symbol used to compare two numbers. It shows that the first number has a lower value than the second.

line plot a graph that uses a number line to show measurement data.

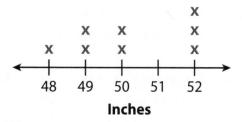

Sea Lion Lengths

Inches

liquid volume the amount of space a liquid takes up.

liter (L) a unit of liquid volume in the metric system. One liter is equivalent to 1,000 milliliters.

mass the amount of matter in an object. Measuring the mass of an object is one way to measure how heavy it is. Units of mass include the gram and kilogram.

measure to determine an attribute of an object, such as its length, weight, or area by comparing it to a known unit.

meter (m) a unit of length in the metric system. One meter is equivalent to 100 centimeters.

metric system the measurement system that measures length based on meters, liquid volume based on liters, and mass based on grams.

minute (min) a unit of time equivalent to 60 seconds.

minute hand the longer hand on the clock. It shows minutes past the hour.

multiply to find the total number of items in equal-sized groups.

nickel a coin with a value of 5 cents.

numerator the number above the line in a fraction. It tells how many equal parts are described.

$$\frac{2}{3} \longleftarrow \text{numerator}$$

odd number a whole number that ends in the digit 1, 3, 5, 7, or 9. An odd number of objects cannot be divided into two equal groups without one left over.

PM the time from noon until midnight.

parallel always the same distance apart.

parallelogram a quadrilateral with opposite sides parallel and equal in length.

pattern a series of numbers or shapes that follow a rule to repeat or change.

penny a coin with a value of 1 cent.

pentagon a flat shape with exactly five sides and five angles.

perimeter the distance around a two-dimensional shape. The perimeter is equal to the sum of the lengths of the sides.

Glossary

picture graph a graph that uses pictures to show data.

Favorite Vegetables	
Carrots	
Beans	
Broccoli	
Corn	

place value the value of a digit based on its position in a number. For example, the 2 in 324 is in the tens place and has a value of 2 tens, or twenty.

product the result of multiplication.

Q

quadrilateral a flat shape with exactly four sides and four angles.

quarter a coin with a value of 25 cents.

quotient the result of division.

R

rectangle a parallelogram with four square corners. Opposite sides of a rectangle are the same length.

regroup to put together or take apart ones, tens, or hundreds. For example, 10 ones can be regrouped as 1 ten, or 1 hundred can be regrouped as 10 tens.

rhombus a parallelogram with all four sides the same length.

round to find a number that is close in value to the given number by finding the nearest ten, hundred, or other place value.

row a side-to-side line of objects in an array.

rule In a pattern, a rule describes how to get from one number or shape to the next.

S

scale on a graph, the difference between the numbers labeling the graph.

second (s) a unit of time. Sixty seconds is equivalent to 1 minute.

side one of the line segments that form a flat shape.

square a flat shape that has four sides of equal length and four square corners.

square unit a square with a side length of 1 unit that is used to measure area.

standard unit any commonly used unit of measure, such as an inch or a centimeter.

subtract to take away one quantity from another, or to compare two numbers to find the difference.

sum the result of addition.

thirds the parts formed when a whole is divided into three equal parts.

three-dimensional solid, or having length, width, and height. For example, cubes are three-dimensional.

trapezoid a type of quadrilateral. A trapezoid always has a pair of parallel sides.

triangle a flat shape with exactly three sides and three angles.

two-dimensional flat, or having measurement in two directions, like length and width. For example, a rectangle is two-dimensional.

unit fraction a fraction with a numerator of 1. Other fractions are built from unit fractions. For example $\frac{1}{4}$ and $\frac{1}{8}$ are unit fractions.

Venn diagram a drawing that shows how sets of numbers or objects are related.

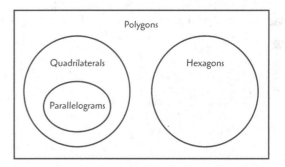

yard (yd) a unit of length in the U.S. customary system. One yard is equivalent to 3 feet.

Common Core State Standards Coverage by *Ready* Instruction

The chart below correlates each Common Core State Standard to the *Ready® Instruction* lesson(s) that offer(s) comprehensive instruction on that standard. Use this chart to determine which lessons your students should complete based on their mastery of each standard.

Common Core State Standards for Grade 3 Mathematics Standards	Content Emphasis	*Ready® Instruction* Lesson(s)
Operations and Algebraic Thinking		
Represent and solve problems involving multiplication and division.		
3.OA.A.1 Interpret products of whole numbers, e.g., interpret 5 × 7 as the total number of objects in 5 groups of 7 objects each. *For example, describe a context in which a total number of objects can be expressed as 5 × 7.*	Major	1
3.OA.A.2 Interpret whole-number quotients of whole numbers, e.g., interpret 56 ÷ 8 as the number of objects in each share when 56 objects are partitioned equally into 8 shares, or as a number of shares when 56 objects are partitioned into equal shares of 8 objects each. *For example, describe a context in which a number of shares or a number of groups can be expressed as 56 ÷ 8.*	Major	4
3.OA.A.3 Use multiplication and division within 100 to solve word problems in situations involving equal groups, arrays, and measurement quantities, e.g., by using drawings and equations with a symbol for the unknown number to represent the problem.	Major	11
3.OA.A.4 Determine the unknown whole number in a multiplication or division equation relating three whole numbers. *For example, determine the unknown number that makes the equation true in each of the equations 8 × ? = 48, 5 = ? ÷ 3, 6 × 6 = ?*	Major	6
Understand properties of multiplication and the relationship between multiplication and division.		
3.OA.B.5 Apply properties of operations as strategies to multiply and divide. *Examples: If 6 × 4 = 24 is known, then 4 × 6 = 24 is also known. (Commutative property of multiplication.) 3 × 5 × 2 can be found by 3 × 5 = 15, then 15 × 2 = 30, or by 5 × 2 = 10, then 3 × 10 = 30. (Associative property of multiplication.) Knowing that 8 × 5 = 40 and 8 × 2 = 16, one can find 8 × 7 as 8 × (5 + 2) = (8 × 5) + (8 × 2) = 40 + 16 = 56. (Distributive property.)*	Major	2, 3
3.OA.B.6 Understand division as an unknown-factor problem. *For example, find 32 ÷ 8 by finding the number that makes 32 when multiplied by 8.*	Major	5
Multiply and divide within 100.		
3.OA.C.7 Fluently multiply and divide within 100, using strategies such as the relationship between multiplication and division (e.g., knowing that 8 × 5 = 40, one knows 40 ÷ 5 = 8) or properties of operations. By the end of Grade 3, know from memory all products of two one-digit numbers.	Major	6

The Standards for Mathematical Practice are integrated throughout the instructional lessons.

Common Core State Standards for Grade 3 Mathematics Standards	Content Emphasis	Ready® Instruction Lesson(s)

Operations and Algebraic Thinking *continued*

Solve problems involving the four operations, and identify and explain patterns in arithmetic.

3.OA.D.8 Solve two-step word problems using the four operations. Represent these problems using equations with a letter standing for the unknown quantity. Assess the reasonableness of answers using mental computation and estimation strategies including rounding.	Major	12, 13
3.OA.D.9 Identify arithmetic patterns (including patterns in the addition table or multiplication table), and explain them using properties of operations. *For example, observe that 4 times a number is always even, and explain why 4 times a number can be decomposed into two equal addends.*	Major	7

Number and Operations in Base Ten

Use place value understanding and properties of operations to perform multi-digit arithmetic.

3.NBT.A.1 Use place value understanding to round whole numbers to the nearest 10 or 100.	Supporting/ Additional	8
3.NBT.A.2 Fluently add and subtract within 1000 using strategies and algorithms based on place value, properties of operations, and/or the relationship between addition and subtraction.	Supporting/ Additional	9
3.NBT.A.3 Multiply one-digit whole numbers by multiples of 10 in the range 10–90 (e.g., 9×80, 5×60) using strategies based on place value and properties of operations.	Supporting/ Additional	10

Number and Operations—Fractions

Develop understanding of fractions as numbers.

3.NF.A.1 Understand a fraction $\frac{1}{b}$ as the quantity formed by 1 part when a whole is partitioned into b equal parts; understand a fraction $\frac{a}{b}$ as the quantity formed by a parts of size $\frac{1}{b}$.	Major	14
3.NF.A.2 Understand a fraction as a number on the number line; represent fractions on a number line diagram.	Major	15
3.NF.A.2a Represent a fraction $\frac{1}{b}$ on a number line diagram by defining the interval from 0 to 1 as the whole and partitioning it into b equal parts. Recognize that each part has size $\frac{1}{b}$ and that the endpoint of the part based at 0 locates the number $\frac{1}{b}$ on the number line.	Major	15
3.NF.A.2b Represent a fraction $\frac{a}{b}$ on a number line diagram by marking off a lengths $\frac{1}{b}$ from 0. Recognize that the resulting interval has size $\frac{a}{b}$ and that its endpoint locates the number $\frac{a}{b}$ on the number line.	Major	15

The Standards for Mathematical Practice are integrated throughout the instructional lessons.

Common Core State Standards for Grade 3 Mathematics Standards	Content Emphasis	Ready® Instruction Lesson(s)

Number and Operations—Fractions *continued*

Develop understanding of fractions as numbers. *continued*

3.NF.A.3 Explain equivalence of fractions in special cases, and compare fractions by reasoning about their size.	Major	16, 17, 18, 19
3.NF.A.3a Understand two fractions as equivalent (equal) if they are the same size, or the same point on a number line.	Major	16
3.NF.A.3b Recognize and generate simple equivalent fractions, e.g., $\frac{1}{2} = \frac{2}{4}, \frac{4}{6} = \frac{2}{3}$. Explain why the fractions are equivalent, e.g., by using a visual fraction model.	Major	17
3.NF.A.3c Express whole numbers as fractions, and recognize fractions that are equivalent to whole numbers. Examples: *Express 3 in the form $3 = \frac{3}{1}$; recognize that $\frac{6}{1} = 6$; locate $\frac{4}{4}$ and 1 at the same point of a number line diagram.*	Major	17
3.NF.A.3d Compare two fractions with the same numerator or the same denominator by reasoning about their size. Recognize that comparisons are valid only when the two fractions refer to the same whole. Record the results of comparisons with the symbols $>$, $=$, or $<$, and justify the conclusions, e.g., by using a visual fraction model.	Major	18, 19

Measurement and Data

Solve problems involving measurement and estimation of intervals of time, liquid volumes, and masses of objects.

3.MD.A.1 Tell and write time to the nearest minute and measure time intervals in minutes. Solve word problems involving addition and subtraction of time intervals in minutes, e.g., by representing the problem on a number line diagram.	Major	20, 21
3.MD.A.2 Measure and estimate liquid volumes and masses of objects using standard units of grams (g), kilograms (kg), and liters (l). Add, subtract, multiply, or divide to solve one-step word problems involving masses or volumes that are given in the same units, e.g., by using drawings (such as a beaker with a measurement scale) to represent the problem.	Major	22, 23

Represent and interpret data.

3.MD.B.3 Draw a scaled picture graph and a scaled bar graph to represent a data set with several categories. Solve one- and two-step "how many more" and "how many less" problems using information presented in scaled bar graphs. *For example, draw a bar graph in which each square in the bar graph might represent 5 pets.*	Supporting/ Additional	24, 25
3.MD.B.4 Generate measurement data by measuring lengths using rulers marked with halves and fourths of an inch. Show the data by making a line plot, where the horizontal scale is marked off in appropriate units—whole numbers, halves, or quarters.	Supporting/ Additional	26

The Standards for Mathematical Practice are integrated throughout the instructional lessons.

Common Core State Standards for Grade 3 Mathematics Standards	Content Emphasis	*Ready®* *Instruction* Lesson(s)

Measurement and Data *continued*

Geometric measurement: understand concepts of area and relate area to multiplication and to addition.

3.MD.C.5 Recognize area as an attribute of plane figures and understand concepts of area measurement.	Major	27
3.MD.C.5a A square with side length 1 unit, called "a unit square," is said to have "one square unit" of area, and can be used to measure area.	Major	27
3.MD.C.5b A plane figure which can be covered without gaps or overlaps by *n* unit squares is said to have an area of *n* square units.	Major	27
3.MD.C.6 Measure areas by counting unit squares (square cm, square m, square in, square ft, and improvised units).	Major	27
3.MD.C.7 Relate area to the operations of multiplication and addition.	Major	28, 29
3.MD.C.7a Find the area of a rectangle with whole-number side lengths by tiling it, and show that the area is the same as would be found by multiplying the side lengths.	Major	28
3.MD.C.7b Multiply side lengths to find areas of rectangles with whole-number side lengths in the context of solving real world and mathematical problems, and represent whole-number products as rectangular areas in mathematical reasoning.	Major	28
3.MD.C.7c Use tiling to show in a concrete case that the area of a rectangle with whole-number side lengths a and $b + c$ is the sum of $a \times b$ and $a \times c$. Use area models to represent the distributive property in mathematical reasoning.	Major	29
3.MD.C.7d Recognize area as additive. Find areas of rectilinear figures by decomposing them into non-overlapping rectangles and adding the areas of the non-overlapping parts, applying this technique to solve real world problems.	Major	29

Geometric measurement: recognize perimeter as an attribute of plane figures and distinguish between linear and area measures.

3.MD.D.8 Solve real world and mathematical problems involving perimeters of polygons, including finding the perimeter given the side lengths, finding an unknown side length, and exhibiting rectangles with the same perimeter and different areas or with the same area and different perimeters.	Supporting/ Additional	30

Geometry

Reason with shapes and their attributes.

3.G.A.1 Understand that shapes in different categories (e.g., rhombuses, rectangles, and others) may share attributes (e.g., having four sides), and that the shared attributes can define a larger category (e.g., quadrilaterals). Recognize rhombuses, rectangles, and squares as examples of quadrilaterals, and draw examples of quadrilaterals that do not belong to any of these subcategories.	Supporting/ Additional	31, 32
3.G.A.2 Partition shapes into parts with equal areas. Express the area of each part as a unit fraction of the whole. *For example, partition a shape into 4 parts with equal area, and describe the area of each part as $\frac{1}{4}$ of the area of the shape.*	Supporting/ Additional	33

The Standards for Mathematical Practice are integrated throughout the instructional lessons.

Acknowledgments

Illustration Credits

page 62, 100, 104, 148, 150, 151, 322, 354: Sam Valentino

All other illustrations by Fian Arroyo.

Photography Credits

page 64: MedicMedic/Shutterstock

page 65: user friendly/Shutterstock

page 106: Angela Waye/Shutterstock

page 107: David Franklin/Shutterstock

page 144: Surrphoto/Shutterstock (blue shirt)

page 144: Ronald Sumners/Shutterstock (green shirt)

page 144: Khvost/Shutterstock (red shirt)

page 200: Blaz Kure/Shutterstock

page 204: Juriah Mosin/Shutterstock

page 206: Venturelli Luca/Shutterstock

page 318: momopixs/Shutterstock

page 324: nito/Shutterstock

page 325: sirastock/Shutterstock

page 358: Milosz_G/Shutterstock (blue paper)

page 358: bahri altay/Shutterstock (green paper)

page 358: Malgorzata Kistryn/Shutterstock (red paper)

page 358: Irtsya/Shutterstock (dot paper)

page 360: Brian C. Weed/Shutterstock

page 361: Mike Taylor/Shutterstock

Background images used throughout lessons by Ortis/Shutterstock, irin-k/Shutterstock, and Kritsada Namborisut/Shutterstock.